T0146402

Praise for
Pickin' Up the Pieces

"*Pickin' Up the Pieces* is a love story—a man's love for his family and his music, and his love and devotion to his Lord and Savior, Jesus Christ. This is an inspiring testimony from one of the great singer-songwriters of all time. I feel fortunate to have worked with Richie and very blessed that he is still a part of my life."

—CHRIS HILLMAN, founding member of the Byrds, the Flying
Burrito Brothers, and the Souther-Hillman-Furay Band

"I consider my friendship with Richie to be as solid today as in the days when I was fortunate enough to be a part of the adventures laid out in this insightful book. Staying true to his nature, my musical mentor has written a candid and refreshingly honest account of his life."

—TIMOTHY B. SCHMIT, member of the Eagles
and former member of Poco

"As a founding member of the Buffalo Springfield, Richie had a front-row seat to the explosion of sixties rock. He went on to form other bands that shaped musical styles for years to come. In *Pickin' Up the Pieces,* Richie chronicles the steps that led to his Christian conversion and his decision to leave rock stardom behind to become the pastor of a church. This book is insightful, moving, and at times quite surprising. You won't want to put it down."

—GREG LAURIE, author, senior pastor of Harvest Christian Fellowship,
speaker on Harvest TV, and host of radio's *A New Beginning*

"Reading Richie's memories of a life filled with love and music brings back all the highs and lows that can be experienced in the world of music. Through it all he has remained a true pioneer and a friend you can count on. One thing's for sure. Richie is the heart and soul of country rock."

—RUSTY YOUNG, founding member of Poco and winner
of *Billboard*'s Song of the Year award for "Crazy Love"

"Richie's story brings back recollections of both glad and sad times during my days with him in Poco. And I learned many things about my Buffalo Springfield bandmates Neil Young, Stephen Stills, Dewey Martin, and Richie—especially those times before my arrival on the scene. But the thing that strikes me most is the honesty Richie conveys. His perceptions and explanation of the emotional rise and fall of each of his musical passages bring out both the joy and sorrow he felt."

—JIM MESSINA, former member of the Buffalo Springfield
and founding member of Poco and Loggins & Messina

"Richie Furay has a pure voice—in song and on the page. This is an honest book of true devotion to rock and roll and to Richie's faith."

—PETER KNOBLER, editor of *Crawdaddy* magazine

"Richie Furay is one of the kindest, most decent, and most talented people I have met in my forty years on the radio. You will find that out for yourself on every page of this terrific autobiography. Hey, Richie, 'You're *still* nothing less than wonderful!'"

—PETE FORNATALE, mixedbagradio.com and wfuv.org

"This book is a wonderful example of how God moves in hearts and lives to bring about His purposes. Richie's story points to a loving God who is with us in times of joy and sadness, success and failure, and sometimes even when we don't consciously seek Him. Richie's life has been a tremendous blessing to many thousands of people, and *Pickin' Up the Pieces* is an unforgettable book!"

—AL PERKINS, friend and original member
of the Souther-Hillman-Furay Band

"Few moments in music history are as fabled as the 1966 traffic-jam encounter between a California van and a Canadian hearse. On board the two vehicles: Stephen Stills, Neil Young, and Richie Furay. From that fated meeting would emerge Buffalo Springfield, one of America's most beloved folk-rock groups, and later, Poco, pioneers of country rock. And the catalyst of both was Ohio-born Richie Furay. His journey from Greenwich Village coffeehouses to the Rock and Roll Hall of Fame is an inspirational story of determination, dedication to family, and devotion to God."

—JOHN EINARSON, author of Desperados: The Roots of Country Rock
and coauthor of For What It's Worth: The Story of Buffalo Springfield

"When I met rock star Richie Furay, he and Nancy were fighting to save their marriage. Richie had arrived in California to meet with Chuck Smith, pastor of the Jesus Movement's most well-known church, Calvary Chapel. And Richie's struggles helped bring him to God. He is not a religious man; he is a *real* man who has found his purpose in life. He is transparent, vulnerable, and honest as he lays out his life on the pages of this book. The story he tells—of glory and defeat and redemption—will challenge anyone who has encountered deep and inescapable hurt."

—MIKE MACINTOSH, author of When Your World Falls Apart and
pastor of Horizon Christian Fellowship in San Diego, California

"*Pickin' Up the Pieces* is more than a nostalgic trip through the pop-music scene of the 1960s and 1970s—though there's enough of that to satisfy the most die-hard fans. This book tells how rock-and-roll pioneer Richie Furay found spiritual redemption. It's also a compelling personal story about the high cost of striving for celebrity."

—JOSEPH FARAH, author of Taking America Back, founder and editor
of WorldNetDaily.com, and a nationally syndicated talk-show host

"Richie Furay's path goes beyond his concert tours with Buffalo Springfield and Poco—and even beyond the Rock and Roll Hall of Fame. Richie's path extends colorfully from a small town in the Midwest all the way to heaven! Music aficionados, rock historians, curious fans, and ardent admirers will love this volume. Richie not only puts all the pieces of his wonderful journey together, but he also tells how God took his shattered life and arranged the pieces to create something more magnificent than Richie could have ever imagined."

—SKIP HEITZIG, author and pastor of Ocean Hills Church
in San Juan Capistrano, California

"Finally, one of rock music's pioneers rolls back the curtains and gives us a rare backstage view. But more than that, this is the story of a man in rock music who had the hand of God upon his life. Richie's perspective of that era is as priceless as the life he now lives in Christ."

—MIKE FINIZIO, senior pastor of Harvest Christian Fellowship NYC

"The music of Richie Furay will forever be etched in my soul. From Buffalo Springfield to his music today, his vocals always inspire me to listen. This is the book I've been waiting for—to hear the story that only Richie can share. Like his songs, I cling to every word, not wanting it to end."

—DEAN FEARING, chef of The Mansion
on Turtle Creek in Dallas, Texas

PICKIN' UP
the Pieces

The Heart and Soul of Country Rock Pioneer
Richie Furay

Richie Furay

with Michael Roberts

WATERBROOK
PRESS

PICKIN' UP THE PIECES

Trade Paperback ISBN 978-1-57856-957-1
eBook ISBN 978-0-307-55079-8

Published in the United States by WaterBrook, an imprint of the Crown Publishing Group,
a division of Penguin Random House LLC, New York.

WATERBROOK® and its deer colophon are registered trademarks of Penguin Random House LLC.

Library of Congress Cataloging-in-Publication Data
Furay, Richie.
    Pickin' up the pieces : the heart and soul of country rock pioneer Richie Furay / by Richie
Furay with Michael Roberts.—1st ed.
        p. cm.
    Includes bibliographical references, discography (p. 241), and index.
    ISBN 1-57856-957-5
    1. Furay, Richie. 2. Rock musicians—United States—Biography. I. Roberts, Michael, 1961
Apr. 2– II. Title.
ML420.F899A3 2006
782.42166092—dc22

                                                                              2005031074

This book is dedicated to the Lord of my life, Jesus Christ, Who has been with me every step of the way. It is also dedicated to the love of my life, Nancy, who has stood beside me—for better, for worse, for richer, for poorer, in sickness and in health—for thirty-eight awesome years. I am blessed.

Contents

Acknowledgments xi

Prologue: The Hall-of-Fame Phone Call 1

1   Yellow Springs, Ohio 11
     Boyhood Dreams and a Summer Tragedy

2   A Folk Singer in the Making 21
     My First Brush with the Big Time

3   Big City Lights and Village Nights 35
     From Passing the Hat to a Record Deal

4   The Move to L.A. 49
     Meeting Neil Young; Hanging Out with Gram Parsons

5   Becoming the Buffalo Springfield 59
     Two New York Folkies and Three Canadians Create Magic

6   Visions of Fame and Fortune 73
     How a Fast Start Drifted into the Slow Lane

7   "Stop, Children, What's That Sound?" 87
     An Unexpected Single Breaks Big

8   A Legendary Band Self-Destructs 99
     The Impossible Challenge of Keeping Things Together

9   A New Type of Rock Music 117
     Finding Three Other Guys Who Love Country Rock

10 The Bottom Keeps Falling Out 133
     Fleeting Success and the Damage of Sexual Sin

11   Will *Deliverin'* Really Deliver? 147
Leaving Poco to Form the First Country Rock Supergroup

12   On the Brink of Commercial Success 161
How "Super" Could This Group Become?

13   A New Life of Faith 173
Traveling the Long Road Back Home

14   A Christian Making Music 187
Striking Out in Another New Direction

15   Finding a New Calling 201
Who Would've Guessed That I'd Become a Pastor?

16   The Challenges of a Poco Reunion 215
At First It Seemed Like Such a Great Idea

Epilogue: The Lord and Me 231
Discography 241
Notes 243
Index 247

Acknowledgments

Where to begin…

My life has been so blessed and enriched by each of the people whose names appear on the pages of this book—yes, every one of you. (I know somewhere, somehow I have forgotten someone, and for that I am truly sorry.) Each of you has been so important to me and to making me who I am!

There are those of you I grew up with in Ohio—oh, the days of innocence. Then there are those who came into my life in that Big City, New York—oh, the anticipation of where the future was leading and the feeling that nothing could ever stop the dream from unfolding. Then it was on to California, where my life began to mature and the music in my heart was given the opportunity to be expressed. And along with you, some of the most talented musicians American rock and roll will ever know, we sure had some fun—and then some. Who could have planned it?

But California gave me more than just the opportunity to express my music; it gave me my bride. Then it was on to Colorado, my place of saving grace and home for thirty-five years now. And, oh, the friends I have come to "settle down with." Home is where the heart is, and it's with you, whether we're servin' in the ministry, makin' music together, or just "goin' fishin'." I want to acknowledge all of you who fit in this paragraph—just write your name in here; it belongs here. You are a part of my life, and I acknowledge you.

Of course, there are some I will mention by name:

- Mike Roberts, for putting forth the idea to write the story and for bringing it to life on the pages of this book. It was a lot of fun; a lot of work, but fun.
- Al Perkins, for taking the time to share the love of Jesus Christ with me and for taking me to Calvary Chapel in Costa Mesa.
- Mark Ferjulian, my good friend.

- To my church family at Calvary Chapel, Broomfield, for "getting it" and understanding that ministry goes beyond the four walls of a church building.
- Scott, Carolyn, and Aaron Sellen, the closest ones I know to a family outside my own personal family.

And that brings me to my family. Life would be utterly meaningless without family—someone to share all of life's experiences with, to laugh with and cry with, to hope and dream with. So God designed life in such a way that we would share the deepest and most personal moments with family. And He blessed me with the most wonderful family anyone could ever go through this life with.

To my mom, Naomi, and my sister, Judy: You've supported me all the way through, even when sometimes it was probably hard to do. But I've gotten only love and support from you. Thank you for being you! I would also like to acknowledge my dad, Paul Charles Furay—I hardly knew you.

To Nancy, my bride: There are no words to say what I feel in my heart toward you. If I could have made a list of everything I wanted in a wife, it would have fallen so short. You are more than I could have ever dreamed of. I'll be yours till the end, however long that may be—and that's a promise I plan to keep. When I say I love you, I mean what I say. And, baby, those words don't come cheap!

Timmie, Katie, Polly, and Jesse: You are your papa's delight—my precious babies who are all grown now into beautiful young women. I love you so much. The Lord has truly blessed me.

To Dave, Vincent, and Tom, my sons-in-law: I finally got some men in the family and the answer to my prayers that my girls would marry godly men who would love them and care for them. Thank You, Jesus. Three down; one to go. I love each of you as my own.

To Jackson, Luke, Kendall, and Parker: Oh my, the joy of grandkids! You make life exciting all over again in your special ways. I love you so much!

—RICHIE FURAY

This is Richie Furay's story, and I'm proud to have played a role in helping him share it. Richie was a rock throughout the writing process, and his wife, Nancy, his sister, Judy, and his longtime friend Bob Harmelink were more than helpful. They contributed memories and observations that make this book even richer. Also invaluable were numerous online resources, ranging from *www.AllMusic.com,* a true Web gem, to sites assembled by devoted fans of Buffalo Springfield, Poco, and Richie's solo recordings. Aficionados will want to visit *www.ChromeOxide.com,* which includes an amazingly comprehensive list of Buffalo Springfield shows, and *www.PocoNut.com,* a treasure-trove of Poco-related information and lore. Another terrific Internet stop is the Poco page maintained by Torbjörn Orrgård, accessible at *http://82.182.182.163/poco,* which overflows with news, lyrics, and links, not to mention a guitar tablature section designed to help budding musicians who are eager to follow in Richie's footsteps strike just the right chord. And Richie's own Web site, *www.RichieFuray.com,* is a great way to keep up with the latest developments, both musically and spiritually.

Other key sources include *For What It's Worth: The Story of Buffalo Springfield,* a book Richie co-wrote with journalist John Einarson in 1997. (An updated edition was published in 2004.)[1] And not to be overlooked are the liner notes to the *Buffalo Springfield Box Set,* released by Rhino Records in conjunction with Atco and Elektra, circa 2001. The liner notes are packed with fascinating details, and the box set's four disks of music provide pure listening pleasure from start to finish.

I would also like to acknowledge my wonderful family: Ellie, Lora, Nick, and Deb. I don't know how I got so lucky, but I'm certainly glad I did.

—MICHAEL ROBERTS

A man's heart plans his way,
But the LORD directs his steps.
—PROVERBS 16:9

The Hall-of-Fame Phone Call

On a beautiful March day in 1997, I came back to my office from lunch to find an unbelievable message on my answering machine: "Hey, Richie. It's Neil. Congratulations there, buddy. In case you haven't heard, you're in the Rock and Roll Hall of Fame, and I'm very proud of you. I'm very proud to be there with you, and I certainly hope you'll be able to break away from your duties there to…to allow for some time to come and celebrate with us.… I wish you all the best. Take care, and our best to you and your family and your children. See ya, Richie. Bye."

"Neil," of course, was Neil Young, a friend who had been part of a very significant time in my musical life. Along with the original lineup of me, Dewey Martin, Bruce Palmer, and Steve Stills, Neil was a member of the Buffalo Springfield, which a lot of people regard as one of the best and most influential rock bands of the sixties. The group wasn't around for long—just a couple of years. Still, we made our mark not only with our version of Steve's anthemic "For What It's Worth," our biggest hit, but also with three albums that inspired generations of folk-rock and country rock musicians.

Our induction into the Rock and Roll Hall of Fame, scheduled to take place in May 1997, was proof that our music had stood the test of time. The founding members of Buffalo Springfield deserved to stand alongside the other artists who'd made the cut that year—a list that included the Jackson 5; the Bee Gees; Parliament-Funkadelic; the Rascals; Joni Mitchell; and Crosby, Stills, and Nash, the trio Steve formed after the Springfield broke up in 1968.

A lot had happened since the breakup of Buffalo Springfield. I cofounded Poco, a pioneering country rock band that's still recording and performing today—often with me sitting in. After I left Poco in 1973, I was one-third of the Souther-Hillman-Furay Band, a supergroup put together by film and music mogul David Geffen. And I later embarked on a successful solo career that I've been able to balance with what I've come to see as my deeper calling—my work as pastor of Calvary Chapel in Broomfield, a community near beautiful Boulder, Colorado.

The activities and commitments associated with my work as a pastor are the "duties" Neil mentioned in his phone message. They're as important to me as anything in the world. But while some people think teaching the Word of God contradicts my earlier days as a rock star, I know better. As I look back on all the music I've made since my folk-music days in New York City in 1964, there's not a song I would be ashamed to sing anywhere, anytime. I'm proud of every single one.

CLERGYMAN AND COUNTRY ROCK LEGEND

When I got started in music, my aspirations were simple: I wanted to be a folk singer and to have fun making music. Twenty-five years later, I was being enshrined with the best ever in rock music. All I could think was, *This is pretty cool.*

Thank goodness for my wife, Nancy. She was thrilled, too, but she has a real gift for keeping things in perspective—both the good and the bad. Our life together has been blessed by four wonderful daughters—Timmie, Katie, Polly, and Jesse—and by our love for each other. But there have been soul-wrenching difficulties as well, times when we struggled with everything from our faith to our future as a couple.

Throughout all the mistakes and hurt and craziness, though, Nancy has stayed rooted in her faith, trusting that God has a bigger purpose in everything that happens to us. She's so good for me, because emotionally I ride a roller coaster. And even with something as terrific as the Hall of Fame vote, I was about to encounter more ups and downs.

Over the next couple of months, conversations went back and forth between various managers about having the Buffalo Springfield play at the Hall of Fame ceremony. This was almost beyond belief because we hadn't performed publicly as a group since 1968. Adding to my excitement was the location of the ceremony, which would take place in Cleveland in my home state of Ohio. This was too good to be true! But due to logistics and a lot of other factors, the decision was made that we wouldn't perform—definitely a bummer. We'd still be getting together, though, and I was eager to see all the guys again.

Then, just two days before Nancy and I were to leave for Cleveland, I received another message from Neil. This time it wasn't directed only to me. Instead, it was a fax addressed to the Hall of Fame Foundation, Atlantic Records chairman and CEO Ahmet Ertegun, VH1—the cable channel that would broadcast the event—and all the members of the Springfield.

In the fax Neil wrote that he was proud to be inducted as a member of Buffalo Springfield, saying,

> I always felt that we were doing something meaningful, that our
> band and audience had a unique bond. Times were simpler then.
> Music was a small business by today's standards. Money was small,
> record sales were just beginning to take hold in a major way. Those
> were innocent days.

He went on to talk about the pride he felt when inducting other performers into the hall, including Woody Guthrie, the Everly Brothers, and Jimi Hendrix, and he recalled fond memories of speeches made by Bob Dylan, producer Phil Spector, and Mike Love of the Beach Boys. "That was the real Rock and Roll Hall of Fame," he said.

Then the tone of his fax changed. He claimed the planned ceremony for 1997 would be nothing but "a VH1 TV show, edited for television and the adult contemporary market served by VH1. Cheapened forever.... This should be a special private moment for those who are on the inside, reported on but not seen or heard outside the Hall itself." He complained that inductees "are forced to be on a TV show, for which they are not paid, and whatever comments they would like to make, dirty laundry they would like to air, thanks they would like to give, are all subject to the VH1 editor. Someone who has absolutely no right to interfere." Neil also griped that "at over a thousand dollars a seat, many of the inductees cannot even afford to bring the family members they would like to accompany them to see the event.

"For these reasons," he concluded, "I regretfully will not be present to accept the honors along with my brothers in the Buffalo Springfield. I wish all the inductees well and congratulate you all. This is only my own opinion, and I realize it may be a selfish one.... Although I accept the honor in the name of Rock and Roll, I decline to take part in this TV presentation and be trotted out like some cheap awards show. There are already too many of those."[1]

BUFFALO SPRINGFIELD AGAIN

In a lot of ways the fax was a flashback, since Neil always marched to the beat of his own drum. When we were in the Springfield, there were many times when he would decide not to do something we'd all agreed upon, and for reasons he almost never bothered to explain. He'd just take off. We learned to live with that part of his character—but that didn't stop me from questioning his timing in this instance. He had attended his Hall of Fame induction as a solo artist in 1995 and had played at the hall itself just a few months earlier for the broadcast of the "MTV Music Video Awards"—a TV show of the same type he criticized in his fax. And sure enough, just two years after the Springfield's moment in the spotlight, he was back at the Hall of Fame inducting Paul McCartney at a ceremony that was later shown on VH1.

Frankly, I understood Neil's complaints about the expense of attending the induction ceremony. I would have loved for my kids to have been there too. After reading the fax, however, I wondered if something else was going on, especially since Steve Stills would be inducted twice that evening—with the Buffalo Springfield and also with Crosby, Stills, and Nash. Bottom line, it was really Steve's night. And since he and Neil are like brothers in the way the competitive spirit drives them, their rivalry could have had much to do with the way things unfolded.

Whatever the case, Neil wasn't planning to show and I was disappointed, but I wasn't going to let it ruin the experience. And what an experience it was.

Rock-and-Roll Royalty

Huge crowds had gathered outside the hall to watch the limousines pull up in front of the Renaissance Cleveland Hotel, where the Hall of Fame ceremony was being held. And inside the hotel, every direction you turned you saw another star. The first morning we were there, Nancy and I headed downstairs for breakfast and found ourselves in the dining room with Maurice Gibb of the Bee Gees and David Crosby, another acquaintance from the Springfield days. David had been a member of the Byrds, whose first album was a huge inspiration for me.

More celebrities, including actor Michael Douglas, were on hand when we were given a private walk-through of the Hall of Fame. Even so, what made the biggest impression on me was the small room at the top of the building, where the plaques of all the inductees are on display. To see the names of performers I'd admired all my life, and then to see my name alongside theirs—among the greatest musicians in rock-and-roll history!—caused me to catch my breath. Was this really happening?

The Hall of Fame ceremony was a whirlwind, and not only because of the heavy concentration of cameras and celebrities. I ended up getting food poisoning from a piece of salmon and spent the evening feeling more and more queasy. Still, I was hoping I'd be able to meet one of my favorite musicians, Brian Wilson of the Beach Boys, who was inducting the Bee Gees that night.

Near the end of the Buffalo Springfield era, we played a number of shows with the Beach Boys. But by then, Brian was suffering from the effects of a rock-and-roll lifestyle lived to extremes, and he had stopped touring. In Cleveland that night, I would have loved to let him know how much his music meant to me and to tell him what a musical and melodic genius I consider him to be. Unfortunately, the Jackson 5 had an enormous entourage that blocked the way between Brian and me, and there was no way to get through the crowd.

At least I was able to greet and shake hands with Felix Cavaliere of the Rascals, one of my favorite bands. I'd covered their song "I've Been Lonely Too Long" on my *I Still Have Dreams* solo album. During the ceremony Nancy and I enjoyed sharing a table with Bruce Palmer and Dewey Martin of the Springfield. I never would have guessed that just seven years later, in 2004, Bruce would die of a heart attack at the age of fifty-eight.

Steve was at a different table; he chose to sit with David Crosby and Graham Nash. But the other three members of the Springfield who were present were joined by Tom Petty, who had been chosen to induct us into the Hall of Fame. I'd never met Tom before, and I found him to be an extremely nice guy—and very nervous. He shouldn't have worried, because his speech that night was wonderful.

"Buffalo Springfield was born in 1966," he said from the stage. "They were blonde and brunette. They were fringe and paisley. They were the city and they were the canyons. They were the Sunset Strip and the Whisky a Go Go. There were three great voices, and they were poets. They were electric and they were an absolutely new acoustic. They were ominous and they were a country morning. They were Cuban heels and moccasins. And they were Gretsch guitars and Fender amps. They were dueling guitar solos: one bluesy, the other fuzzy and angry. They were beautiful harmonies and they were a psychedelic orchestra. They sang of children's claims to fame, of broken arrows, and for what it was worth. They were immensely influential and they begot many more groups that would make more silver and gold music throughout the decades to follow. They were, most of all, Stephen Stills, Richie Furay, Neil Young, Dewey Martin, and Bruce Palmer."[2]

Tom left his notes on the podium when it came time for us to speak. Bruce Palmer went up before me and rambled on and on. After he finished, to relax myself I grabbed the paper and acted as if he had actually written a prepared statement. "Hey, Bruce, here are your notes," I said, drawing laughter from the audience. Part of me wishes I'd kept those notes, but I later found out they had made their way back to Tom. That's where they belonged.

Some of the performances during the evening were absolutely great. I was especially knocked out by the Bee Gees. The last group was Crosby, Stills, and Nash, and when they finished and everyone started to go onstage for the traditional end-of-the-evening jam, I stayed in my seat. Nausea from the food poisoning was making me feel worse by the minute, and I had other concerns as well. While I would never tell another artist what he should or shouldn't do, I'm a Christian and the pastor of a church, so I constantly think about how the things I do and say might affect other people. So as the other inductees took the stage for the closing jam, I gave in to my queasy stomach and quietly went back to my room.

LIFE IN TWO WORLDS

A passage in the Bible says that, in essence, people who follow Jesus are "in" this world but not "of" this world.[3] We live in the physical realm, but we are spiritual beings—inhabited by God's Spirit and invested with a divine purpose. On the night I was inducted into the Rock and Roll Hall of Fame, at no time did I find myself looking around and thinking either *I shouldn't be here* or *I wish I'd never stopped making records or performing concerts.* I had done both, and I was thankful for it all. I had enjoyed the fame, the applause, the honors, and the accolades, but those things can't last forever. So in the end I was able to look at the Hall of Fame induction simply as a great, great moment—an absolutely satisfying and rewarding personal moment, and a lot of fun. But the life I was living in Colorado, with my family and my church congregation, never left an emptiness that I felt needed filling.

In the days that followed the ceremony, I made several stops around Ohio, touching on other elements of my past. First, I headed to the town of Massillon where I'd promised to speak at a school attended by the daughter of my old friend Bob Harmelink. Bob and I were fraternity brothers at Otterbein College in Westerville, Ohio, and we sang together in the school's a cappella choir. We also performed in a vocal group with another friend, Nels Gustafson. The three of us were the Kingston Trio of Otterbein College—the campus crooners. And a trip we took to New York City in 1963 put me on the path to my music career.

After a short visit to Massillon, I went even further back in time, figuratively speaking, spending a few days with my mother at her home in Springfield, near the town of Yellow Springs where I grew up. While I was there, a reporter from the Yellow Springs newspaper interviewed me for a hometown-boy-makes-good article.

In a way, my trip to Ohio took me full circle. Suddenly I had a new perspective on the person I had been and the person I became, and I realized that they were one and the same, even though things had changed. When God steps into your life, He doesn't turn you into someone else. He uses who you are to make you into the person He wants you to be—the unique person He created you to be.

Growing up in Ohio, life was simple. Most people were satisfied and pretty complacent. But something inside told me there was more waiting in the world beyond the limits of my hometown. That must be why I had dreams of being a successful musician from a very early age—maybe eight or nine. And no matter what else was happening in my life, this dream, this passion was something that never let up.

During the first part of my career, I lived on a horizontal level. I was a musician, and success was my main focus. I looked straight ahead, wondering what I needed to do next to attain my goals. My vision extended no further than what I was able to see directly in front of me. But that changed when I accepted Jesus into my life. All of a sudden, life had so much more meaning than I could ever have imagined.

In the years that followed, I learned that the Lord had been looking out for me much longer than I realized. For one thing, I was blessed with strong moral values from the very beginning—solid midwestern values that my parents passed along to me. This gave me a grounding that served me well during the sixties and seventies. Even when the music business was at its wildest (and it got really wild), I tried to live my life as a good person, and I put a premium on taking care of my family. Today when I look at the lyrics to the songs I wrote back then, I realize that some of them were calling out to me in ways I wasn't aware of at the time—stirring up things that went well beyond a life that operates only in the physical realm.

Take "Pickin' Up the Pieces," the title song from the debut album by Poco, released in 1969. The first verse is a fairly straightforward celebration of the music I was making at the time:

Well, there's just a little bit of magic
In the country music we're singin'
So let's begin
We're bringin' you back down home where the folks are happy
Sittin', pickin' and a-grinnin'
Casually, you and me
We'll pick up the pieces.

The second verse, though, contains images that can be read in a couple of different ways:

Somebody yelled out at me
Country music and company kind of makes it
On a Sunday afternoon

Picnic lunches of yesterday
Should still have a place in your heart today
Think it over
'Cause we'll all be goin' home so soon.[4]

Today I understand that the lines about company on a Sunday afternoon could easily refer to a fellowship of believers who gather after a morning church service. Likewise, "We'll all be goin' home so soon" echoes the idea that after Christians have lived their earthly life, they look forward to "going home" to their eternal life with Christ. The song has a double meaning that I was unaware of when I wrote it.

I was able to spell out the message more plainly in "I've Got a Reason," the 1976 title song from the first album I wrote after giving my life to Christ. As I sang, "Music was my life, finally took everything. Ain't it funny how you got it all and not a thing."[5] Those words express the ultimate lack of fulfillment in a person's life when Jesus is excluded.

Was I destined to walk in the light of the Lord? Definitely. Looking back on my exciting, challenging, but ultimately wonderful journey through life, I realize that He's been with me every step of the way. Even when I wasn't looking for Him.

1

Yellow Springs, Ohio

Boyhood Dreams and a Summer Tragedy

On paper, my story begins at 5:30 p.m. on May 9, 1944, the day I was born. To get a clear idea of all that has made me who I am, though, you have to go back to my parents. Both of them were strong, determined, and morally principled people, and I am blessed to have been their son. If there were any regrets, it was that I got to know only one of my parents— a hard fact of life that I'm still coming to terms with.

My mother's maiden name was Naomi Coffman, and she came from a big family. Her father was both a constable and a farmer, and when my mom was a child, he died in a terrible accident. A threshing machine he was using broke down, and when he tried to fix it, he was pulled into the mechanism and his head was crushed. My dad's father also died before I came along, so I never had a chance to meet either of my grandfathers.

As my mom grew up, she didn't grow very tall. If I said she eventually hit five feet, I might be giving her an inch or two. But in spite of her lack of stature, she was very athletic, playing basketball, tennis, and many other sports. She played golf into her eighties.

My dad, Paul Charles Furay, was less of an athlete than my mom was. He wasn't fat, but he was stout. His hair began turning gray when he was in high school, around the time he met my mom, and he was a smoker, which probably didn't do his long-term health any good. He was a gifted artist who loved to doodle. His pencil and chalk portraits were impressive. I have a sketch he made of my mom that I keep in my office, and also one of his self-portraits. These are some of my most prized possessions.

My parents, who were high-school sweethearts, got married after graduating and set up housekeeping in Yellow Springs, Ohio. My sister, Judy, came along first, on September 9, 1941. I followed three years later. We had the typical sibling rivalries, but I definitely looked up to Judy. She went on to attend Otterbein College in Westerville, Ohio, where she met her future husband, Tony Hugli. Today they live in San Diego.

LIFE IN A SMALL TOWN

Yellow Springs was quite small back then, with a population around two thousand. It looked very much like Mayberry, but it was quite a progressive community, thanks in part to the presence of Antioch College, a liberal-arts school that was sort of an Ohio version of the University of California at Berkeley. Antioch has had its share of famous graduates, including Rod Serling, who created and hosted *The Twilight Zone.* Actor John Lithgow, who starred in *Third Rock from the Sun,* also grew up in Yellow Springs.

The town's economy was driven by manufacturing plants. One big employer was Morris Bean and Company, which specialized in producing tire castings that would be shipped to Akron, a center of tire and truck production. My dad worked for a while at another factory, which made parts for military equipment. Plenty of people who took these jobs never moved on to anything else, but my dad was more ambitious. Having grown up during the Depression, he was determined that his family would never want for anything. He decided to go into business for himself, and he and my mom took over management of the local Rexall store.

Running the drugstore was a perfect job for my parents. My dad, in particular, could remember the name of every person who came into the store—

not only the adults but also the names of their children. He truly enjoyed talking with his customers, and they in turn liked spending time with him. He was always smiling and would head to work every day wearing one of his trademark bow ties. I think this part of my dad's personality rubbed off on me. He had a pioneering spirit, and he was a people person.

The building that housed my parents' drugstore was one of the oldest in Yellow Springs. My mom has a photo from approximately 1900 that shows the building, and two more on either side, looking just as I remember it—and I remember it very well. A couple of steps led inside. To the right, customers could find beauty supplies, over-the-counter medications, and a big variety of other goods. At the rear of the building was a full-service pharmacy.

My mom pitched in on the sales floor and kept the books. She had to do the store's accounting on a bulky adding machine—the type with a long handle on the side. Unlike me, she was very sharp with numbers. I was more interested in the rack of magazines and comic books on the left side of the store. Past the racks was another of my favorite spots, the candy counter, where the cash register was located, and the soda fountain just beyond it. Predictably, I remember the fountain mainly for the ice cream and the milk shakes, but my parents also offered a lunchtime menu. There weren't any booths, but there were stools at the counter that were almost always filled during the lunch hour, with lines of people stretching out behind them. When it was crowded, my sister and I could go to the front of the line to get our lunches and then eat them in the back room. While I was eating, I could read any new comic book I wanted. And yet I don't remember feeling special as a result of these privileges—they were just part of my everyday life.

Because of Yellow Springs's size, the two houses where I spent many of my formative years—both located on Xenia Avenue—were close to the drugstore. The first was right next-door, and the second was only about a mile away. There was always a lot going on in the first house because a doctor's office occupied half of the main floor and a beauty shop the other half. We lived upstairs, above the doctor's office. The attic of the house was filled with stuff from the drugstore—spooky stuff, I thought as a kid. There was many a time I went exploring in that attic. The floors would creak as I moved through the maze of boxes, and I had to use a flashlight because the two bulbs dangling from overhead provided only dim lighting. When I found something that interested me, I would sit down and stay for what seemed like hours. If I was feeling brave, that is.

A New Business Venture

As I approached my teenage years, my parents closed the drugstore and started another business, which they called Furay's Gift Shop. They built it across the alley that led to our first house on Xenia Avenue. When people think of gift shops today, they generally picture places that specialize in greeting cards, knickknacks, and so on. Furay's certainly carried such items, but in other respects, it was really a smaller variation on a modern department store.

The nearest sizable town was at least a thirty-minute drive from Yellow Springs, so my dad, being a visionary, stocked a variety of items that would appeal to townspeople and Antioch College students alike: jeans, jewelry, dishes, shoes, and much more. The store also included a used-book department and a large toy section. But I was more interested in the collection of sports equipment. Furay's carried tennis rackets, golf clubs, basketballs, baseball gloves—pretty much anything I or anyone else needed. And on the odd chance that something wasn't in stock—such as when my sister needed red shoelaces—my dad was happy to order it.

Like the drugstore, the gift shop was the kind of place any kid would love to spend time—and I did. Even so, there were drawbacks, owing to the long hours my parents had to work. My dad usually left the house at 6:00 a.m. and on most nights didn't return home until after 10:00 p.m. On many days I didn't see him at all unless I went to the store.

My mom wasn't gone as much as my father was, but close. So for the most part, Judy and I were raised by my dad's mom, Grandma Furay. She lived with us, prepared meals for us, and was there when we got home from school. My mom's mom, Grandma Bertie, was around sometimes too. She divided her time among several relatives who lived in the area.

I appreciated everything Grandma Furay did for us, but still I was hungry to spend more time with my parents, particularly my dad. Back in the forties and fifties, responsible fathers were expected primarily to take care of providing for their families, and my dad certainly did that. Today, however, we know that in addition to food and shelter, kids benefit from being around male role models, and I'm sure I would have too. On top of that, my dad was a great guy, as everyone in Yellow Springs knew. I wish I'd had a chance to get to know him.

Because of my dad's frequent and long absences, my memories of him are a bit hazy, although I know he tried to be there for me. A few episodes of father-son bonding stand out, like the time we drove to LeSourdsville Lake, a recreational area that resembled an early theme park. It had a beach, rides, and a range of attractions. Tired after a long day, I thought I would tease my dad a bit. I was in the backseat, tickling him as he drove, and somehow his glasses got broken, badly. Some glass actually got in his eye, which made the ride home extremely tense.

If this had happened to most kids, the next part of the story would involve a lot of yelling and some kind of severe punishment, but I don't remember anything like that. While it's possible I've buried any memory of the consequences, chances are good that my dad handled this injury the way he handled most things—in an upbeat, let's-make-the-best-of-it way.

Typically, fathers in the 1950s were disciplinarians who taught lessons with a belt or a hairbrush, but I didn't get swatted very often. That may have been because I was a kid who usually did what I was told. Then again, it's just as likely that my father didn't treat me that way because he wasn't that kind of man. He seldom got angry. One time when I was seven or eight, I decided to play a trick on my dad. Knowing how terrified he was of spiders, I sneaked up behind the couch where he was sitting. I dangled an eight-legged tarantula toy in front of his face as he was reading a *Life* magazine, and the sight of it scared him so much that he ripped the magazine in half. Right down the middle!

A more poignant memory dates back to a family trip to Traverse City, Michigan, when I was about ten. I went fishing for smallmouth bass with my dad and a friend of his, Dale Cook. I hadn't done much fishing before, but on that day we caught so many fish that people gathered on the shore to watch us reel in one bass after another. We had a boatload! I don't remember a lot of interaction with my dad as we were making our haul, but I know he was excited, and seeing him that way was a big thrill for me.

ATHLETE OR MUSICIAN?

Like my mom, I was very into sports. I enjoyed playing basketball so much that when I was in junior high school, my parents put up a minicourt in our backyard, complete with blacktop and a mounted hoop. My friends would come over to play all the time because no one else in town had his own basketball court. Because my height was somewhat of a disadvantage to me when it came to basketball, baseball became my main sport. I loved playing the game, and I was pretty good, too.

My interest in music played second fiddle to sports during that time, but it was always there. Today I feel that I was intended to become a musician in much the same way I was destined to devote my life to serving the Lord. Not that anyone could have guessed how things would turn out. For one thing, we weren't an extremely religious family. We went to the Methodist church in Yellow Springs, but my parents were too busy running the store to do much more than attend Sunday services. (In 1953 I received a New Testament from one of my relatives, but more than two decades would pass before that gift would hold any real meaning for me.)

My mom sang in the church choir—she had a beautiful voice—but neither of my parents played an instrument. My father, however, was a big music fan. There was always a lot of music around the house, and around the drugstore, too. We had a jukebox there that played oversized 78 rpm records, not the seven-inch, 45 rpm singles that were used in jukeboxes in later years. When the people who maintained the jukebox loaded up the latest hits, the old records came home to our house. From a very early age, I was able to identify all the songs, and not just from the melody. My sister says I memorized all the labels so I could tell what was what just by looking at them.

In addition to my fascination with records, there was the Revere reel-to-reel tape recorder that my dad bought for my mom. To this day I have no idea why he gave it to her. Maybe he thought she'd like to sing songs into it that she was learning in the church choir. If so, she didn't get much of a chance, because I confiscated it. I took the tape recorder to my room, where I'd spend hours listening to early rock and roll and rhythm and blues on my radio. My favorite station was WING-AM—known as "Wingy Wing"—out of Dayton. I'd sit beside the radio for hours, the tape recorder at the ready, listening for one of my favorite tunes to come on so I could record it. If the disc jockey decided to play Gene Vincent and Eddie Cochran, or vocal groups like the Five Satins, you can bet the tape was rolling. (I loved those tapes so much that I kept several of them. I guess that makes me one of the original bootleggers!)

An even more significant story involves my first guitar—and my second. We were coming up to the Christmas of 1952 when I was eight years old, and I wanted a guitar more than anything in the world. My parents were reluctant to get it for me, thinking I was too young, but I made it clear that I wanted nothing else under the tree that year. So when I went downstairs on Christmas morning and saw the shadowy outlines of a guitar, my heart soared. But it quickly sank when I realized it wasn't a real guitar. The one under the tree had six strings, but the pressed–particle board construction, not to mention the cowboy scenes printed on the front, marked it as more of a toy than a real instrument. So did its color. I'm color-blind, yet somehow I could tell it wasn't just green; it was puke green.

What I wouldn't give to have that guitar today, but back then I was repulsed by the sight of it. My parents weren't out of bed yet, so they missed seeing my initial disappointment. I wanted them to know how I felt, though, so I raced to their room and told them all about their terrible mistake. I'm sure they were devastated, especially considering that it was Christmas morning. But I was inconsolable, and they agreed to head down to Morelli Music in Springfield after the holiday to see about buying a "real" guitar.

At Morelli's I found that I couldn't even get my hand around the necks of most of the guitars they had in stock, let alone play a chord. But I promised my parents that I'd take lessons from Lois Northeim, a teacher at the store, if they would just buy me a real guitar. My dad had something else in mind. He insisted that if he bought me a guitar, I had to agree to play trumpet in the school band, which my parents probably saw as a lot more practical. That sounded like a fair trade to me, and before the day was done I had the guitar of my dreams—a Gibson hollow-body electric, an ES295!

I kept my end of the bargain, signing up for guitar lessons at Morelli's and practicing diligently on numbers such as "The Rustic Dance," a tune that probably every beginning guitar student in the fifties learned to play. Before long I was good enough to keep up with my friend Roger, who had a steel guitar, and two other buddies, Bill Black and Rob Randall. Somehow, the four of us wheedled an invitation to perform at a senior-citizens' home affiliated with the local International Order of Odd Fellows chapter. My earnings for that performance consisted of a one-dollar bill—a silver certificate—that I still have framed to this day.

TRAGEDY ENDS A GROWING BOND

Tales like these make the Furays seem like a real *Ozzie and Harriet* family—loving parents of two adoring kids, with the younger one playing guitar. Of course, the truth is more complicated. Whereas the Nelson clan regularly ate dinner together, we did so only on rare occasions. Nonetheless, our family life would have been considered "normal," until the unthinkable happened.

By the time I turned thirteen in the spring of 1957, I think my dad realized that if he didn't spend more time with me, he'd miss my childhood. When he could, he began taking a few moments to toss a baseball back and forth with me in our yard. I was a Little League pitcher, and after one session of playing catch, my dad's hand was swollen. His little boy was growing up—and was able to bring on the heat. I might have really impressed him with my athletic ability in future years, but due to the events of August 13, 1957, I never got the chance.

The day before had started out like any other and had ended better than most. For some reason, my dad was home early, and we had a chance to roughhouse a little, which was rare. I'm sure I went to bed happy, especially since the next day, a Sunday, we'd be going to a family reunion at my Uncle Johnny's farm. Relatives from Yellow Springs, as well as ones from nearby Green and Clark counties, were expected to attend.

When I awoke very early that morning, my thoughts suddenly were crowded out by confusion. My mom had called an ambulance because my dad was experiencing severe chest pains. I remember looking out the window as the ambulance drove off, not knowing what was going on. My father was a healthy man as far as any of us knew. Besides, he was extremely easygoing—much more than I am. And he was just forty-five years old. He had his whole life in front of him.

But he had been taken away in an ambulance, and my mom and other relatives did all they could to downplay the situation. My sister and I went to my uncle's farm for the family reunion. I was playing with my cousins as if nothing was wrong, when one of my relatives pulled me aside and told me that my dad had died. I subsequently learned that he'd suffered an aortic aneurysm, the sort of catastrophic injury to the heart that is all but impossible to treat, even today. (Actor John Ritter died of the same condition.) My father never had a chance.

I was allowed to go through the entire range of emotions that such a shock triggers. Mixed up in all these feelings was the sense that the relationship between my father and me, which had recently begun moving in the right direction, was over. His death prevented us from continuing to strengthen the bond that I had longed for my entire life.

The town of Yellow Springs joined us in grief. Family lore has it that my dad's viewing was the second largest in the history of the town, ranking behind the funeral of a local senator. Undoubtedly that provided comfort for my mom, who suddenly faced the prospect of raising two children and running a business on her own. My dad may have died long before he should have, but he spread a lot of goodwill and fellowship during the relatively brief period he was here.

At the same time, I was aware that with my dad's death, everything had changed. My life would never be the same again.

2

A Folk Singer in the Making

My First Brush with the Big Time

hortly after my father's funeral, my family moved from our home on Xenia Avenue to a new ranch-style house on Spillan Road. In a bigger community, this location would have been in the suburbs, but Yellow Springs was so small that we were putting down roots in the country.

The Spillan Road house was smaller than the one we were leaving, but we didn't move to save money. The real motivation was emotional. Simply put, my mother found it difficult to stay in the house where her husband had just died. Everywhere she looked there were memories—many of them wonderful memories. But because of my dad's fatal heart attack, even recalling the good times was painful. My mother and my sister needed a fresh start.

I didn't share their urge to move. This was a confusing time for me, and at age thirteen I didn't realize all the repercussions of my dad's death. It affected me deeply, of course, but I didn't have the tools I needed to deal with it. For one thing, my religious training had been quite superficial. Going to church was nothing more than a weekly routine. We didn't have a Christian community around us that served as a spiritual family to help in a time of crisis. Nor was I aware of the deeper spiritual truths that would one day be so significant in my life, or how such truths could help me gain inner strength. So I had to deal with losing my dad without having the knowledge and understanding of

Scripture that help put the issues of life and death into context—other than the idea that good people went to heaven and, well, bad people didn't. I had no awareness of the ramifications that life continues beyond this life. With only this general understanding to draw upon, I got by in the short term because I didn't know my dad that well.

When we moved I was keenly aware of the great things about the Xenia Avenue house that we were leaving behind. For one thing, there was the black-topped basketball court my father had installed, where my friends and I spent hours playing one-on-one. Just as meaningful to me was the cement siding over a cellar that led down into the house's basement. When I wasn't at a nearby field hitting ground balls or shagging flies with my cousin Jim Johnston or with Dale Schaub, a neighbor who played catcher on the Little League team, I'd be at home tossing balls against that cement pad.

A NEW PHASE OF LIFE

During this time of transition, my strong home life helped me adjust, and eventually I agreed that the move had been the right thing to do. Even better, I discovered that my recreational opportunities were just as great at the new house as they'd been on Xenia Avenue. Noel Ashbaugh, a neighbor who was a few years older than I, had a blacktopped driveway with a basketball hoop, and he let me shoot baskets whenever I wanted to. As a bonus, the Spillan Road house had an enormous yard, which meant plenty of space to practice chipping golf balls. According to the old saying, you drive for show and putt for dough. But you can't putt unless you get the ball on the green. Over time I also got better at not taking divots out of my mom's lawn!

At Spillan Road, my sister and I took care of ourselves more than we'd done previously—in part because my Grandma Furay wasn't around to keep an eye on us. Instead of joining us in the new house, she chose to split her time between the homes of her other children. She and my mom weren't at odds; it just made more sense for her to stay with her kids rather than with her daughter-in-law.

Judy and I were getting older, and after our dad died, we attended fewer gatherings with our extended family. The trips to my Uncle Johnny's farm, which had been so much fun until the one when I learned my dad had died, were pretty much over. But another tradition—the family vacation—lived on, and in the summer following my dad's death, it had special importance. Traveling has a strong beneficial effect on people even at the best of times because it provides new experiences and new perspectives on life. When people are grieving, the benefits are magnified, because travel serves as a diversion from grief and sadness. That's probably why my mom didn't plan just one vacation but three. On top of that, she chose unusual destinations, guaranteeing that each one of us would experience something memorable and exciting.

We had never traveled in the western United States, so it was a special thrill to visit California, where a friend of my mom's had moved. Just as thrilling was our mode of transportation. We flew in a TWA Constellation, which, as a budding model-plane buff, I fully enjoyed. We also took a couple of driving trips, one to Washington DC and the other to Colorado, where I saw for the first time what would become my future home. I remember crossing the Kansas plains, which were featureless and seemed to go on forever. Then the majestic Colorado mountains slowly rose to dominate the horizon. While I don't remember feeling that I wanted to someday live in this part of the world, the scenery made a huge impression on me.

My dad had taken us on some great vacations to such destinations as Michigan, Florida, and Virginia, but because he was such a workaholic, I always had a sense that he needed to get back home as soon as possible. My mom had a different approach. She knew that after my dad passed away, we needed to clear our heads so we could look toward the future with optimism. Likewise, she was confident that the people she left in charge of the gift shop, including my Aunt Treva and Eleanor Miller, a family friend and longtime employee, would keep things going. I wish my dad could have relaxed and fully enjoyed our family vacations. Maybe if he had, he would have lived longer than the forty-five years he was given.

Years later I needed to learn this same lesson. When I became a pastor, I began to notice my own workaholic tendencies. I tried to do everything myself, which left little time for my family. Finally, I took a step back and realized that I could better serve my congregation, my family, and myself if I learned to delegate. I know the gifts and abilities that I have, and a natural skill of administration isn't one of them. By passing on such responsibilities to other people, and by putting a structure in place that allows everyone to do what they do best, I'm able to serve the Lord more effectively. It's a matter of faith and trust—and it's something I wish my dad had learned to do when I was young.

A SONGWRITER IS BORN

As I adjusted to life without a father, I began to explore other budding interests. For instance, my first girlfriend was Diane Bingham, who lived not far from my house on Spillan Road. Our relationship was wholesome even by 1950s standards. I'd usually walk her home from school, and when I did, I would carry her books. More significantly, she was my incentive for writing my first song. I called it "Bubby," after my nickname for her. It wasn't a big hit or even a minor hit, since the only two people who ever heard it were her and me. But it set me on a path that I continue to follow to this day.

Even though sports remained my main obsession, a musical foundation was being laid with the help of some important inspirations—the biggest being Ricky Nelson. *The Adventures of Ozzie and Harriet* was one of my favorite TV shows—so much so that when we visited California, I insisted that we drive by the house where this TV family lived. Ricky, the Nelsons' guitar-playing younger son, was the family member I identified with most strongly. One episode in particular stayed with me. Ricky was at home, quietly singing "Be-Bop Baby" to a baby in a crib. All of a sudden there was a transition, and Ricky was belting out the same song at a high-school dance, backed up by a terrific band led by guitarist James Burton, who went on to play with Elvis Presley.

At the time I couldn't have imagined that, in the future, Burton would contribute to an album by my band; he can be heard playing Dobro on the second Buffalo Springfield album *Buffalo Springfield Again*. Years later I heard through the grapevine that he might not have gotten paid for that session. If that's true, it's a shame, because he's one of the all-time greats—definitely a member of the A-team. So was Ricky Nelson, and he stirred my imagination in more ways than I can measure. I didn't stop to think that he was only acting and that his music career had been given a huge boost by his parents, who were powerful Hollywood celebrities. All I knew was that I wanted to be in his place.

It would be several more years before I could pursue my fantasy of making it big in the music world. But I got a taste of the excitement Ricky Nelson's character experienced while I was still in junior high. A group of students at Bryan High School formed a doo-wop group that they christened the Barons, and through friends of friends and other small-town connections, I came to their attention. Before long I was made the lead singer, acting like Little Anthony while the older guys oohed and aahed in the manner of the Imperials. The Barons played dances at the high school, so in a sense I got to walk in Ricky Nelson's shoes. Plus, Diane and I were admitted to dances that we wouldn't have been able to attend otherwise because we were too young.

The Barons' repertoire was made up of the great doo-wop songs of the era, by vocal groups such as the Crests and Dion and the Belmonts, whose classic "Teenager in Love" was always a show-stopper. Many years later, after I became a Christian, I went on a tour to Israel with Dion DiMucci, the Belmonts' leader and namesake, who had also become a follower of Jesus. In Solomon's Quarry we had a chance to talk, and I told him how much I had idolized him in the fifties. Not long afterward, Dion recorded a song called "I Put Away My Idols." Maybe he was trying to give me a hint!

TEENAGE REBELLION

As I was preparing to enter Bryan High School, I went through a particularly rebellious phase. It wasn't that I did anything criminal, or even particularly dangerous. That kind of behavior just isn't in me. But whether it was due to unresolved feelings about losing my father or the typical teenage changes that everyone undergoes, I started giving my mom fits.

I remember one cold winter morning. My mom was driving me to school, and whatever we were talking about got me so upset that I slammed the dashboard with my fist, causing the simulated vinyl to shatter. My mom was rightfully upset. "If you can't control your emotions," she said, "you're going off to military school."

She never made good on that threat, even though I kept pushing the envelope. By the time I was sixteen or seventeen, it was just the two of us in the house, since my sister had left Yellow Springs to attend college. But rather than sticking close to home, I'd stay out late with a group of friends—usually Kippy Eckroad, Mike Sparks, Bruce Dwyer, Dick Hathaway, and John Hughes, a friend dating back to kindergarten. We would get together and drink, either at one of the guy's houses if no parents were around, or else we'd hang out in Kippy's truck, nursing quart bottles of Pabst Blue Ribbon and talking about how cool we were. Afterward I'd sneak home, trying (and often failing) to get into bed without my mom hearing me.

I'm grateful that the Lord had His hand on me back then, even though I didn't know it. With my dad gone, I didn't have a male role model to follow. But in the end, my buddies and I came through this period very well, and we've gone on to lead productive lives. For instance, Mike Sparks is a prominent dentist in New Hampshire, John became a financial counselor in Minnesota after serving as a Navy SEAL, Bruce worked at the Pentagon for years, and so on.

In high school I devoted very little energy to scholastic achievement. I got by, but I didn't put any more effort into schoolwork than was absolutely necessary. As I mentioned earlier, I was much more interested in playing basketball, at least until it became clear that my size and my very ordinary ballhandling skills would keep me on the bench most of the time. After that, baseball was my primary focus, and throughout high school I entertained fantasies that I had a future in the sport. But I finally had to face the fact that I didn't have enough talent to attract the attention of college coaches, much less major-league scouts.

GOOD-BYE YELLOW SPRINGS

After graduating from Bryan High, I was accepted at Otterbein College, a school seventy or eighty miles from Yellow Springs. The only problem was that I didn't know what degree to seek. I was sure a major that required constant study and heavy bookwork wasn't for me, yet the idea of concentrating on music hadn't fully formed.

Since I had a natural aptitude for entertaining people, I decided to give drama a try. I'd performed in small, background roles at Antioch College's famous summer Shakespeare Festival and always enjoyed the experience. So I thought, *How hard can this be?*

Pretty hard, actually. At Otterbein, students with similar interests were often paired as roommates, which helps explain why I shared a dorm room with Pat McGinnis, another drama major. When tryouts were announced for the first production of the year, *The Pajama Game,* Pat and I auditioned. I was sure I'd land a good part, so when the cast list was posted, I started reading from the top. With a crowd of aspiring actors surrounding me, I had to work my way down—*way* down. I read almost to the bottom of the list before I saw my name. I'd been put in the chorus. And Pat? He got the lead. What a blow to my ego.

That was the end of my drama career, and with sports no longer an option, I was at loose ends until a freshman talent contest pointed me in the direction I'd been destined to head all along. My love of early rock and roll, rhythm and blues, and doo-wop had lately led me to folk music, the most popular style of the day. Such groups as the Kingston Trio and Peter, Paul, and Mary appealed to young people because of their thoughtful and sometimes political lyrics, not to mention their beautiful vocal harmony. I had become a big fan, which is why, before I went off to college, I traded that hollow-body Gibson for an acoustic, my first and only Martin D28.

At the talent show I played my acoustic guitar and sang "They Call the Wind Mariah," and everyone loved it. Not only did I win first prize, but the audience insisted that I play the song again. I'd been searching for an identity at Otterbein, and that night I found out I was a musician who seemingly could appeal to a universal audience.

One of the other competitors in the talent show was Bob Harmelink, a freshman from Massillon, Ohio, who had a great ear for singing harmony. He performed with a barbershop quartet in the contest, but he remembers my solo performance. He says I put every ounce of my energy and passion into the song—a terrific compliment.

Bob and I didn't get to know each other until the following semester when we were pledges at the same fraternity, Lambda Gamma Epsilon. One of the fraternity's nicknames was "the Monks" because it attracted a large percentage of Otterbein students who were majoring in theology or were otherwise eyeing a life in the ministry. However, the fraternity also prized musicians, which is where I fit in. Today I'd qualify in both categories.

Like most fraternities before and since, Lambda Gamma Epsilon put pledges through a series of tests and rituals, one of which brought Bob and me together with another key person in my life, a sophomore named Nels Gustafson. At one point Nels ordered Bob and me to sing a song to his girlfriend. When we delivered one of the folk songs I knew so well, Nels joined us, singing in a tremendously deep, rich bass voice. Together, we had a special sound. The blend was incredible.

We enjoyed the sound so much that we traveled to Ohio State University and convinced the members of a sorority there to let us serenade them. We stood in the foyer of the large house, with me playing guitar and singing lead, and Bob and Nels contributing terrific harmonies. The sound drew every girl in the house out of her room. They gathered on the stairways and all around us, hanging on our every note. What a great feeling. Experiences like these were beginning to light a fire in my heart for bigger things.

Before long, the three of us—performing as the Monks, appropriately enough—were officially recognized as the Otterbein campus crooners. We weren't getting many paying gigs, although we did perform a few, including a memorable dance for students at the Columbus School for the Blind. Mostly we showed up at parties, campus events, and sororities, singing and strumming just for the fun of it. Nonetheless, the acclaim made an impression. I began to realize that we had something special.

If I hadn't yet decided to devote myself to music as a profession, I was moving in that direction. I even began writing songs for the Monks to perform. One I remember is "The Ballad of Johnny Collins," a Civil War tune of the sort that was popular in the folk scene at the time. It wasn't particularly original, I admit. People say I've been a musical innovator, someone who was always ahead of my time, and I take that as a tremendous compliment. But back then I was basically imitating my heroes while trying to find a style of my own, which is the way all artists develop. You have to follow before you can lead.

My musical education got another boost when I joined the A Cappella Choir, a musical unit associated with Otterbein. The choir specialized in classical music, a form I didn't know much about, and getting into the group was difficult. It was essentially a class, and the director was a taskmaster who required everyone to audition. (After my experience with *The Pajama Game,* I didn't take that process for granted.) The students who tried out for the choir often were music majors already well versed in reading music. As for me, I had raw talent, but I wasn't musically trained by any stretch of the imagination. But Bob and Nels wanted to participate, and I knew that doing so would broaden my musical horizons. So I gave it a try.

Upon passing the audition, I soon learned how valuable it was to be one of the fifty or so members of the ensemble. I greatly improved my ability to read music, picked up innovative ways to harmonize, and discovered new ways of thinking about my own music. The choir also gave me another opportunity to sing, which I loved to do. This was clearly a moment of destiny in my life, as you will see, because there's *no way* I should have been accepted into the choir.

The choir performed at Otterbein and other locations in Ohio, but a trip planned for spring break of my sophomore year would take us to Maryland, Delaware, Pennsylvania, and New York. For me, only one stop on the tour really mattered—New York City.

Greenwich Village was the center of the folk-music universe, and the thought of being able to go there was electrifying. Even better, the schedule had an open weekend night when we would be in the area. That would give Bob, Nels, and me—the Monks—a chance to talk to some coffeehouse owners. *Who knows?* I thought. *We might even get a chance to perform.*

Bob and Nels thought it would be fun to give it a try, but for me this was much more than just a lark. I wanted to be where Bob Dylan and Peter, Paul, and Mary were making history—and maybe make some history of my own. But making history is never easy, and months before the choir left on the spring break tour, I was blindsided by an emergency that threatened to destroy my dreams of performing in Greenwich Village.

APPROACHING DEATH'S DOOR

The trouble started the night before the beginning of Christmas break. To celebrate, I joined some friends at the Dublin Inn in nearby Dublin, Ohio. The next morning I woke up feeling so bad that I knew I had much more than just a hangover. Something seemed to be gnawing at my solar plexus, which only made my heavy-duty indigestion more severe, and I had major cold symptoms. A fever was burning me up, and I suffered the alternating extremes of the chills and the sweats.

I managed to make it back to Yellow Springs, but things went sour very quickly. My temperature kept rising, but the doctor who examined me thought I was suffering from nothing more serious than a bad case of the flu. He sent me home, where my condition deteriorated so quickly that I had to be rushed to the hospital in Springfield.

My memory of all that happened next is a blur. I remember being taken into a cold, sterile room where I was laid on a metal table. When the table was tilted so that I could be x-rayed, everything suddenly got very bright before going completely black. I passed out, and when I awoke I learned why. My appendix had ruptured.

This condition was dangerous under the best circumstances, and these weren't the best circumstances. I didn't have gangrene, but I'd progressed to the point of peritonitis, which made getting my appendix out extremely urgent. To complicate matters, I was on the verge of pneumonia, preventing doctors from giving me a general anesthetic. The situation was critical; I could easily have died.

Obviously, I pulled through, but the recuperative process was a lengthy one. I spent nearly two weeks in the hospital, and for much of that time, I had a tube up my nose and a drain coming out of my side. When I got out, I was told that it would take me much longer to get up to speed, making an immediate return to Otterbein impossible. As a result, I missed all my exams. The health crisis and lengthy recuperation caused so much anxiety that I had a spate of nightmares that remain vivid to this day.

Even worse was the prospect of not going on the A Cappella Choir trip to New York. The choir director was a disciplinarian of the old school: If you didn't meet all the standards, you were out. There was real doubt about whether he'd let someone participate who wasn't currently enrolled at the college, and even if he could be persuaded to overlook that requirement, he would insist that I attend the twice-weekly practices. How on earth could I pull that off in my weakened condition? But looking back, I can see that God was there to help. I believe that what happened next was inspired by His providence, not to mention His perfect plan for my life. He was orchestrating all the events that would inevitably lead me to Him.

I didn't understand any of this at the time, of course. I just knew I needed to find a way to remain in the choir—and I did. As soon as I was able, I began making the drive from Yellow Springs to the Otterbein campus for choir practice on Tuesdays and Thursdays, even though I wasn't enrolled in any classes that semester. My dedication and devotion persuaded the choir director to let me go on the choir trip.

When spring break rolled around, I headed east with the rest of the choir. We performed in numerous churches, often staying with members of the congregation before continuing on to the next location. From all reports, our singing was well received. But to me, the journey was of secondary importance to what I saw as the ultimate destination: Greenwich Village.

FOLK-MUSIC MECCA

The Village was just as alive as I'd pictured it. Musicians were everywhere, and so were venues catering to the folk-music crowd. In this environment there seemed little chance that three boys from Ohio would get permission to play, especially since we had just one night to make it happen. But we had a secret weapon: Nels. At well over six feet tall and possessing a powerful voice, combined with his overwhelming personal confidence and quick-thinking banter, he could talk anyone into anything.

Nels convinced not one, not two, but *three* club managers to give us a shot during intermission between the main shows. And these weren't just any nightspots. One was the Café Wha? a legendary Village venue next-door to the theater, where the first group I would record with, the Au Go-Go Singers, would soon perform an off-Broadway play. Another was the Four Winds, where just a few months later I would meet Steve Stills.

Several fraternity brothers who were also in the A Cappella Choir came to cheer us on. I'm sure we must have been nervous, but that's not what I remember. Instead, what sticks in my mind is the kick I got out of being onstage in such storied places. And everywhere we played, the audiences loved us. We weren't doing anything all that unusual—just playing popular folk songs— and we didn't get paid for the privilege. Not that we cared. We were living the dream, and it didn't have anything to do with money.

After we completed our set at the Four Winds, the manager, John Hopkins, mentioned that our performance impressed him. In turn, we asked if we could perform at the club again if we returned that summer. Hopkins didn't hesitate. He said yes right away.

I couldn't believe this was happening. Only a year earlier I'd been lost, with no real clue about what I was going to do with my life. Now I was beginning to see the road ahead. I had a guaranteed summer gig at a club in Greenwich Village—and a clearer vision about where my life was leading.

I loved Ohio, but from that point on, I only had eyes for New York City.

Big City Lights and Village Nights

From Passing the Hat to a Record Deal

As we walked out of the Four Winds that glorious evening, Bob, Nels, and I could hardly believe what had just happened. If the mere fact that we'd been able to talk our way onto three Greenwich Village stages in a single night didn't confirm how good the Monks were, the applause we received certainly did. From then until the end of our trip with the A Cappella Choir, the topic of returning to New York was never far from our lips.

Of course, John Hopkins wasn't offering us a job in a formal sense. The Four Winds was a pass-the-basket joint, where musicians were paid whatever customers thought they were worth. I figured Bob and Nels were aware of that detail, and if they weren't, I sure wasn't going to tell them! I wanted the three of us to go to New York as a team, and in my mind any obstacles that might stand in the way of that goal—such as money—weren't worth dwelling on.

Today Bob says he honestly thought we would be receiving a salary—not just spare change. Whether he would have chosen not to join us had he known the truth, I don't know. But had he stayed home, he would have missed a wonderful adventure.

After the college choir trip, Bob and Nels returned to Otterbein while I went back to Yellow Springs. Although I hadn't decided to drop out of college, it was clear that I wouldn't be returning until fall semester at the earliest. And since I'd need a bankroll to survive in New York over the summer—and beyond, if I could convince Bob and Nels to stick around—I needed a job.

The employment opportunities in Yellow Springs were limited. Since my mom had all the help she needed at the gift shop, that left Morris Bean and Company, a tire-castings manufacturer. This wasn't my idea of a great time, but I figured I'd only be there for a few months. How bad could it be?

Pretty bad at first. When I started the job, I was introduced to the person I'd be working with on the 3:00 p.m. to 11:00 p.m. swing shift. He was a country boy by the name of Ronnie Sams, and when he walked into the foreman's office, he took one look at me and, without saying a word, immediately turned and walked back out.

Ronnie probably wasn't as tall as I was—he might have been five feet eight. But his stocky, muscular build was perfect for the job, which required lots of heavy lifting. As for me, I typically weighed in at about 125 pounds, but because I'd just gone through a serious illness, I was even skinnier than that. Ronnie undoubtedly figured that having to partner with someone built like me would be worse than doing everything himself, which explains why he cornered the foreman, Bob Doerson, the first chance he got. I remember sitting in a small windowed cubicle, watching the two of them go at it. The foreman must have won the argument because I kept the job. Still, I could tell Ronnie was far from happy.

The next two weeks were among the most awkward of my life. First of all, the work was extremely tough. We made the sand backs—"backs" for short—into which boiling aluminum was poured to make tire castings. Because they literally weighed almost a ton, the backs had to be moved with a hoist, and accidents were a constant threat. Once, my finger was nearly crushed underneath one of the backs. I was able to move it out of the way at the last second, but some of my skin was shaved off, and I had to wrap it in bandages before I could continue. As a guitar player eager to break into the music industry, an injury to a finger could have been catastrophic, since it was on the left hand—the hand I use to play chords.

When we weren't moving backs, we were making them, and that process was exhausting. We called it "digging sand." Ronnie and I would stand at a table that held an enormous ring five to six feet in diameter and two feet deep. We'd then be given a pattern and a mold with smaller fiberglass rings coming out of it. The two of us would fill the main ring with sand and then use a carbon-dioxide process to harden the sand. Next we'd pour hot aluminum into the mold. When it cooled, the resulting slab of metal would be shipped to Akron to make tires.

What bothered me about the job wasn't the work itself, but the atmosphere. Ronnie obviously wasn't happy to be paired with me, so there was very little communication between us. Most days I wound up eating dinner by myself. I now realize that Ron was testing me. He wanted to see if I was going to make it or if I'd simply fold like the scrawny, no-account college boy he thought I was. Whatever the case, I felt horrible. I was only a few months away from leaving for New York, but the departure date seemed to be an eternity away.

Setting your mind to something and following through takes perseverance and character. You may be the only one with a vision for what could become reality. You may have to go it alone. But in the end, what really matters is that you don't give up. Obstacles are guaranteed; success depends on your commitment to seeing your dream become reality. I admit that this is kind of a trial-and-error process. But the Lord has ways of watching over us through it all.

Around the start of my third week at the tire-castings plant, Ronnie began to loosen up and open up. I'm not sure what led to his transformation. Maybe he was pleasantly surprised at how well we wound up working together, since before long we were turning out more backs than the day shift. Or perhaps he simply realized that the differences between a blue-collar type like him and a music-loving kid from Otterbein College weren't as insurmountable as he might have feared. We wound up hanging out together and becoming good friends, and we recently enjoyed a reunion.

Strange as it might seem, I began looking forward to going to work at the plant, which helped the next couple of months pass more quickly. Toward the end of June, when it finally came time for me to leave for New York, Ronnie drove me to the airport in Vandalia (now Dayton International Airport) to catch the flight that would deliver me to my future. When I said good-bye to him, it was truly the end of a chapter in my life.

THREE MONKS IN NEW YORK CITY

I was the first of the Monks to arrive in New York, armed with a book about how to live in the city on five dollars a day. Nels and Bob followed shortly thereafter, and we spent the first few nights with a fraternity brother who lived in Bedford-Stuyvesant, known as Bed-Stuy for short. He was an African American whose church in Brooklyn had hosted Otterbein's A Cappella Choir that spring. His church was a rip-roaring place, which helped make the Monks' show one of our most enjoyable. His neighborhood, however, was a scary place for three white guys from Ohio. When we would walk with him in the area, I remember him saying, "Stay close to me."

From there we wound up at a youth hostel in the Bowery, which was hardly an improvement over Bed-Stuy. The place was essentially a large room filled with cots, which made sleeping difficult, privacy a lost cause, and storage of personal items impossible. As a result, we had to rent a locker at the Port Authority. Whenever we needed to brush our teeth or change our clothes, that's where we had to go.

This situation continued until I heard about an apartment that folk singer Allan Jacobs was going to sublet. He was part of a duo called Bunky and Jake that released a couple of albums on the Mercury label during the sixties, and he was planning to be out of town for a while. The place was on the top floor of a six-story building. There was no elevator, so simply getting to it required a considerable trek, and it was infested with king-size New York cockroaches. Whenever we'd turn on the light after walking home from the Four Winds, the entire floor seemed to be moving. Bob, Nels, and I quickly worked out a strategy to combat the problem. One of us would twist the key in the lock, one would hit the light switch, and the other would lunge into the room with a newspaper, ready to swat anything with more than two legs. It looked like a Three Stooges routine, and most of the cockroaches were in better shape by the end of it than we were!

Not that we were complaining, especially after experiencing Bed-Stuy and the Bowery. We were official Greenwich Village residents, which sounded pretty cool when we talked to the folks back home. The apartment offered easy access to the building's roof, where we spent a lot of our time contemplating the New York skyline, working on our harmonies, and thinking about our purpose in life. It was a great place to beat the heat of a "hot town and summer in the city" as another New York folkie, John Sebastian, would later describe an East Coast summer.[1] We had to be careful up there, dangling our feet over the side, since the roof didn't have a guardrail. In the end, though, the prospect of toppling over the edge to the pavement below was the least of the dangers. Shortly after we moved out, a section of the roof collapsed right over the spot where one of us usually slept. But as far as I know, there were no injuries from the accident—not even to the cockroaches.

John Hopkins let us perform almost on a nightly basis at the Four Winds, and we invariably got a good reception. Most of our set was made up of covers, but on occasion we'd toss in songs I'd written, such as "The Ballad of Johnny Collins" and a newer effort, "Hear Our Song." It was gratifying when audiences responded as favorably to my music as they did to old favorites. Even so, the hours were long. We had to play multiple twenty-minute sets between about 8:00 p.m. and perhaps 2:00 or 3:00 a.m., when the last stragglers would head out. Through the night we'd rotate with three or four other acts.

The Monks and the other acts at the Four Winds were hardly the only show in town. The Village was hopping, particularly on weekends, and there were lots of entertainment options at places like the Café Wha? the Night Owl, and the Bitter End. Bob Dylan, who had helped put the Village on the folk-music map, was gone by that time, but a lot of singer-songwriters followed in his wake, including Tim Hardin, Tim Buckley, Vince Martin, Fred Neil, and Patrick Sky.

To make matters even more challenging for us, the Four Winds was a fairly small venue, with a seating capacity of around thirty people. Even when it was packed, there were never all that many wallets or purses in the vicinity. And when the basket was passed during the week, the payoff could get really slim. One night we walked out with nineteen dollars, which we had to split three ways. The book I brought with me about how to live in New York on five dollars a day definitely came in handy!

To make sure we didn't have too many paydays like that one, we came up with different techniques intended to coax people into putting change or bills into the basket. We'd try to make a lot of eye contact and would often launch into tales of woe about our being college students struggling to make ends meet. Sometimes our pitches, and our performances, would inspire uncommon generosity, but we were never in a position where we had a surplus of cash. I ate a lot of bouillon-cube soup that summer, and when I could afford a slice of pizza, I felt like I was sitting down to a meal at a five-star restaurant.

We were far from the only starving musicians in the Village in those days. Plenty of others were in the same boat. Peter Tork, who would go on to television and pop-music stardom as one of the Monkees, traveled in the same circles we did, and so did Charlie Chin, a banjo player we subsequently used on *Buffalo Springfield Again*. Charlie later contributed to the first album by Cat Mother and the All Night News Boys. The group had a Top 40 hit in 1969 with "Good Old Rock and Roll," from an album that was coproduced by Jimi Hendrix.

Steve Stills was also part of the Greenwich Village folk-music crowd, and he definitely stood out from the pack. He was working at the Four Winds when we got to New York, having arrived there from New Orleans, one of the many places he'd lived. His father was in the import-export business, which gave Steve an opportunity to travel at an early age. He always had intriguing stories to tell about his experiences. Maybe that's why he seemed a little more worldly than we did, despite being about our age. But he wasn't all talk; he had the talent to back up his words. He was blessed with a distinctively gruff voice, and he was a very good guitar player. He played a twelve-string acoustic using finger picks and got a great sound.

A New Type of Folk Group

Around this time a manager named Eddie Miller approached the Monks, and he immediately made an impact. Before I met him, everyone called me Richard. But he called me Richie, and it's been that way ever since.

Eddie was something of an entrepreneur. He had experienced some success as a tunesmith, having co-written a couple of songs for the Serendipity Singers, a folk group out of Boulder, Colorado. He wrote what is arguably their biggest hit, "Don't Let the Rain Come Down." He also co-wrote "After Loving You," which was performed by both Elvis Presley and Bobby Vinton.

Like the New Christy Minstrels, who helped inspire them, the Serendipity Singers were a big folk ensemble with nine members. Given how popular this setup was at the time, Eddie wanted to assemble a combo of his own, using the same big-group model. Starting with the Monks and a larger group called the Bay Singers, he had the raw materials. But even if the two groups were combined, we were still two performers short of nine. Eddie made up the difference by recruiting Steve Stills and Kathy King, Roy Michaels's girlfriend. (Roy was in the Bay Singers and would later join Cat Mother and the All Night News Boys.) That gave Eddie what he saw as a perfect combination: seven male singers, two female singers (Kathy and Jean Gurney of the Bay Singers), three guitarists (me, Steve, and Fred Geiger, who now goes by Rick Geiger), a stand-up bassist (Mike Scott), and Roy on banjo.

Next, Eddie presented us with an idea that would make us different from the other plus-sized folk groups. He envisioned an off-Broadway play that would tell the history of folk music, and he wanted the nine of us to serve as the cast. The venue was to be the Players Theatre, which was next-door to the Café Wha?

This proposal appealed to me largely because Eddie offered to pay each of us about fifty dollars a week for rehearsing. The deal was so good that Bob and Nels, who'd only committed to staying in New York through the summer, decided to skip the fall semester at Otterbein and stick around. From my point of view, it couldn't have worked out any better.

Despite what we saw as a generous salary, we soon came to realize that the budget for the production, titled *America Sings,* was fairly limited. Our costumes came from a discount clothing store and probably looked it. The girls were put in black dresses, while the guys wore black pants, blue-striped oxford shirts, and gold vests.

The nine of us spent the next few weeks learning the songs Eddie had assembled and rehearsing dance steps with a choreographer. Then, as our theatrical debut neared, Eddie rented an open trolley that drove through the streets of the Village with us on board, in full costume, singing for passersby! That was Eddie's way of letting people know the show featured a bunch of fresh-faced youngsters who were having fun.

Unfortunately, these promotions didn't lure enough paying customers to make *America Sings* a legitimate hit. The production ran for only about two weeks, and we were off off-Broadway before we knew it. But by the time the curtain was drawn for the final time, we had another opportunity. Howard Solomon, the manager of two Village hot spots, the Café Au Go-Go and the smaller Café Bizarre, saw the group and got very interested very quickly. I'm not sure what happened behind the scenes, but Eddie Miller was soon out of the picture, and Howard was in charge. He signed on as our manager and let us use the Café Bizarre to rehearse. There we wound up in close proximity to another pair of newcomers who would go on to great things, comics Flip Wilson and Richard Pryor. Howard obviously had a thing for comedians, since we subsequently opened for the late Vaughn Meader, whose impersonations of President John F. Kennedy made him one of the biggest stars in the country.

The First Record Deal

When Howard thought we were ready, he moved us over to the Café Au Go-Go, where we performed as the Au Go-Go Singers. He also began to look for ways to garner us more attention, and luckily he had a lot of connections. In short order, Howard lined up a record contract with Roulette Records, a label started in the fifties that scored quite a few pop and R&B hits over the years, including "The Peppermint Twist" by Joey Dee and the Starlighters.

Roulette's history includes more than just music. The company was headed by Morris Levy, a former nightclub owner with a shady reputation. Two years before his death in 1990, Levy was convicted of extortion and sentenced to a decade in jail.[2] But in 1964 we didn't know anything about Levy's less-than-spotless reputation. Since Howard handled all of our business matters, we met Levy only once. Besides, we were more interested in the opportunity to record an album with the production team of Hugo Peretti and Luigi Creatore. Hugo and Luigi, as they were known, produced an amazing range of artists over the years, among them Sam Cooke, Sarah Vaughan, Etta James, Perry Como, and Elvis Presley. They were also composers, with perhaps their best known credit being "The Lion Sleeps Tonight," a reworking of an African melody that became a smash for the Tokens.

Too bad we had so little interaction with Hugo and Luigi. The two of them rounded up a collection of folk songs for us, including "Where I'm Bound," which I sang, and "High Flying Bird," featuring a vocal by Steve. They also hired professional musicians to perform on the recording, standard practice at the time. Steve may have been the only one of us to actually play guitar on the finished album *They Call Us Au Go-Go Singers*. For their part, Hugo and Luigi mostly stayed in the recording booth during the several days' worth of sessions that led to the finished product.

The album was released in late 1964, featuring a stylized, black-and-white drawing of the nine of us in performance, with Roy and his banjo at the center. (The album was reissued on compact disc in 2000 by Collector's Choice

Music. The reissue came complete with a highlighted announcement added to the original cover artwork boasting the "First Recordings of Stephen Stills and Richie Furay.") Upon listening to the album again, I realize that it definitely was a product of its time. It gave only the barest hint of what Steve and I would go on to create in future years.

Around this period Howard introduced us to another important music figure, Jim Friedman, and Jim wound up having a much more profound impact on me than Hugo, Luigi, and Morris Levy. Jim, who became our musical director, was perhaps best known for working with poet and humorist Shel Silverstein, and he soon proved himself to have a tremendous understanding of music. The nine of us would rehearse at his apartment, gathered around his piano, and Jim would make up terrific arrangements right off the top of his head. He wasn't the best singer in the world, so he would play the vocal parts on the piano to demonstrate what he wanted: "Steve, you sing this. Fred, you sing this. Bob, you sing this…" And when we did, the results were always impressive. Jim was amazing to watch.

With Jim's help we developed a sound that had a jazzier feel than the Serendipity Singers or the New Christy Minstrels and was edgier than what we'd been doing for Eddie Miller. If anything, it was reminiscent of the Modern Folk Quartet, whom we played alongside on a number of occasions. Talk about a talented group of musicians. The quartet included Jerry Yester, Cyrus Faryar, future world-class photographer Henry Diltz, and Chip Douglas, who went on to work with both the Monkees and the Turtles.

As much as I enjoyed the Modern Folk Quartet's style, jazz wasn't really my thing. So even I was surprised by how much I liked the results when we added some of this flavor to our sound. That's how good Jim was; plus, he was just as nice a person. (We'd been out of touch for many years when we reconnected in New York around the time my daughter Jesse was going to school there, and he couldn't have been more gracious. I'm glad I was able to tell him how much he meant to me then, since he passed away not long afterward. Jim was a real father figure to me, musically speaking.)

As we were honing our sound with Jim, Howard shifted into promotional overdrive. Before long he'd arranged for us to travel to Texas in November for a series of one- or two-week runs in Houston, Austin, and Beaumont. The venues we played were far removed from the Four Winds. The one in Beaumont was called the Petroleum Club, and it catered to customers who'd struck it big in the oil business.

We traveled to Texas by train, sleeping upright in our seats as best we could. The farther south we traveled, the more I learned about the racial tensions that wracked the region. Nothing in my past had prepared me for this. Aside from one minor incident years earlier involving my mother's less-than-enthusiastic reaction to my dating a Japanese girl, I was blissfully unaware of racial and ethnic prejudice. After we pulled into New Orleans, I stopped by a rest room at the train station. While I was there, two African Americans watched me warily, and I soon discovered why. I had used a rest room designated for use by "colored" people only.

Enforced divisions between people offended my sensibilities. Our country was founded on the premise that all people are created equal. After becoming a Christian nearly ten years later, I learned that this principle is found in the Bible. Any distinctions that are drawn between people of different nationalities, languages, cultures, or ethnicities are merely human creations. There is nothing inherent in humanity that justifies separating us for any reason.

The Beginning of an End

Before long, divisions began to appear within the Au Go-Go Singers, but I didn't see the warning signs. This should have been a great time for us. Our album had just been released, and while sales weren't astronomical, the first print run of five thousand copies sold out, requiring a second run. And thanks to Jim, we were assembling material for a second album that was far superior to anything we'd done previously. Yet the Texas tour was the beginning of the end for the group.

The reasons for these divisions were complicated and a bit ugly—especially those having to do with certain business matters. Jim, who traveled with us, and Howard got into a dispute over creative matters and money for touring expenses. In the end, there was a huge blowup.

Our association with Howard didn't end there, however, and in January he secured a booking for *On Broadway Tonight*, a nationally broadcast TV show hosted by crooner Rudy Vallee. This TV appearance prompted an article about me in an Ohio newspaper, and it certainly was exciting for everyone in the Au Go-Go Singers. Diahann Carroll was also a guest on the show, which followed a variety format something like *The Ed Sullivan Show*. If only we'd been able to give a real performance. Instead, the music was recorded ahead of time. We were required to lip-synch, with the technicians asking us not to make any noise at all. Live, it wasn't.

Another prestigious show Howard landed for us was more musically gratifying. We played for New York mayor Robert Wagner at his official residence, Gracie Mansion. In addition, we played a few gigs in the Catskills, singing and strumming for nightclub visitors in what is known as the borscht-belt circuit.

Nonetheless, the strain between Howard and Jim was taking its toll, and eventually Howard decided that he was finished with the Au Go-Go Singers. This turn of events didn't seem to be fatal at first, since Jim was our real musical mentor. But his attempts to get us a deal with another label ran afoul of Roulette Records. Morris Levy was not a figure whom people in the industry wanted to cross.

Making things more complicated were the emotional undercurrents that ran through the group. For Kathy King, the stress of touring and performing ultimately became too much. She was stricken with bouts of stage fright that got increasingly worse over the course of our Texas dates, and by the time she returned to New York, it was clear that she was in no shape to continue with the band. Suddenly our soprano and one of the focal points of our live presentation was gone.

Nels and Bob soon followed Kathy out the door due to the untimely arrival of their draft notices. I received my notice too, and while I certainly loved my country, I wasn't eager to join the military. My cousin, Jim Johnston, had just returned from Southeast Asia with a slew of horror stories. Besides, I was determined to do what I could to keep my musical career on track. I wouldn't do anything foolish; I wasn't going to embarrass anyone by breaking the law or running off to Canada. But I was determined to stay focused, though, and that trait has paid off for me again and again.

But no matter how firm my personal resolve, things looked grim. We had lost the support of Howard Solomon, we were unable to perform as the Au Go-Go Singers, and getting a new record contract under another group name was made impossible by the Roulette situation. On top of that, we'd lost a key member (Kathy) and our regular gig, leaving us in disarray and practically destitute.

In fact, we were so short of funds that five of us were staying in a small apartment at 171 Thompson Street, which was largely furnished with items other people had discarded. One day I spotted a chest of drawers and a mattress that had been left curbside on Sullivan Street. I took the mattress first, and as I carried it on my head back to the apartment, I was hoping with each step that the chest would still be there when I got back. I was so happy during the several trips more it took to get the chest and its drawers to the apartment that I don't think I spent a second wondering what may or may not have crawled into the mattress during its time on the pavement. I'd been sleeping on the floor, so I was concerned only with getting some padding beneath me.

Even living in such humble circumstances indicated progress, as far as I was concerned. In less than a year, since arriving in New York with only a few dollars in my pocket and no permanent place to stay, I'd been part of recording an album with a major record company, performed on national television, appeared in an off-Broadway play, and gone on a concert tour halfway across the country. Those accomplishments were more than enough to fuel my optimism.

Nevertheless, I can understand why Bob and Nels saw things differently.

I was much more serious about making music my lifetime pursuit than either of them were. With the Au Go-Go Singers having run their course and the draft board looming, it made perfect sense for them to go back to Otterbein, since being enrolled in college exempted them from the draft. They returned to Otterbein, and they both went on to fine careers. Nels was an executive with Sylvania for many years before retiring, and Bob runs his own cleaning-supply business.

I had other ideas, and despite the draft, college wasn't part of my plan—much to my mom's chagrin. She'd been quite supportive when I announced that I would be spending the summer in New York City, and she stood by my decision to extend the stay after good things started happening. We were working, she knew, and the record album and the TV appearance showed how well things were going. But she always expected that after I got music out of my system, I'd earn a degree and find work in a more reliable profession. When I told her I wouldn't be returning to Otterbein, she made it clear how disappointed she was.

She let me know that by choosing such an unpredictable path, I was running enormous risks. But in spite of the threat of being drafted, or even starving to death, I had no choice but to pursue my passion for music. That's how focused I was. At the time I gave God little thought, but had I known then that He was guiding and protecting me, the hazards that loomed directly ahead would have been much easier to navigate.

4

The Move to L.A.

Meeting Neil Young; Hanging Out with Gram Parsons

I knew it was possible to avoid the draft because Steve Stills, who had also received his draft notice, had managed to stay out of olive drabs without heading to college. We were all on the edges of our seats when Steve went for his army physical, knowing he might be inducted immediately and shipped to parts unknown. We shouldn't have worried, though. Steve was as devoted to a music career as I was, and he came up with a way to convince the army doctors that the military would be better off without him. I don't know exactly what he did, but it must have been an Academy Award–worthy performance.

Steve's success reassured me to some degree, and so did the knowledge that, as an only son in a family without a father, I could make a good argument against being inducted. Yet I was still terrified when I had to report for a physical. And when I was singled out to meet alone with a sergeant, my anxiety only increased. Luckily, my worries proved to be my deliverance.

For some reason, the sergeant asked to see my hands, and when I held them up, they were shaking uncontrollably. On top of that, my fingernails were a bloody mess due to my nervous habit of chewing on them. When I saw how strongly the sergeant reacted to this sight, I played up my apprehension. For one thing, I never made eye contact with him. Instead, I stared out a window, looking dazed.

My acting that day was a lot better than it had been during my audition at Otterbein for *The Pajama Game,* because the sergeant decided I wasn't ready to enter the army. But he let me know that I wasn't out of the woods either. As I left, he said, "We'll see you again in six months," meaning that I'd have to report for another physical.

Between that moment and my next brush with the army, my life was almost constantly in flux. The first challenge involved making a living, and as much as it pained me to admit it, the odds that I could support myself through music seemed to be growing longer. The remaining members of the Au Go-Go Singers couldn't perform together because of the Roulette contract and our falling out with Howard Solomon, whose Café Au Go-Go was part of the group's name. Had Bob and Nels stuck around, the three of us could have gone back to singing and strumming as the Monks, but with them back in Ohio, I was left on my own. I could have hit the folk circuit as a solo performer, but in early 1965 I wasn't ready to go it alone.

I've always felt most comfortable when I'm around other people. Even though my dad was often absent, I grew up with a love of family and community. The small size of Yellow Springs probably had something to do with this. All these years later, I remain close with friends I first got to know in school. Likewise, I've generally had strong relationships with my musical collaborators, and I'm convinced that our regard for one another elevated our music.

In many ways, a band is a family, much like a church congregation. The settings are very different, of course, but working together with a common cause and toward a shared goal is one of life's greatest rewards. In a sense, the lessons I learned as a musician paid dividends years later when I became a pastor.

THE AIRPLANE PLANT

During those chaotic months, my passion for music never diminished, but I had to make a living somehow. Being a starving artist is cool up to a point, but eventually I had to eat. I wanted to stay on the East Coast, and I remembered that my cousin Don Conrad was an executive at Pratt and Whitney, a major aircraft manufacturer, which had a plant in East Hartford, Connecticut. With his help, I was able to land a job there, but I had to exaggerate to get one. During my interview, Don asked if I was looking at Pratt as a genuine career rather than just a stopgap that would keep me going until something musical came along.

"Absolutely," I told him.

Several months earlier I'd started dating Ann Gurney; her sister Jean had sung in the Bay Singers, which had been folded into the Au Go-Go Singers. Ann's parents allowed me to stay with the family at their home in Wilbraham, Massachusetts. I'd usually travel to work in East Hartford from Wilbraham or the nearby community of Monson, Massachusetts, where Ann and I spent a lot of time.

The Gurneys made me feel like one of the family, which I appreciated since I was so far from my own home. During that time I also got to know a local Wilbraham boy named Skip Goodwin, who would figure in my music in future years. He co-wrote three songs with me that were included on *Pickin' Up the Pieces*, the first Poco album: "Tomorrow," "Consequently So Long," and "Calico Lady," which Jim Messina helped on too.

But while I was working at Pratt and Whitney, I had little time for music. (The only link between Pratt and Whitney and music, aside from yours truly, was the on-staff presence of singer Gene Pitney's brother.) At the factory I oversaw a tool crib, which might sound like a simple task, until you give it a try. I had to learn my way around the biggest toolbox you can imagine. The crib contained five or six aisles lined with shelving that stood approximately eight feet high and ran thirty feet in length, and every inch of shelving was crowded with precision tools. A lot of them looked identical, but they differed in minor but consequential ways. When workers from various parts of the factory came to me needing something, such as a specialized type of Allen wrench, I had to quickly find what they needed. I knew that if I gave someone a tool that was off by even a millimeter, he'd be very unhappy when he came back.

As it turned out, I earned a reputation for keeping my customers satisfied. When a fill-in was needed at another crib, I'd often be picked because my superiors knew I would go out of my way to do the best possible job. It also kept a boring job interesting.

While I was working at the plant, I got back to New York and the Village music scene as often as I could. I went on several auditions, including a tryout for a TV show being put together by Fred Weintraub, the owner of the Bitter End. There was also a cattle call to fill an opening with the Chad Mitchell Trio. I came close to getting the gig but lost out to a guy named Henry John Deutschendorf Jr. Shortly thereafter he changed his name to John Denver.

Another group put together around this time might have seemed like a better fit for me. Called the Company, it featured the original members of the Bay Singers—Jean Gurney, Mike Scott, Fred Geiger, and Roy Michaels, plus Steve Stills. The quintet was put together to take advantage of a three-week tour of Canada they'd been offered.

The Bay Singers didn't have a dominant lead vocalist, so it made a lot of sense to include Steve in the group. Jean recalls that I wasn't asked to join because Steve and I were at odds. I don't remember that, but it may have been true, musically speaking. Around that time, Steve was beginning to make a break from the pop-oriented folk music he'd been producing. He had grown fond of the Lovin' Spoonful, a sort of modern jug band that gave folk music a jolt of electricity, and he quickly formed a different group in its image. At one point he invited me down to hear this other project with an eye toward signing me up. But after hearing the new group's sound, I definitely wasn't interested. It was quite possibly the worst thing I'd ever heard—a garage band that shouldn't have been allowed out of the garage. Steve was, and is, an immensely talented guy, but this wasn't his best moment. Given the choice between making that kind of noise or going back to Pratt and Whitney, I decided to stick with Pratt and Whitney. Steve must have felt that way too, because he left that unnamed band and moved on to the Company.

NEW INFLUENCES, MUSICAL AND OTHERWISE

In the end the Company wasn't destined for great things, but it's a footnote in musical history because of its first show. The band was on the same bill as Neil Young and the Squires, and the meeting of Steve and Neil, a Canadian, was a historic moment, since it pushed the formation of Buffalo Springfield that much closer to reality.

After the dates in Canada were completed, Steve decided to move to California, which he felt had a hotter music scene. He was "already gone" (sounds like a good song title) by the time Neil arrived in New York City, having been invited by Mike and Jean to crash at the Thompson Street apartment. I got a chance to meet Neil then, and I was immediately impressed by his music. He played an original tune that turned out to be a future classic: "Nowadays Clancy Can't Even Sing," which is a highlight of the first Buffalo Springfield album. When I met Neil, I liked his song so much that I recorded it using the old Revere reel-to-reel that I'd hijacked from my mom many years earlier. (It's a pity that I lost track of the tape. I'll bet a lot of music collectors would love to hear Neil playing that early rendition of "Clancy.")

This brief brush with Neil occurred around the same time I was getting to know another musician with whom I would continue to cross paths: the late Gram Parsons. He lived across the street from the Thompson Street apartment, and when I would get together with fellow musicians, he'd usually be part of the mix.

Gram had just dropped out of Harvard, where he'd majored in theology, and he was in the midst of working up material that would appear on 1968's *Safe at Home,* an album by his group, the International Submarine Band. He was playing music that would come to be known as country rock, and one of his songs, titled "Brass Buttons," really knocked me out. I remember thinking that it was an incredibly sensitive song to have been written by someone so young. I asked Gram to teach me how to play it, and it stuck with me for many years. When I was in Poco, we included our rendition of "Brass Buttons" on

Crazy Eyes, which came out in 1973. That was the same year Gram's own version appeared on *Grievous Angel,* his last studio album.

It was clear that my own musical sensibilities had a lot in common with what Gram was doing. We became fast, if casual, friends, and if he had been around longer, we might have collaborated professionally. Even in those early days, he lived with reckless abandon, routinely taking risks with his health and his mental well-being that would cost him dearly. He died of an overdose in 1973 at the age of twenty-six, depriving the world of a great musician and robbing his friends and family of his active presence in their lives. Gram is one of the truly tragic figures in popular music history.

Could my legacy have been the same? Easily, had I not avoided many of the same pitfalls into which Gram stumbled. On one occasion, in fact, Gram tempted me to follow his lead. Only my strong sense of personal values and the Lord's mercy prevented me from taking him up on his offer. In the sixties and seventies in particular, drugs of all kinds were everywhere in the music business, and I indulged in them on occasion. At the same time I never became obsessed with doing drugs, and I stayed clear of the hardest of the hard stuff. In retrospect, I think I feared that by going too far I might be jeopardizing essential parts of my character and personality—the qualities that made me who I am. Even in settings where everyone around me was pushing the edge of the envelope, I knew where to draw the line.

My first test took place at Gram's apartment—a considerably nicer space than ours. (Gram's family was very well off; his grandfather, John Snively, owned a huge number of citrus fields in Florida.) He was staying with several musicians associated with the Highwaymen, a longtime folk group that was going through a transition around that time.

One evening when I was the only person at the Thompson Street apartment, Gram called and invited me to a party at his place. I assumed he meant that we'd be drinking the night away, but when I got there, I saw that something far more unexpected was on the menu. Before I quite knew what was happening, Gram had gone to his refrigerator and removed a batch of sugar cubes laced with LSD.

I was naive about hallucinogens. While I was growing up in Yellow Springs, alcohol was the substance of choice, and the same was true at Otterbein. Later there were whispers among some of the Au Go-Go Singers that Steve, and perhaps others in the group, smoked marijuana, but I hadn't witnessed it. I suppose I had heard of LSD, or otherwise I wouldn't have been startled by its presence in Gram's refrigerator, but it certainly wasn't something I'd encountered firsthand.

When Gram put a cube in my hand and said, "We're all going to take these and get high," my heart started pounding—and I'll bet my hands were shaking. Everyone else was eager to swallow this stuff, and in such a peer-pressure situation, even the most self-possessed people will often do things they ultimately regret. All of us have been in situations where we don't want to look bad in front of our friends.

In some ways I'm amazed that I found the strength to say, "Man, I can't do that." But I got the words out, and I remain grateful that I made that choice. In the years that followed, I never once took any hallucinogenic drugs. Who knows how they might have affected me. Perhaps I didn't have the emotional makeup to handle LSD, or maybe I would have survived just fine. Either way, I see my decision to avoid taking acid as another example of the Lord protecting me. His hand of grace was upon my life even at moments like these. He watches over all of us, and some of us respond even when we don't know exactly who God is, while others don't. I fit into one category; Gram fell into the other.

To Gram's credit, he didn't pressure me to change my mind, but he did offer me some marijuana as a substitute. "Here," he said, "smoke this and keep an eye on us. Make sure we don't fall out the window." No one did. It was actually a pretty mellow night, with everyone just sitting around playing music and acting dumb. For my first experience smoking marijuana, it was quite uneventful. Had it been otherwise, I might not be here to tell you about it.

INSPIRED BY THE BYRDS

The other major incident in my life involving Gram was much more positive. I see it as a major turning point, an event that propelled me toward the next stage of my musical development. I had invited Gram to come to the Gurneys' house in Wilbraham for a visit, and he didn't arrive empty-handed. He brought with him an album that changed everything for me.

"You've got to hear this," he said before putting *Mr. Tambourine Man,* the debut album by the Byrds, onto a turntable. In a matter of minutes, I was completely blown away. The LP had great songs on it, among them the title track, one of several compositions by Bob Dylan, plus first-rate material by the Byrds' guitarist-singer Gene Clark and the band's leader, Roger McGuinn. And the sound! McGuinn and Clark, along with Chris Hillman, David Crosby, and Michael Clarke, had come up with a completely original hybrid of folk music and rock and roll that was unlike anything the world had ever heard.

Of course, Gram was just as amazed by *Mr. Tambourine Man* as I was, so it was only appropriate that both of us would eventually have personal connections with members of the band. Gram actually joined the Byrds, contributing to their classic 1968 album *Sweetheart of the Rodeo.* Afterward he and Chris Hillman formed the Flying Burrito Brothers. As for me, I got together with Chris and J. D. Souther years later in the Souther-Hillman-Furay Band.

But as I listened to the Byrds that day, I couldn't have conceived of getting a chance to team up with any of them. Indeed, *Mr. Tambourine Man* inspired a much more down-to-earth reaction. The album was totally cutting edge, and as I sat there absorbing it, I realized that I wanted to get back to making music. No, I *had* to get back to making music. I had a good job, a nice girlfriend, and a comfortable life, but I was unfulfilled. And I was certain that only music could put all the pieces together. I didn't want to copy what the Byrds had done; I wanted to do my own thing, and I was confident that I could come up with music that would be every bit as good.

SEARCHING FOR STEPHEN STILLS

When I started considering various strategies to get back into music, my thoughts naturally drifted toward Steve, who was extremely gifted and just as driven to make music as I was. I couldn't picture him giving up until he achieved his goals, which made him exactly the kind of person I wanted by my side.

There was just one problem: I had no idea how to reach him. Last I'd heard, he was heading to California, which appealed to me as well. Ever since going there on vacation in my early teens, I'd regarded it as a kind of dreamland—warm, beautiful, exciting. But it was also big, and Steve hadn't left an address or a phone number with any of us back on the East Coast. Finding him would be next to impossible.

My only clue to his whereabouts was his dad, William Stills, who Steve had said would always be able to find him. Too bad his dad was also tough to track down. William's most recent address was in San Salvador, El Salvador. I sent him a letter in Central America, asking if he could help me get in touch with Steve, but my letter came back because I hadn't put enough postage on it. How was I to know how many stamps it took to get a letter to El Salvador? The second time around the letter reached Steve's dad, but he didn't know where Steve was. In his reply he gave me an address for Steve's mom, who made her home in San Francisco. So I wrote another letter and hoped for the best. At least she was in the right state—California.

Any number of things could have prevented me from reaching Steve, but in this case, persistence paid off. One day the phone rang, and Steve was on the other end, calling from Los Angeles. He sounded as cocky and confident as ever.

"I've got a band together out here," he said. "All I need is another singer." And the singer he wanted was me. I suppose I should have seen warning signs in this invitation, since Steve's jug-band experiment had given me an earache. But I'm not sure the thought of being stuck in the lousiest jug band imaginable even crossed my mind. It was time to move on, and Steve was inviting me into his world.

MOVING TO THE WEST COAST

I told Don Conrad that I wouldn't be around for the gold-watch anniversary as a Pratt and Whitney employee, which probably didn't come as a big surprise to him. I also had to break the news to Ann. We didn't split up immediately, but over time I found that keeping a long-distance relationship going would prove to be impossible.

After packing up my belongings, I caught a plane that brought me to Los Angeles International Airport, where Steve was to meet me. When I walked out of the terminal, however, I saw plenty of palm trees but no Steve. I waited in the passenger pickup area for several hours, watching unfamiliar cars drive past, but still no Steve. One type of car really caught my eye, though: a Porsche. Watching them go by helped me pass the time while I waited, and before long I fell in love with this sleek sports car.

The car that finally did arrive for me wasn't a Porsche, and it wasn't Steve's, either. Its owner was Dickie Davis, the stage manager at the Trouba-dour, a destined-to-be-famous club in West Hollywood. He and Steve had roomed together for a while, but they weren't bandmates. In fact, Steve admit-ted, the band he'd told me about on the phone consisted of only two people. Him and me.

I was disappointed, of course, but moving to L.A. without having a band to join ended up being only a temporary challenge that turned into the oppor-tunity of a lifetime. As I pursued my musical dream, I was learning a lot about life and how to succeed in it. The important thing in any endeavor is to not give in to discouragement. In music and in life, I lean toward being an opti-mist—and my optimism ensures that I don't stay down for long. Steve had lied to me about having a band, but the two of us would form the foundation of a great one.

5

Becoming the Buffalo Springfield

Two New York Folkies and Three Canadians Create Magic

In some ways, it was good that Steve and I were the only members of the "band." Steve's apartment on Fountain Avenue in West Hollywood was so small that no one else could have stayed there. Steve did have a bedroom, but I had to stay in the outer room—which was every other room in the house except the bathroom.

Given Steve's circumstances, we were lucky to have any kind of roof over our heads. He'd arrived in California in August 1965, and he was still a long way from the big time. The closest he'd come was auditioning to become a member of the Monkees, a group created to star in a TV series. Steve failed to make the cut, but in an odd quirk, Peter Tork, an acquaintance from Greenwich Village, did. Also picked were Davy Jones, Micky Dolenz, and Mike Nesmith, and the four of them became a music and television phenomenon. Imagine how differently Steve's career would have turned out had he been cast as a Monkee. Instead of Crosby, Stills, Nash, and Young, it might have been Jones, Stills, Dolenz, and Nesmith.

When not attending casting calls, Steve was making connections in the L.A. music scene, and somewhere in his travels he'd run across Van Dyke Parks. Van Dyke would subsequently collaborate with Brian Wilson of the Beach Boys on *Smile,* a famous project that wasn't completed until 2004 due to Brian's personal problems. Van Dyke also made interesting solo albums such as *Song Cycle* and *Jump!* (*Jump!* is an adaptation of the Uncle Remus folk tales.) But in 1966 he and Steve were just two more obscure musicians trying to make a name for themselves. They wrote a few tunes together, including "Hello, I've Returned," which we played for a while in Buffalo Springfield; a demo version of the song is on the *Buffalo Springfield Box Set,* released in 2001.

More significant to the future of Buffalo Springfield were two other people Steve had befriended: Dickie Davis and Barry Friedman. Barry (no relation to Jim Friedman) was and is a real character. He currently lives in Canada, where he runs a small recording studio under a truly eccentric name, Frazier Mohawk. His weird pseudonym is appropriate considering his out-landish background. He grew up around the Ringling Brothers Circus—his godfather was the ringmaster. As a teenager he worked on a television series starring Chucko the Clown. Later he created the Mother Goose Menagerie, a touring show that featured fairy tales and live baby animals. Maybe Barry's experience with wildlife is what led him to start working with L.A. musicians!

Barry served a stint as publicist for the Troubadour, which is where he met Dickie. In addition, he was grooming bands under the auspices of Randy Sparks, a former member of the New Christy Minstrels who'd gone on to found another large-scale folk group, the Back Porch Majority. Barry's base of operations was a house on Fountain Avenue not far from Steve's apartment, but a whole lot nicer. It had high ceilings, stained-glass windows, and a huge sunken bathtub that was practically an indoor pool. Around the tub were dec-orative tiles that told the story of Don Quixote. Only in Hollywood.

When the average person first arrives in Hollywood, it's easy to get caught up in the glitter and glamour. Hollywood loves to promote these "values," if you can call them that, and given the images of limos and red carpets that are part of every TV awards show, it's no wonder so many people fantasize about this kind of life. Certainly, we did. But the sad truth is that the glitz is only a facade that disguises a sort of modern Babylon. Years later, after I left Cali-fornia for Colorado, I reflected on this reality in a song called "Seasons of

Change": "Big stars, boulevards, a boardwalk of pawns. Hollywood seemed more nightmare than dream."[1]

Actually, when I first saw Barry's place, I was as impressed as anyone. His property included a small guesthouse, and Barry would let musicians he was working with stay there. The main occupants when I hit town were Mike Brewer and Tom Mastin, who performed as Mastin and Brewer, folk singers whose phrasing was terrific. Barry teamed them with bassist Jim Fielder and Billy Mundi, a drummer who went on to play with an incredible variety of acts from Barry McGuire to Frank Zappa and the Mothers of Invention. Jim would also be part of many different groups, including the Association and, briefly, our band, the Buffalo Springfield. He can be heard on "Everydays," a song written by Steve that's on our second album, *Buffalo Springfield Again*.

SEARCHING FOR A SOUND

Although Mastin and Brewer didn't last long, Mike and Tom inspired Steve and me with their professionalism and great sound. After going their separate ways, they each made a mark. Tom wrote "How Do You Feel," which ended up on the Jefferson Airplane album *Surrealistic Pillow*, while Mike went on to form Brewer and Shipley with another songwriter, Tom Shipley. The two of them had success from the late sixties to the late seventies (their biggest hit was "One Toke Over the Line"), and they released a couple of comeback albums in the nineties.

Obviously, Barry knew talent and good music, and he heard something in both Steve and me. At first I was upset at having been lured to California under false pretenses, and there were plenty of times when I considered leaving. Eventually, though, I calmed down enough to appreciate how good Steve and I sounded together. I could never walk away from that.

Our lack of cash forced us to spend most of our time in Steve's apartment, and the only way to make it tolerable was to play music. From early in the morning until late at night, we devoted ourselves to learning and performing

songs. Some, like "Nowadays Clancy Can't Even Sing," which I'd learned from
Neil Young in New York, were songs from various composers we admired. The
others were original with us. And the more we rehearsed, the tighter our vocals
became.

Fortunately, Steve was writing some great songs, several of which ended
up on the first Buffalo Springfield album. He sold one of them, too, after
Barry put him together with Chuck Kaye from Screen Gems. That tune, "Sit
Down, I Think I Love You," became a hit for the Mojo Men. In another of
those seemingly random events that litter the Springfield's story, Van Dyke
Parks was the arranger on their version.

Not that Steve got rich from the single's success. He received a piece of the
publishing from the Mojo Men cover and also from the rendition we put on
the first Buffalo Springfield album, as did Screen Gems. Yet at the time of the
initial transaction, I think he was paid a grand total of one hundred dollars.

I sold Screen Gems a song as well, titled "Loser." I suppose the real loser
was me, because nothing ever happened with it. But I did make one hundred
dollars. Other songs I wrote around that period, including "Sad Memory" and
"Can't Keep Me Down," had longer lives. Demos of those songs are on the
Buffalo Springfield Box Set as well.

Many of our demos from this period, recorded on my trusty Revere reel-
to-reel, featured just Steve and me singing and playing acoustic guitars. But
the lack of polish and shortage of additional instrumentation doesn't diminish
them in the slightest. The sound of our harmonies was as amazing to me then
as they seem to me now. The contrast between our styles was a big reason our
voices worked so well together. Steve's singing was somewhat gruff, and he had
a really nice feel for phrasing that, in my opinion, had a lot in common with
the work of folk singer Tim Hardin. In contrast, my singing was smoother in
texture. So when the two of us would sing unison songs à la Beatles, it created
a unique sound that expanded the variety of our two-part harmonies.

But once the music stopped, life wasn't always so harmonious. Although
I had more money than Steve—thanks to saving up wages from my job at

Pratt and Whitney—I didn't want to be put in the position of financially supporting him. It may seem cold of me, but when I was desperate for a real meal, I'd sometimes sneak out of the apartment while Steve was still asleep and buy myself breakfast at a nearby Thrifty drugstore on the corner of Fairfax Avenue and Sunset Boulevard. Yeah, yeah, I know what you're thinking.

After a few weeks of making this trek, I had an experience that said a lot about the widening gap between mainstream society and the counterculture and told me what side of the divide I was drifting toward. When I worked at Pratt and Whitney, I'd worn my hair short and conservative, but after I reached Los Angeles, I let it grow out because that was the style among the musicians of the day. Apparently, doing so made me an unacceptable customer in the eyes of the drugstore's management, because one morning I sat down at my usual place at the counter, ready to buy my bacon and eggs, and no one would wait on me. I guess it was their way of letting me know they didn't like my kind—whatever kind that was.

THE L.A. MUSIC SCENE

Los Angeles was filling up with outrageous performers who wanted to take music to new places, and many of them were banding together in groups such as the Doors. Steve and I tried to follow suit, but despite meeting lots of people on the local club scene, we could never find the right match. This led us to begin looking beyond L.A. for collaborators, and naturally Neil was one of the first people who came to mind. Getting in touch with him proved impossible, but we were able to reach Ken Koblun, one of Neil's best friends, in Canada.

As it turned out, I'd met Ken before. When Neil came to New York looking for Steve—the trip when he taught me "Clancy"—Ken was with him. That wasn't unusual; the two of them had been practically inseparable for several years. Ken was a bass player with the Squires, Neil's band in Canada, anchoring the lineup as far back as 1962. When the Squires broke up in 1965,

Ken and Neil remained close, but they went off in different musical directions. While Ken gigged with a popular folk-rock combo called 3's a Crowd, Neil began playing with a group called the Mynah Birds, which featured Bruce Palmer, our future bandmate, and the late Rick James, who went on to become a funk-music star known for such songs as the appropriately named "Super Freak." The combination of Rick James and Neil has got to be one of the weirdest pairings ever, and it didn't last long. After the Mynah Birds signed with Motown Records and cut some songs in early 1966, James was busted for being absent without leave from the U.S. Navy. At loose ends, Neil and Bruce took off together, bound for parts unknown.

Back in Los Angeles, Steve really wanted Neil in the band, but he also decided that Ken would be a worthy addition. Steve wound up using the same tactics on Ken that had worked on me, and he was just as successful. By the time Steve finished talking, Ken had agreed to come to Los Angeles, even though 3's a Crowd was doing quite well. If Steve hadn't made it as a musician, he could have made a nice living selling cars.

Too bad the pitch was better than reality. As was the case with me, Steve made our circumstances sound better than they actually were. For one thing, the apartment on Fountain Avenue was tiny, and Ken was anything but—he was around six feet eight inches tall. Worse, the only place for Ken to sleep was the floor, a cramped space that was not nearly big enough for him.

In a futile attempt to impress Ken, we invited him over to Barry's house. Barry would let us stay there when money was short, which it almost always was. We eventually gave up the Fountain apartment to stay with Barry on an open-ended basis. Ken, meanwhile, must have been wondering when we were going to put together a real band.

Billy Mundi and Jim Fielder made up a competent rhythm section, and Steve and I would jam with them every once in a while. Nonetheless, Barry wanted them to concentrate on Mike and Tom, who he felt were farther along than we were. The problem was that if Barry believed we needed more seasoning before making our debut, how could Ken expect to earn any money?

Convinced that 3's a Crowd was a better bet, Ken decided to head back to Canada. But he didn't tell us. One night, about a week after his arrival, we took him out to Pioneer Chicken on Sunset Boulevard, which specialized in the best cheap chicken in town—not too nutritious, but mmm-mmm good. For us this qualified as a feast, and we hoped it would help persuade Ken to stay. It didn't. The next morning I awakened to find a note from Ken on Barry's coffee table. "Steve, I can't make it," it read.

How Ken managed to leave without me hearing him is still a mystery. I'm a light sleeper, and I wasn't far from where Ken had bedded down for the night. He must have really wanted to get out of there.

Neil Comes to Town

With Ken's departure, Steve and I were back to square one, but a solution was just down the road—literally. Some might say it was a miracle. For sure, it was an example of destiny. I've seen it again and again. Time after time God has put me together with people who turned out to be important to me at exactly the right point and at the ideal time. And the story of how Steve and I found Neil and Bruce is so unreal that it's capable of making a believer out of almost anyone.

Unbeknown to Steve and me, Neil and Bruce had been looking for us and had made their way to Los Angeles as part of their search. They'd been in town for a while, and as they were heading west on Sunset Boulevard toward the 405 freeway, they were just about to give up. We happened to be driving down Sunset at the same moment, heading in the opposite direction in Barry's van.

Now Sunset Boulevard is hardly a country lane. It's a major east-west route that cuts across a big chunk of L.A., and the area known as the Sunset Strip is almost always packed with cars heading to clubs, restaurants, and trendy shops. No one could expect to spot someone driving in the other direction under those conditions, and we probably wouldn't have been able to if it hadn't been for Neil's peculiar taste in automobiles. As we knew, his chosen mode of transportation was a 1953 Pontiac hearse, which stood out even on Sunset, particularly given its Ontario license plates. It certainly hadn't come from the funeral home down the street.

As with any rock-and-roll story this famous, there are many different versions of it. One story holds that I was brushing a fly off my shoulder when I caught sight of the Canadian plates shrinking in the distance behind me, which doesn't have any basis in truth, but it's colorful. Whatever the case, Steve and I recognized the hearse and the strange-looking character behind the wheel, so we immediately executed an illegal U-turn in the middle of heavy traffic. When we pulled up alongside the hearse, shouting to get Neil and Bruce's attention, they began screaming with excitement. We pulled into the parking lot of a Ben Frank's restaurant and had the most unexpected of reunions.

Think of all the coincidences that led to this moment, not to mention the geographic distances that separated the series of coincidences. Steve met Neil in Canada. I met Neil in New York. And we both encountered Neil in Los Angeles on one of the busiest thoroughfares in the world, after Neil's friend, Ken, had been unable to give us a clue as to his whereabouts. Had cell phones been available, things would have been much easier, but we had no such technology to assist us. And had any one of these seemingly random encounters failed to happen, the Buffalo Springfield might never have existed.

By the time we got back to Barry's house, we were well on our way to being a band. If Neil had any doubts about whether he should hook up with us, they were allayed as soon as he heard what we'd done with "Clancy." Our arrangement wasn't fancy. In fact, it was every bit as simple and lovely as it appeared on our first album. By letting the song speak for itself, Steve and I sent Neil a message that we respected his creativity and would do whatever we could to nurture it.

Bruce also turned out to be a good fit. Not only did he have a good rapport with Neil, but he was also an excellent bass player with a unique approach to his instrument that supported the music instead of overwhelming it. This quality was reflective of his personality. When Buffalo Springfield began play-ing live, Bruce never needed to dominate the spotlight. He remained in the background, and because his focus was entirely on the music, he didn't seem to notice or care that others were getting more attention. Bruce's quiet per-sonality made him come across as mysterious, but I never got the sense that he was playing politics. Steve might not like a song of mine or Neil's, but it didn't seem to matter to Bruce. If it was music, he wanted to play it.

Neil was built differently. He may always have looked at the band as his vehicle to a solo career—or this conclusion might have slowly dawned on him. But initially his tendency to think first about what was good for him and then to consider the band as a whole afterward wasn't evident. What came across instead was his extreme confidence and ambition. He knew he was talented, and he wanted to do whatever he could to be recognized for it.

Over the years people have said that Neil was insecure about his singing, which helps explain why the Squires started out doing instrumentals and why I took the lead vocals on some of the songs he wrote for the Buffalo Spring-field's debut album. There's no question that his voice isn't as good in the con-ventional sense as Steve's or mine. Yet I never thought he shouldn't sing. When he sang to me in New York, I was captivated. If his voice was a little idiosyn-cratic, it perfectly conveyed the emotions in his songs, which is what mattered most.

Deep down, I think Neil knew that, and the more we played together, the more the drive to express himself personally and to call all the shots came to the fore. But in the beginning he seemed like someone who wanted to be part of a team, and that was just what we needed. We knew we had the makings of a unique band.

But being confident in our potential as a band didn't put a roof over our heads. The apartment on Fountain was gone, and as supportive as Barry was, he didn't have room for Steve and me plus Neil, Bruce, and Billy Mundi, who'd agreed to drum for us. So we moved to one of the city's least attractive inns, the Hollywood Center Motel, on Sunset just east of Highland Avenue.

The building dates to the 1920s, and it had long since gone into decline. In *L.A. Confidential,* a movie set in the fifties, the filmmakers chose the Hollywood Center Motel as the location where a young actor in a particularly unwholesome relationship is found with his throat slashed. Talk about typecasting. By the time we got there, the motel was even seedier than it's pictured in the film. It was a crash pad for musicians like us who had to pool their cash to rent even the crummiest excuse for shelter.

Although nothing life threatening happened while we were at the Hollywood Center, its sleaziness immediately went to work on my imagination. Billy and I were bunking together—our room had actual bunk beds—and one night I awoke out of a deep sleep, leaped to my feet, ripped the curtains from the window, and screamed, "They're coming to get me!" Billy was scared to death. He probably wished that whoever was after me would hurry up and get there.

As for who was stirring up this anxiety, it wasn't a single person but a whole group of them: the United States Army. Another draft notice had arrived, and I had to get a physical and undergo a reevaluation to determine if I was now fit to be a soldier.

I really didn't know much about the Vietnam War, but it didn't seem to me that it was on par with World War II. Besides, I was eager to get on with music. I got myself high on "black beauties" for about three days and then went off of them. By the time I arrived at the draft board, I was really wiped out. But that's when the real show began.

The personnel there escorted me to a room with just a few other young men in it, and I was given forms to fill out. When I came to the questions about homosexuality, I crossed out the answers several times. A sergeant watching me asked, "Which is it?" I said, "What do you mean?" After I told him I had some girlfriends and some boyfriends, he decided I needed to have an interview with the psychiatric staff.

Next I was told to follow the red line on the floor to reach the proper office. When I told the sergeant I couldn't see a red line (I'm color-blind), he made me wait for another person in the same group of potential enlistees. As soon as that guy put his hand on my shoulder, I knocked it off as dramatically as I could. From there I went to the interview room and finally to the health department, an elevator ride away. On the way up I fell down on a military staff woman. Before long I was told, "Go home." Only then did it hit me: I wasn't going to be drafted.

COMPLETING THE LINEUP

We thought the band was complete, but Billy decided to work on other projects. Losing our drummer could have sent us back to square one, so it's good that Barry was willing to call upon another of his connections. He was friendly with Jim Dickson and Ed Tickner, managers of the Byrds. When he asked if they could recommend a drummer, they suggested Dewey Martin—the person who would complete the picture that became Buffalo Springfield.

Born Walter Milton Dwayne Midkiff, Dewey was another Canadian. This is ironic since Buffalo Springfield is regarded as being such a quintessentially American band. Before coming to our attention, Dewey was playing for the Dillards, a bluegrass-oriented act built around brothers Doug and Rodney Dillard. The group had been kicking around Los Angeles for several years, even making a handful of appearances on *The Andy Griffith Show* in the early 1960s. Fans of the series will remember them as musicians called the Darlings.

Over the years the Dillards went back and forth between old-time and contemporary formats. Around the time Billy left us, the group was moving into one of its traditional periods, and since pure bluegrass doesn't include drums, Dewey was left out in the cold. That made him available, but there was a rub—and it was the same one we'd encountered with Ken. Dewey was accustomed to playing with bands that actually made money, not ones, like ours, that were nearly starving. We figured that talking him into signing up with us would take all of Steve's considerable powers of persuasion.

We were wrong. Dewey heard us and realized right away that our sensibility was close to his. His only demand was that he be allowed to sing every once in a while. "I sing like Otis Redding," he told us, and while no one really sang like Otis Redding, we bought into it. We added the late Wilson Pickett's "In the Midnight Hour" to our repertoire just for Dewey. He was a crazy, entertaining guy, and a terrific addition.

The Buffalo Springfield—Steve, Neil, Bruce, Dewey, and me—was finally together, and from the start the chemistry was incredible. Many years later, when I was working on my own, I tried to assemble a band using the very best musicians I could find, but it didn't add up as I'd hoped. I learned that often what looks good on paper doesn't always translate into good chemistry or great music. With the Springfield, on the other hand, we had a weird mix of Canadians and Americans with different levels of experience, and none of us could be considered virtuosos. Dewey, for example, was a really straightforward drummer with no frills, no bells and whistles. Maybe that's why Steve became enamored with the drumming of Buddy Miles, a flashy player who went on to work with Jimi Hendrix. Buddy played exceptionally well on "Special Care," a Springfield track on the box set and our final studio album, *Last Time Around*. Yet without Dewey keeping the beat, the magic was missing from the song. In later periods with the band, we had to replace members on occasion, and no matter how hard we tried, we could never replicate the chemistry of the original Springfield lineup.

Part of the secret was the way our guitars played off each other. I'm capable of playing lead guitar, as I did a number of times on solo records and on one particular song with Poco. But in the Springfield I concentrated on rhythm guitar. I developed into a melodically oriented supporting player almost by necessity because of the competition between Neil and Steve. Neil must have felt that because he wasn't singing, he had to stand out somehow, and lead guitar was a good way to do it. Steve wasn't going to stand for that, so he played lead too. On the surface this battle for supremacy should have led to disaster, but their playing was so different that it meshed instead of clashed. The result was a sound that no one else had. We were unique. No one sounded like us, and we didn't sound like anyone else.

SEEING A SIGN

With the band finally together, we needed a name. And truth be told, we lifted it from somewhere else—literally. One day a steamroller was resurfacing Fountain Avenue in front of Barry's house. It had a metal plate on the back of it that read "Buffalo Springfield." We took the plate, put it on Barry's mantel-piece, and adopted the words on it as our own. To put it another way, we saw a sign!

I didn't realize at the time how close to home the name was. The Buffalo Springfield Roller Company, which built the steamroller that had inspired us, was headquartered in Springfield, Ohio, only nine miles or so from Yellow Springs. In 2002 the city of Springfield opened its Heritage Center, and one of its main exhibits is a vintage steamroller that had been made nearby.

The company is no longer in existence, but it was still a going concern in 1966. Today it's hard to imagine a corporation that would allow musicians to borrow its name. A band whose members decided one morning to perform as Coca-Cola, for instance, would probably be in court that afternoon. So it's surprising that we not only got away with calling ourselves Buffalo Springfield, but we even received a blessing from the company. Somewhere along the way we received a letter from one of its representatives that basically said, "Cool to see the name going around again. Enjoy it and have fun."

We certainly did. Buffalo Springfield jelled quickly, and in a matter of days, even Barry had to admit that we were now more than ready to make our public debut. He was so positive about our prospects that instead of slotting us into some obscure club on a weeknight, where we could work out the kinks in front of a small audience, he pushed us straight into the big time. Again, he contacted Jim Dickson and Ed Tickner, and after a single warmup show at the Troubadour, we were booked to open for the Byrds for a half-dozen dates around Southern California.

We should have been intimidated going into our first concert at Swing Auditorium in San Bernardino on April 15, 1966. After all, we were not only introducing the Buffalo Springfield to the public, but we were doing so by opening for one of the most popular bands in Los Angeles. For me, the headlining group meant even more than that. The Byrds' example had helped spur me on to leave an unfulfilling job in the East and take a shot at a career in music, and here I was on the same bill with them. I'd not only moved across the country; I was living in an entirely different world. And they were a big reason why.

So why weren't we nervous? And why did we sound so good, so strong, from the first note until the last? Because, I know now, Buffalo Springfield was meant to be.

The great adventure of life is not only how it all will turn out in the end but also what's waiting around the next corner. Just because we never know until we get there doesn't mean that the things in our lives happen randomly or without a reason. I had a dream to make it big in music, but day to day I had no idea where I was headed. People and circumstances would come into my life, things I could never have arranged on my own, and only later did I realize how crucial those things were. Little did I know that everything that was happening—all the events, all the relationships—was being orchestrated by Someone other than me. God had a perfect plan for my life, just as He does for yours, and He was unfolding it one step at a time. Where's life leading you?

6

Visions of Fame and Fortune

How a Fast Start Drifted into the Slow Lane

When it came to the Buffalo Springfield, everything was fast. How could it not be, considering how much we accomplished in just two years? We came together quickly, and within just a few weeks, we went from being totally obscure nobodies to being the toast of the Los Angeles rock-and-roll scene. Not long after that, we were signed to a record deal by one of the most famous record executives the music business has ever known. Those months went by in a blur—but it was one of the most exciting blurs I could have ever imagined.

Once we'd completed our minitour with the Byrds, we needed a place where we could play more regularly. The premier rock venue in L.A. at the time was the Whisky A Go Go, so it was at the top of our list. Unfortunately, every other up-and-coming group in Southern California wanted to gain a foothold at the Whisky too. As the most famous club on the Sunset Strip, it had a well-deserved reputation as a launching pad for talent.

Luckily, we got in with a little help from a new friend: Chris Hillman of the Byrds. He knew the Whisky's crusty owner, Elmer Valentine, and its manager, Mario Maglieri, a former Chicago cop who didn't seem like the type of person who should be running a rock hot spot. But somehow he fit in perfectly. Chris went to bat for us, and because of his good word, we were given an opportunity to audition for Elmer and Mario. That chance was all we needed. We knew we were good enough to pass the test, and we did. Shortly thereafter we were chosen to open a string of gigs for Johnny Rivers.

Rivers put the Whisky on the map. His first album in 1964, *At the Whisky a Go Go,* was a huge hit thanks to his versions of rock classics, including the Chuck Berry songs "Memphis" and "Brown Eyed Handsome Man," and Lloyd Price's "Lawdy Miss Clawdy." He was a Las Vegas–style entertainer who made rock music palatable to a larger audience, not the kind of performer who would come to be associated with the Whisky in later years. Still, he had a terrific career, scoring hits with cover versions of "Maybelline," "Mountain of Love," "Rockin' Pneumonia and the Boogie Woogie Flu," and "Blue Suede Shoes," among many others.

GOOD NIGHTS AT THE WHISKY

Because the Springfield went over well with Rivers's fans, Elmer and Mario extended our run. Before long we were essentially the Whisky house band, playing alongside an incredible variety of groups. One of the most unforgettable was the Doors, whose story is also closely linked to the Whisky. I got along fine with the backbone of the band, keyboardist Ray Manzarek, guitarist Robby Krieger, and drummer John Densmore, and I thought all of them were extremely talented. On a personal level, though, lead singer Jim Morrison was a different story. He was friendly enough, but because his dark side made me uncomfortable, I kept my distance. Down deep, I was still a small-town Ohio boy, and Morrison was too far over the edge for me.

Another excellent band we played alongside was Love, fronted by Arthur Lee and featuring Bryan MacLean, an underrated guitar player and songwriter who became a Christian later in life before he died on Christmas day in 1998. We actually sing a worship song at our church today that's credited to him: "If You Want Love in Your Heart." Love was a huge band in L.A., and they recorded several critically acclaimed albums, including 1967's *Forever Changes.*

But Arthur could be a difficult individual. Years later, during the nineties, he was arrested on an illegal firearms charge and spent several years in jail.[1] Personnel issues and personal problems prevented Love from becoming all it could have been.

If shows that put Love or the Doors alongside Buffalo Springfield seem like a bizarre mix, there were stranger combinations to come. On one occasion we shared the stage with Captain Beefheart, whose blues-hollering leader Don Van Vliet was a pal of Frank Zappa. Obviously, the folks at the Whisky didn't go out of their way to pair up bands that were compatible. Rather, they scheduled groups that were in vogue at the moment. The results could be odd, but more often than not, they were also fascinating.

We didn't let any of the other artists steer us off course. The Buffalo Springfield was creating a sound that was all our own, and it didn't matter to us what other bands were doing. So many groups are pressured into sounding like "so-and-so" to be accepted, but most of them never get beyond the club stage because they're not true to themselves. They're afraid to be original or unique, and when they give in to the pressure to conform to someone else's idea of what they should be or sound like, they lose their identity. In music, just as in the rest of life, it's a mistake to follow the crowd simply for the sake of following the crowd. It may be going somewhere you don't want to go.

Living according to this truth early in life helped me later on when I became a Christian. As a follower of Christ, I realized that I was different— not necessarily on the outside, but on the inside, where the real change had taken place. In order to resist outside pressure that would compromise my life of faith, I had to be confident of who I was in the Lord and not worry what others thought about me. Since I had always been comfortable just being myself, getting to know God only reinforced this characteristic in my life. The longer I follow Him, the more I realize that I have nothing to prove and nothing to lose. The only One I have to please is Jesus.

The audiences that came to the Whisky A Go Go were just as eclectic as the bands. Fans of electrified folk music, of the type popularized by the Byrds, would wind up elbow to elbow with crazily costumed dancers from the Zappa crowd. At times it felt as if we were inside a cuckoo clock. But no matter who was there, how they were dressed, where they'd come from, or where they were going, all of them went wild for what we were doing—and they spread the word about us. The crowds kept growing, to the point where there'd be lines down the block and around the corner whenever we were slated to perform.

Those who got inside heard Buffalo Springfield at its peak. I don't think we ever sounded better than we did during those first weeks at the Whisky. Why? For one thing, we had first-rate material. Our sets usually consisted of the tracks that would end up on our first album, all of which were strong. The songs were as unique as they were fresh, and everyone knew it.

Just as important, we were completely unified, despite being five very different people. Without even thinking about it, we developed an effective stage dynamic, with Steve and me up front and Neil behind us generating all sorts of commotion on his guitar. Bruce would turn his back to the audience so he could concentrate on his bass lines, and Dewey laid down a driving rhythmic foundation that allowed everything else to happen. Back then no one was thinking about playing with other musicians or why another writer's song was released as a single instead of his. At least I thought so at the time. It seemed as though we were a team, pure and simple, and we performed like one.

If you've ever been part of such a tight-knit team—in music or sports or any other endeavor—you know the power that is generated by that type of unity. You have to be a group player in those situations, and by understanding your strengths and weaknesses, the whole becomes stronger than the separate parts. The minute that bond starts to fail, though, everything begins to unravel, and before you know what's happening, you're beyond the point of rescue. Sadly, the dynamic in the Springfield would soon change, but at the moment we were producing original music with a power that few other bands could match.

Our sound was enhanced by the club's acoustics, which were exceptional. When we recorded our first batch of material, we did so in a fairly sterile studio environment. At the Whisky, on the other hand, we were in front of several hundred people whose energy was contagious. Even when Arthur Lee was nowhere to be found, there was a lot of love in that room, with more to come. Enough love to last my entire life, in fact, because that's where I met the love of my life, Nancy, my wife of thirty-nine years.

THE BLOND GIRL IN THE CROWD

Nancy Jennings wasn't a typical music fan. The way she tells it, she wasn't really a music fan at all. She grew up in the San Fernando Valley and was raised by her mother, a financial manager at Pacoima Junior High School—Ritchie Valens's alma mater. Nancy's mom provided for the two of them, since her husband died when Nancy was just seven. Years later, as a student at Granada Hills High School (the alma mater of Colorado's most famous athlete, John Elway), Nancy never felt the need to buy the latest record or to go see the groups that had all the kids talking. She'd watch *American Bandstand,* but that was about it. One of her favorite TV shows of recent years was *American Dreams,* which used *Bandstand* as a centerpiece.

So how did she wind up at the Whisky during a Buffalo Springfield show? As the old saying goes, the Lord works in mysterious ways. And thank goodness He does, because His decision to bring Nancy and me together has been the true blessing of my life.

Our meeting was literally years in the making. During a trip to the beach, Nancy had met Bill Rinehart, a surfer who would go on to become a member of the Leaves, another L.A. band from the period. The group had its biggest success with a cover of "Hey Joe" that predated Jimi Hendrix's. Nancy and Bill were an item for a couple of years before breaking up. That was fine by Nancy, but Bill wanted a reunion, and in an attempt to make one happen, he invited her to come see the Leaves play the Whisky with an outstanding new band— Buffalo Springfield.

Talk about a plan that backfired. Nancy came to the club with a friend,

Pam Swaton, but she had no interest in Bill after she saw me onstage with the Springfield. Our eyes probably met, but I can't say for sure because I never wore my glasses onstage. Picking out specific faces in the audience over banks of stage lighting was difficult.

Nancy returned to the Whisky many times with another friend, also named Nancy, and they resembled each other: blond hair, similar height. By then we had seen each other in passing. But since it was never easy to pick her out from a distance, Nancy still jokes that when I thought I was singing "Sit Down, I Think I Love You" to her, I couldn't be sure which Nancy was really in my field of vision. I tell her that at least I chose the right one to marry!

Although the magic was there from the start, there was a complication. Not only was I still officially involved with Ann Gurney, but she had traveled to L.A. to spend time with me. If I wasn't convinced already that my relationship with Ann wouldn't last much longer, seeing Nancy sent me a very clear message. Even so, I wanted to do all I could to avoid hurting Ann, a wonderful person. I was torn between my past and my future.

Then one night as I was driving away from the Whisky with Dewey, I saw my future standing on the corner and couldn't hold my tongue any longer.

"What's your name?" I asked.

"Nancy Jennings," she answered back.

"I'll see you tomorrow night," I said.

I was wrong. Unbeknown to me, Nancy and her friend Pam had tickets to fly to Hawaii the next day. It wasn't just a vacation, either. They were planning to live in Hawaii, maybe for good. Worse, I had no way of getting in touch with her.

Our relationship might have ended before it even got underway if Pam hadn't gotten homesick three months later and decided to head back to the mainland. Not long after she returned to Los Angeles, she began dating Dickie Davis. Dickie and I were sharing a small apartment on Formosa Avenue near Fountain. By then, Ann and I had gone our separate ways, and I told Dickie that I would love to see Nancy. He told Pam, who called Nancy in Hawaii. Nancy responded by catching the first plane she could to L.A.

What happened next was more like a situation comedy than a romance. Nancy was met at the airport by her mother, her grandmother, and her aunt, but rather than heading to her home in the valley, she took her loved ones with her to the Whisky because she thought I was going to meet her there. Too bad the message never reached me, because she wound up bringing her family to one of the wildest night spots in the country, and I was nowhere to be found! We caught up with each other the next day, and almost before we knew it, we were a couple.

I really believe it's true: God has the perfect match for each of us. If we're patient and wait for God to bring the right person into our lives, we will be blessed by His love. That's what happened for Nancy and me, though we were not believers at the time. God's providential grace was working behind the scenes. Nancy was that special one, and I wasn't going to let her get away.

THE BUSINESS OF MUSIC

While I was romancing Nancy, the members of the Springfield, me included, were being sweet-talked by every wannabe band manager and record-label talent scout in the business. All the industry pros who saw us knew we were bound for bigger things, and they wanted to get a piece of the action. We were constantly meeting people who told us how terrific we were, and every one of them insisted that only he or she could make us into the giant celebrities we deserved to be.

That we bothered to listen to these pitches may seem peculiar, since we already had a manager: Barry Friedman. In a lot of ways, he was the reason we'd gotten to the point we had. He supported Steve and me when no one else in the music business would have lifted a finger on our behalf, even letting us stay at his place. And he'd been the one to hook us up with the Byrds' managers, Jim Dickson and Ed Tickner, who not only put us in touch with Dewey but also allowed us to open for their most famous clients. The Byrds connection, which led to our success at the Whisky, would never have been made without Barry.

Then again, Barry wasn't a powerful mover and shaker at that point. He knew people who were capable of making big things happen, but he couldn't do it on his own. He operated on a grass-roots level, not the upper echelon of entertainment. We were ambitious, and it was clear even to novices like us that loyalty was rare in the music business. So when high rollers began talking, we listened.

The frenzy was overwhelming. We received not just one or two offers of a record deal but well over a dozen—including several from some of the most powerful people in Los Angeles music. Dunhill Records, run by Lou Adler and featuring such acts as the Mamas and the Papas, waved some cash around, and so did Elektra Records, which subsequently signed the Doors. The buzz about us was almost deafening.

We desperately needed some guidance, and Charlie Greene and Brian Stone were eager to provide it. Looking back on it today, embracing what they had to say could have been the worst decision we made. According to legend, Charlie and Brian launched themselves as talent managers by sneaking onto the lot at Universal Studios, finding a vacant office, and using it as a base of operations until they were discovered and ejected. Years later a young Steven Spielberg pulled the same stunt, and look how things turned out for him.

By the time we came along, Charlie and Brian were proven star makers, having turned a young singer named Cherilyn Sarkisian and record-promo man Salvatore Philip Bono into the ultra-popular act Sonny and Cher. In person, Charlie and Brian made quite a one-two combination. Charlie was the more casual of the pair, favoring hip clothes and a mod hairstyle sort of like the one Sonny wore. A master at glad-handing, he would come on strong in person, trying to convince anyone and everyone that he had their best interests at heart. Brian, in contrast, was the quintessential businessman, the brains of the operation who kept his eye on the bottom line. He'd stand in the background, watching as Charlie put on the hard sell.

In retrospect, I suppose we should have been wary of this fast talker and his quiet sidekick, especially since Sonny and Cher found other representation shortly after we signed on. But we were easily impressed, and Charlie and Brian had a fancy office and a huge limousine—just the kinds of things that would turn our heads. Certainly, nothing I experienced with the Au Go-Go Singers had prepared me for the whirlwind that Buffalo Springfield would stir up.

For these and many other reasons, we decided to cast our lot with Charlie and Brian, who quickly bought out Barry's interest in the band. From that point forward they were in charge of our careers, for better or worse. Before the band folded, we would live through both of these extremes—the better and the worse, and in that order.

Whatever could be said about Charlie and Brian, they had the ear of a major record-company executive, Ahmet Ertegun, the head of Atlantic Records and its sister label, Atco. A native of Turkey, Ertegun cofounded Atlantic in 1947, and in the years afterward, the company put out some of the best R&B and jazz albums ever made by artists such as Ray Charles and John Coltrane. Ertegun was already a legend, and his stature would only grow in the coming years. In 1995, a couple of years before Buffalo Springfield was inducted into the Rock and Roll Hall of Fame, the hall's directors named the museum's main exhibition area after him.

Ahmet was looking to beef up Atlantic's rock roster. That same year he signed Cream, featuring Eric Clapton, Jack Bruce, and Ginger Baker. Earlier he'd put Sonny and Cher under contract with Atco, and because that deal had worked out so well, he had faith in Charlie and Brian. Ahmet realized the potential of the Buffalo Springfield, and he put an offer on the table right away.

The rate at which all this took place left me breathless. It hadn't been all that long since I'd been working in the tool crib at Pratt and Whitney, and the Springfield had been together for just over six weeks when we were being offered a major record deal. We started playing the Whisky in May, and in June, Ahmet presented us with a contract that included an advance higher than any the other companies had offered. The sum was puny by today's standards—it was in the low five figures—and after Charlie and Brian took their cut, we had to split what was left five ways. In those days, however, it struck me as a huge amount, especially considering how recently the idea of breakfast at a drugstore had seemed like an incredible luxury.

Beyond that, I was extremely impressed with Ahmet. He was very cool, very smart, and a very snappy dresser, and his track record spoke for itself. With him in our corner, I saw us moving a step closer to all of our goals. Pretty soon, I could imagine us being as popular as the Byrds, and after that, the Beatles had better start looking over their shoulders. Deep down, I felt we were every bit as talented as these groups, and if anyone was able to help us prove that to the world, it was Ahmet. Everyone else in the band felt the same way. When the Atco contract was put in front of us, we happily signed it.

INTO THE STUDIO

Ahmet and Atco didn't wait long to get us into a studio to start recording our first album. Sessions were set up at Gold Star, which was *the* L.A. studio at the time. Producer Phil Spector used Gold Star as his base of operations, creating the style that came to be known as the Wall of Sound.

We didn't have anyone nearly as accomplished as Spector overseeing our recording. Officially, our producers were Charlie and Brian, and their musical and recording credentials wouldn't have impressed many people. They received co-writing credits on some Sonny Bono material from 1965, and in the years that followed, they supposedly produced albums by groups they managed, such as the Springfield and, several years later, Iron Butterfly.

Whether they actually did much producing is another question. They'd talk to us between takes, complimenting us on this or that. Yet they had little real input on the arrangements or instrumentation, which we'd worked out during our shows at the Whisky. And since the material was ready in advance, they didn't have much say about that, either. They mainly hung out in the control room with our engineer, Doc Siegel, who was doing the real work. Doc was a great guy, and he knew his way around a mixing board better than Charlie or Brian ever would.

Richie's parents,
Naomi and Paul Charles
Furay. Richie's dad
died in 1957 at age
forty-five.

Richie at ten months.

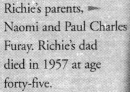

Richie as a fourth grader, 1953.

Richie in 1962 as a senior at Bryan
High School in Yellow Springs, Ohio.

The second Furay
home on Xenia
Avenue, about a mile
from Furay's Gift Shop
in Yellow Springs.

Richie, age eight, with his first guitar—a Gibson ES295.

Ron Sams, the co-worker who gave Richie a ride to the airport so he could fly to New York to launch his music career.

Richie's first regularly paying New York gig, a production called *America Sings*, lasted two weeks at the Players Theatre.

During an East Coast tour with his college choir, Richie and two friends performed during intermission at Café Wha? and other Greenwich Village folk clubs.

The Au Go-Go Singers, from left: Fred "Rick" Geiger (partially hidden), Roy Michaels, Jean Gurney, Bob Harmelink, Richie, Nels Gustafson, Stephen Stills, and Kathy King (partially hidden). Mike Scott is not visible in this photo.

The Buffalo Springfield, from left: Richie, Stephen Stills (standing), Neil Young, Bruce Palmer, and Dewey Martin.

Richie, Neil Young, Stephen Stills, and Dewey Martin (from left) gathered in 1988 to rehearse Buffalo Springfield songs. Sadly, the band's reunion never materialized.

A retired road-building tractor similar to the one that inspired the name of a Hall of Fame rock band, the Buffalo Springfield.

Photo © 2006 Henry Diltz

▲ The Souther-Hillman-Furay Band, from left: Jim Gordon, Al Perkins, J. D. Souther, Chris Hillman, Richie, and Paul Harris.

Photo © 2006 Henry Diltz

◄ Chris Hillman joins Poco in the studio. From left: Hillman, Timothy B. Schmit, George Grantham, and Richie.

Poco (from left): ◄ Paul Cotton, Timothy B. Schmit, George Grantham, Richie, and Rusty Young.

Photo © 2006 Jim Marshall

Nancy and Richie, soon after they met in L.A. in 1968.

Nancy and Richie today, married thirty-nine years.

Nancy and Richie with Jim Messina and Michaela Laza, Jim's girlfriend.

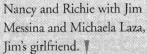

Dave Aragon, Timothy B. Schmit, Timmie Aragon (Richie's daughter), Nancy Furay, Katie Rodriguez (Richie's daughter), and Richie.

◄ Richie and Nancy with Cathe and Greg Laurie.

▲ Richie at a Dallas fund-raiser hosted by Chef Dean Fearing (fifth from left) of the Mansion on Turtle Creek. Standing next to Richie is Wynonna Judd, the event's other musical guest.

▲ Richie performing with Scott Sellen, his current musical collaborator.

From left:
Aaron Sellen,
Parker Lily
Rodriguez (Richie's
granddaughter),
Richie, Kendall Jayn
Aragon (Richie's
granddaughter),
Scott Sellen, and
Alan Lemke.

Richie's sister, Judy, and her
husband, Tony Hugli.

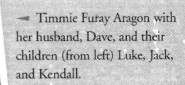
Timmie Furay Aragon with
her husband, Dave, and their
children (from left) Luke, Jack,
and Kendall.

Katie Furay Rodriguez with
her husband, Vincent, and
their daughter, Parker Lily.

Naomi Furay (Richie's mom).

Polly Furay (Richie's daughter).

The Furay girls, from left: Polly, Katie, Timmie, Nancy (Richie's wife), and Jesse.

Jesse Furay Lynch with her husband, Tom.

Because we were novices at recording, we weren't able to match the sound we got onstage. But we worked hard in the studio, with the recording sessions stretching over a couple of months. Neil was never really satisfied with the finished item; that's why he did so much remixing and remastering of our first album for the *Buffalo Springfield Box Set*. Nonetheless, the recording has inspired generations of musicians, and that kind of influence speaks for itself.

The songs by Steve and Neil that we put on the album are a big reason for its longevity. Steve wrote "Sit Down, I Think I Love You" and "Go and Say Goodbye," a number that had a country rock flavor before there was such a thing as country rock. I liked the song so much that I rerecorded it for Poco's *A Good Feelin' to Know* album. Also included were five other impressive compositions from Steve: "Hot Dusty Roads," "Everybody's Wrong," "Leave," "Pay the Price," and "Baby Don't Scold Me." Neil wasn't quite as prolific, but there's no arguing with the quality of his five songs. "Clancy" set a very high mark that was nearly matched by "Flying on the Ground Is Wrong," "Burned," "Do I Have to Come Right Out and Say It," and "Out of My Mind." No wonder the album is considered a classic.

The process of getting these tunes down on tape didn't generate as much tension as future trips to the studio would. Down the line, Steve and Neil, in particular, brought in other people when they were recording. Steve always wanted to jam with the latest instrumental sensation, while Neil was eager to collaborate with Jack Nitzsche, who'd scored an early sixties hit with a song called "The Lonely Surfer" before branching out into experiments with orchestration. But our first album was mainly made with just the five of us. We were still a close-knit unit then. All for one and one for all.

At Gold Star we'd set up in one little room and play live to produce backing tracks, adding the vocals later. Overdubbing was kept to a minimum, partly because the technology was so limited. That first recording was made on a 4-track, a far cry from the 24-track and 48-track setups that would become commonplace in the not-too-distant future. But recording live in the studio wasn't a problem since we were so tight as a band. The rhythm section of Dewey and Bruce had really locked in, Neil's lead playing was getting more distinctive, I'd developed into a good rhythm guitar player, and Steve's soloing was coming into its own.

Just as important, the ego trips that would flare up later weren't yet out of control. An example is how willing everyone was to let me sing or share the lead vocal on songs I didn't write. I think everyone in the group thought my biggest asset was my voice. I could always harmonize well, but I'd developed into a much more dynamic performer than I'd been with the Au Go-Go Singers. That made the unison songs that paired me with Steve even stronger, and it helped increase the accessibility of several that Neil had written: "Clancy," "Flying on the Ground Is Wrong," and "Do I Have to Come Right Out and Say It," three of the songs on which I sang lead. (Today, in my live performances, I put these songs in a medley that I sing as a tribute to Neil.) Taking the lead on Neil's songs worked well within the whole scheme of the band when we were just starting out, and I accepted the opportunity as graciously and gracefully as I could.

Neil would eventually want to sing all of his own songs, but at this stage, he seemed perfectly fine with having me do it. He didn't object, anyway, and he hadn't started disappearing, which is how he would demonstrate his unhappiness in future months. In the meantime, his silence gave us the feeling that he agreed with the direction we were heading.

There wasn't much tension between Neil and Steve at that point. No one had any doubt that Buffalo Springfield was Steve's band, and the programming of the songs on the album reflected that. More of his songs than Neil's were included, and Steve's were more prominently placed. Reflecting that, we picked one of Steve's songs, "Go and Say Goodbye," as the first single, with Neil's song "Clancy" as the B-side. In due time this order was flipped, with "Clancy" being declared the "plug side," as people in the radio business used to say, but that wasn't because Neil insisted on it. The move was made by Ahmet, who thought "Clancy" had the best chance of becoming a smash.

Ahmet has been right about many, many things in his career, but not about "Clancy," which never broke into the Top 100 on the nation's sales charts. When it ran out of gas, I was mystified. We were so popular and so acclaimed in Los Angeles that I assumed any of our songs would be embraced. "Clancy" wasn't, yet tunes from bands no one had ever heard of—such as "Black Is Black," by a Spanish group called Los Bravos—were all over the radio dial.

Looking back I realize that "Clancy" was the wrong choice for a single to introduce us to a wider audience. Sure, it was a striking song that gave listeners an indication of Neil's enormous abilities, but it was a bit too esoteric coming from a new group. Another of Neil's songs, "Do I Have to Come Right Out and Say It," covered more bases from a commercial standpoint, both lyrically and musically. It was a love song, it was a ballad, and it was very simple, with an easily understandable sentiment and a very nice melody.

The weak response to "Clancy" led to some of the first serious friction in the band. Steve had never wanted it to be the single, and he started arguing even harder that his songs should be given greater prominence—something that couldn't help but rub someone as ambitious as Neil the wrong way. These arguments led to distrust and competition, with Steve and Neil keeping track of who sang what, who played the most leads, and so on. Petty disagreements like these were bound to lead to trouble—and they did.

Regardless of these setbacks, the early months after signing with Atco were filled with glorious moments. For instance, Charlie and Brian got us on the bill to open for the Rolling Stones at the Hollywood Bowl toward the end of July. We hadn't even finished our first album by then, so the opportunity to play for nearly twenty thousand people in support of one of the most popular bands in the world was nothing short of amazing.

A more telling concert, though, may have been an early September appearance at the Melodyland Theater in Anaheim, where we played with Chad and Jeremy, a folk-pop duo who had hits with "Yesterday's Gone" and "Willow, Weep for Me." We were the ones who should have been weeping, because Bruce was arrested that night for marijuana possession and taken away by police. This foreshadowed Bruce's problems with the authorities that would crop up during the next year, but his problems were usually due to his immigration status, not drugs. In Bruce's absence, Jim Fielder, our buddy from Mastin and Brewer, filled in on bass.

Then, as if things weren't crazy enough already, Neil suffered an epileptic seizure in the middle of our set. He was stricken by such attacks so frequently during subsequent shows that they became almost routine. He'd never fall with his guitar but would hand it to me right before he collapsed. And because our guitars were grounded differently, I'd always get a terrible jolt. The same sort of thing would happen with Steve and me. When we'd play stuffy little clubs, we'd work up such a sweat that drops of moisture would drip down our noses as we'd sing into the same microphone. If we happened to touch each other—*zap!* I came to hate that shocking feeling so much that today I won't even test a nine-volt battery on my tongue to see if it's still good.

Aside from the unwelcome shocks, though, most of my memories of this period are phenomenal. Our rise was as electrifying as any jolt from Neil's guitar, and none of us thought we'd ever come back down to earth. We did, of course, but not before creating a song that would come to define the era.

7

"Stop, Children, What's That Sound?"

An Unexpected Single Breaks Big

When our first album, *Buffalo Springfield,* was released in October 1966, we had stratospheric hopes that very quickly settled back to earth. "Clancy" hadn't been well received, and our follow-up single, with Neil's "Burned" on the A-side, hardly caused a ripple. The title of the song that was paired with "Burned"—"Everybody's Wrong," written by Steve—definitely reflected how we felt. We knew we were a lot better group than our sales tallies or airplay indicated. That left us with the challenge of convincing the music lovers of the world that they were missing something special.

Our reputation didn't precede us much beyond the L.A. music scene, and even after signing with Atco, money was tight. During much of the time that we were playing regularly at the Whisky, I didn't have a car. On those occasions when I couldn't catch a ride back to the apartment I was sharing with Dickie, I'd have to walk—a distance of two miles. I may have seemed like a rock star when I was onstage, but I was probably more strapped for cash than most people in the audience.

The Sunset Strip had become a mecca for growing legions of hippies, and as they descended on the area, tensions escalated between them and members of the older generation. I usually avoided the Strip for this very reason. I wanted to keep a low profile and not get caught up in a bad scene. But while walking down Fountain Boulevard early in the morning on my way home from the Whisky, a couple of officers from the Los Angeles County Sheriff's Department stopped me. Why, I don't know. Maybe an alarm had gone off in the vicinity. More likely they suspected I was guilty of something simply because of my appearance, even though I was hardly the most outrageous-looking person out that night.

At any rate, one of the officers said, "Let me see your driver's license."

Without thinking, I replied flippantly, "I'm not driving."

That wasn't the right thing to say. With a very intimidating tone, the officer said, "If I didn't want to see your driver's license, I wouldn't have asked for it. Now let me see your license before I knock you on your _____." (You can fill in the blank.) I knew I'd better comply, and fast, or I'd get to know the officer's night stick up close and personal. My license was in my hand and on the way to his in the time it takes to blink.

This incident was a real eyeopener for me. I'd never crossed the law beyond indulging in the occasional illicit substance in the privacy of someone's apartment. And even after moving to Los Angeles, I was something of a homebody. When we weren't performing, I generally avoided the bright lights of the Strip in favor of playing music with my friends. If anyone should have been immune to harassment by the sheriff's deputies, it was me. This unprovoked run-in with the law came to mind later when events on the Strip served as inspiration for Buffalo Springfield's best-known song.

LIVING WITH A TURTLE

The Springfield played a couple of early October dates with the Turtles at a Redondo Beach club named the Third I. At those shows I got to hang around with Mark Volman, who shared frontman duties for the Turtles with Howard Kaylan. I must have mentioned to Mark that my living situation wasn't ideal. He was living in a house that had plenty of room, and he invited me to move in, even though I hardly knew him. I accepted right away, and we became good friends.

Mark's place was on Lookout Mountain Avenue, just off Laurel Canyon Boulevard in the hills that separate Los Angeles from the San Fernando Valley. I enjoyed spending time with Mark, a gregarious and energetic person whom I bonded with right away—in spite of our contrasting musical sensibilities. After moving on from the Turtles, Mark and Howard became part of Frank Zappa's traveling circus, performing under the names Phlorescent Leech and Eddie, later shortened to Flo and Eddie. The music they made in the seventies had practically nothing in common with mine. Even so, I could easily recognize and admire Mark's gifts. I remember the day he came home after the Turtles had just finished recording a song called "Happy Together." We smoked up a storm as Mark played the song at "10" on his state-of-the-art sound system, and we both agreed that it was bound to be a number-one smash. In this case, the stuff we were smoking didn't impair our judgment too badly. "Happy Together," which was released in early 1967, topped the Billboard singles chart for three weeks and remains a staple of rock-oldies radio.

This achievement and others like it undoubtedly impressed the students Mark taught years later at Loyola Marymount University in L.A., where he served as a music professor before moving to Nashville in 2004. His class attracted a lot of interesting pupils, including a young woman who was writing a paper about me. The student was Catherine Hillman, Chris Hillman's daughter. This coincidence helped me and Chris reconnect after having lost touch and reminded me again how glad I am to have Mark as a friend.

I have to admit, though, that the best thing about living on Lookout Mountain Avenue was one of my neighbors: Nancy. She and her friend Pam had moved into a basement apartment on Laurel Pass Avenue, only a couple of blocks from Mark's house. The walk to her door was a lot shorter than the one from the Whisky to Dickie's apartment—and even if it had been longer, I wouldn't have minded one bit.

Living in the basement apartment was Nancy's next step toward independence. She'd lived at home even after enrolling at San Fernando Valley State College, now known as California State University, Northridge. After a year and a half of study, she decided that college wasn't for her, and by late 1966 she was working at a dress shop on La Cienega Boulevard known as the Hole in the Wall. She supplemented her income with modeling assignments, and when she found the apartment on Laurel Pass, she decided to move in. The place came with bare pipes along the ceiling that doubled as clotheslines, and there was no extra charge for the noise provided by the Hard Times, a band whose members occupied the rest of the house. The Hard Times released only one album, 1968's *Blew Mind*, but the group was fairly well known around Los Angeles because of its frequent live shows and appearances on an ABC pop-music TV series *Where the Action Is*.

The proximity between Mark's place and Nancy's led to a memorable mix-up during our courtship. One evening I decided to surprise her with a bouquet of flowers. I walked to her place and put flowers on what I thought was her car, knowing she'd be thrilled when she saw them. But I hadn't factored in my color blindness.

Nancy and her friend Pam both had Volkswagen Beetles that were exactly the same except for their color: Nancy's was red; Pam's was green. My eyes are red-green color-blind, and in the dark the cars looked the same. As a result, I put the flowers on Pam's car. Now, Pam had just broken up with a guy she'd been dating, and when she saw the flowers, she thought he wanted to get back together with her. That made her so mad she threw the flowers on the ground and ran them over with her car. When I walked over to the apartment the next morning, I couldn't imagine why anyone would hate those flowers so much. Nancy was baffled too. But later, when we figured out what had happened, we had something to laugh about.

STILL SEEKING A HIT

Because the Buffalo Springfield had so little control over how our music was marketed, the best way for us to get the word out about our album was to perform as frequently as we could. With that in mind, in the fall of 1966 we headed to San Francisco, where a musical renaissance was taking place. Bands such as the Grateful Dead had risen to prominence, bringing with them a musical sensibility fueled by a love of adventure, improvisation, and lysergic acid diethylamide, better known as LSD. The sound didn't have a lot in common with what we did in Buffalo Springfield, but we were befriended by many of the musicians in the city. We played shows at the Fillmore Auditorium, the Avalon Ballroom, and the Ark, a venue in nearby Sausalito, with such groups as Big Brother and the Holding Company, which was anchored by the terrific vocals of Janis Joplin, and Moby Grape, an act that some people believe imitated the sound of the Springfield.

When we weren't onstage, we were hanging out at a rooming house where we stayed with most of the members of Jefferson Airplane, another San Francisco band that would go on to stardom. The drug scene in the Bay Area was much heavier than anything I'd ever come across, but for the most part I resisted the temptation and was able to maintain what I thought was a good balance. It really wasn't, though, since it was all illegal.

As much as the members of Buffalo Springfield loved creating music and performing together, we still needed money to live on. And that meant, among other things, that we needed a hit single. Around that time, young people who were drawn to the Sunset Strip in Los Angeles were facing heightened opposition to their presence. Owners of businesses that catered to older residents complained to law enforcement, saying their customers were staying away in droves rather than confront the ever-growing number of hippies who spent their time on the Strip. The police responded to the complaints by using L.A.'s curfew laws to cart away anyone who was underage. Dozens upon dozens of arrests took place, causing fear and unrest among the young people being targeted. On November 12 they demonstrated their frustration in a particularly dramatic way.

That night, hundreds of teenagers gathered at a psychedelic club called Pandora's Box, at the intersection of Sunset and Crescent Heights Boulevard. Teens resisted arrest and generally created mayhem in an incident that inspired a movie called *Riot on the Sunset Strip*. Steve felt the police were out of line, and he quickly wrote a song to express his outrage. At first he didn't have a title for the song, but a conversation with Ahmet would give it one. When Ahmet was asking us about new material for future recordings, Steve said, "Here's another one, for what it's worth." Consequently, the expression "for what it's worth" supplied the title for the song that would become our biggest hit.

Steve's fury over police activity on the Strip notwithstanding, "For What It's Worth" wasn't a loud, rage-filled tune, which may explain why it made only a modest impression on me when he first played it for the rest of us. I heard it as more of a folk song, and during that period we were moving in a rock-and-roll direction. Besides, Steve and Neil were coming up with other songs that were much more exciting. Steve had written "Bluebird" and "Rock and Roll Woman," both of which knocked me out; and Neil had "Mr. Soul," a great track that's probably more popular today than it was when Buffalo Springfield was still together. "For What It's Worth" struck me as a pleasant little song, but not much more than that. Good thing I wasn't the one in charge of the record label!

Ahmet, the person who was, immediately recognized "For What It's Worth" as a song capable of breaking Buffalo Springfield. Perhaps he thought a tie-in with the riots, which had received national news coverage, provided a unique marketing opportunity. Or maybe he simply sensed that the tune was a surefire hit. Either way, he switched into high gear, urging us to record the track as soon as possible. We put it down on tape in early December, and Ahmet arranged to put it on our album in place of "Baby Don't Scold Me," another of Steve's compositions. Atco rereleased the album with even more hoopla than before.

This move demonstrated Ahmet's commitment to us, because it wasn't cheap to replace a song on an album that had already been shipped. Approximately 250,000 copies of the original version of *Buffalo Springfield* had been delivered to stores, and recalling them was a big job. (It also turned albums from the first print run that had already been sold into instant collector's items. Not long ago I heard about one listed for sale on the Internet at four hundred dollars. If only I'd kept more copies for myself...)

With "For What It's Worth" in the can, the buzz around Buffalo Springfield was getting louder. Hollywood celebrities began attaching themselves to the band, with two of the biggest—Steve McQueen and Dean Martin—hiring us to play parties at their respective houses. Television producers were paying closer attention too. Just before year's end we performed or lip-synched "For What It's Worth" on *American Bandstand* and *Where the Action Is* (the show that had featured the Hard Times) over a stretch of just a few days.

Even more important, radio stations that had ignored "Clancy" and "Burned" picked up on our latest single, boosting it to number seven on the *Billboard Hot 100* singles chart. And even after it began to slip from that peak, its influence continued to build. A generation of young people protesting the Vietnam War, as well as untold thousands of soldiers serving in it, embraced the song's message. In fact, a lot of people think "For What It's Worth" was written about the war in Southeast Asia, not a scuffle over curfews on the Sunset Strip. Today it's one of a handful of songs that musicologists and social critics point to as defining the 1960s.

THE NEW YORK INCIDENT

For all its lingering influence, the truth is that "For What It's Worth" didn't have the impact during 1966 and 1967 that most people assume. From a sales and airplay perspective, it was a slow mover, becoming popular in widely scattered markets and regions of the country at different times, instead of taking the nation by storm. Our touring schedule during 1967 reflected this reality. Because we couldn't appear just anywhere and expect a large audience to show up, we tended to visit areas where our music was already doing well. In some places this helped build momentum, but not always. Even after "For What It's Worth" made the Top 10, things were still hit-and-miss.

New York City is a good example. After "For What It's Worth," we had enough of a following back east to justify the expense of getting there, but we were still at an almost underground level. The best venue Charlie and Brian could find for us to play was Ondine's, a club under the Fifty-ninth Street Bridge. It had an extremely low ceiling, a scattering of dumpy tables and chairs, and a capacity that was considerably smaller than the Whisky's. We'd been booked for a ten-day run as a support group for Mitch Ryder and the

Detroit Wheels, beginning the day after a one-shot performance at the Night Owl Café, the one-time home base for the Lovin' Spoonful.

In many ways it was great to get back to New York. I hadn't actually been gone that long, but it felt as if a lifetime had passed since Bob, Nels, and I made our debut in a Greenwich Village club. I saw old friends like Jean Gurney, and I got to meet musicians such as Otis Redding, who came to one of our shows with Ahmet Ertegun. Redding hadn't enjoyed huge success at that point; his biggest single, "(Sittin' on) The Dock of the Bay," would be released following his death in a plane crash in late 1967. Yet he was widely respected by hip music fans and performers like Dewey, who thought Redding was untoppable. Remember that Dewey thought he could sing like Redding, and he joined Buffalo Springfield only after we said he could take the lead on a cover of "In the Midnight Hour." It was a dream come true for him when his hero joined us onstage and shared vocals with him on the song.

Later, Redding heard Neil's "Mr. Soul" and asked if he could record it. That may seem surprising, since, aside from its title, it's not really a soul number. On the other hand, Redding's signature song was another "mister" tune— "Mr. Pitiful," released in 1965—and he had shown he could make rock numbers his own when he cut a very interesting version of the Rolling Stones' "(I Can't Get No) Satisfaction." Neil, however, wouldn't give Redding the first shot at his latest creation. He was proud of "Mr. Soul," and he didn't want anyone else to put a stamp on it until he got the chance—a typical Neil reaction. I understood where he was coming from, but I would have loved to hear what Redding might have done with the song.

Redding's visit to the show was one of the highlights at Ondine's, but unfortunately the lowlights were more plentiful. Having traveled to New York from Southern California, we felt as though the weather was especially cold and gloomy. Beyond that, the strain was starting to show in our relationship with Charlie and Brian. Everything came to a head during a visit to Atlantic Studios to record "Mr. Soul" as well as "We'll See" and "My Kind of Love," one of my songs. (These last two tracks weren't commercially available until the release of the *Buffalo Springfield Box Set* in 2001, although the Hollies had once asked me about "My Kind of Love.") Charlie and Brian were in the studio again as producers, but it had become clear to everyone that they weren't adding anything to the music. Far from it. The poor recording quality they were getting may have been partly responsible for our first album failing to meet expectations. We felt we could do better ourselves and told Charlie and Brian that they were no longer producing our records.

Despite this change, however, they continued to be our managers. At least in name. Since our declaration of musical independence, they no longer gave us the level of personal attention we'd previously received, and the difference became obvious before we left New York.

Bruce was the key person in the drama that followed. Friction between him and other members of the band was increasing, and at Ondine's, things got physical. The stage at the club was a double-decker setup that was so small that the five of us couldn't perform on the same level. Steve and I lined up on the bottom platform, with Bruce, Dewey, and Neil the equivalent of a step up behind us. One night Bruce was playing with his eyes closed, as usual; he'd get lost in the music and never look where he was going. This wasn't a problem in roomier venues, but the quarters were so close at Ondine's that when Bruce rocked back and forth, the top of his bass would smack Steve in the head, messing up the cowboy hat he liked to wear.

The first time this happened, Steve tried to ignore it. The second time he turned and yelled, "Watch what you're doing!"—which had absolutely no effect on Bruce. Finally, after Bruce whacked him a third time, Steve turned around and decked him.

I don't know if Bruce was high that night, since he could be oblivious to everything but the music even when he was stone-cold sober. Still, there's a good chance he was on something, considering what happened next. Bruce was arrested at our hotel for drug possession just as we were scheduled to leave for Los Angeles. With the tickets already purchased and shows in L.A. waiting for us, we couldn't stick around to help. To make matters worse, Charlie and Brian were less than enthusiastic about coming to the rescue, considering we had just dismissed them as our music producers. Before any of us quite knew what was happening, Bruce was deported to Canada, and he couldn't get back into the United States for months.

Steve was upset over the deportation and unhappy with Charlie and Brian, blaming them for letting it all happen. Back in L.A., we headed down to their office on Sunset, and Steve expressed his frustration by throwing rocks at the windows. Undoubtedly, that kind of behavior alienated Charlie and Brian even more, but it didn't stop them from taking our money. They'd locked up a sizable chunk of our publishing, and they continued to reap the benefits of our success long after they'd stopped doing much to earn their keep.

A more immediate concern was finding a bass player to fill in for Bruce. We were scheduled to appear on a TV show called *Hollywood Palace,* but it was lip-synched instead of live, so we recruited Dickie Davis to pretend to play bass. Next, we used Love's bassist, Ken Forssi, for a few shows before we brought back Neil's old friend, Ken Koblun. Ken was available and eager to hook up with the very group he'd rejected the previous year, so we decided to give it a try. But it wasn't long before it became obvious that Ken wasn't working out. After just a few dates, we parted ways and replaced him with Jim Fielder. Jim was a fine bassist who'd performed with us the last time Bruce was in trouble with the law. He fit in with the rest of the band, but he also had other responsibilities he had to juggle. Clearly, Bruce was more indispensable than we'd thought. Buffalo Springfield with him was a lot better than Buffalo Springfield without him.

ROAD TO MATRIMONY

The band left on a tour of the Southwest, beginning in Southern California. The headliner was the Seeds, a sort of psychedelic garage band whose biggest hit was "Pushin' Too Hard." Once the tour began, we found the transportation, by bus, to be subpar and the accommodations consistently poor. And the challenges didn't end there. The crowds were small, and the financial compensation was nonexistent—literally. After a couple of terrible shows in New Mexico and an even worse one in Lubbock, Texas, Dickie Davis told us it was time to pull the plug and head home. The tour was a disaster, but our early return to L.A. opened up a life-changing opportunity for me. I decided to ask Nancy to marry me.

Nancy and I had gotten very serious very quickly, and I wanted to make our relationship permanent. At first she was reluctant to take the plunge. Her ugly breakup with Bill Rinehart was still too fresh in her mind for her to suddenly agree to marry a musician. Thank goodness for Michael Miller, a mutual friend who told Nancy to stop being so wishy-washy. She finally accepted my proposal with a heartfelt yes, and we made plans to marry.

Of all the incredible things that have happened in my life, nothing compares to what I found in Nancy. She is truly a gift from God. He certainly knew what He was talking about when He told Adam, "It is not good that man should be alone,"[1] and created a woman to be his companion and partner for life.

Our years together have been hard at times, and sometimes even heartbreaking. When I asked Nancy to marry me, neither of us could have imagined the trials that would test our relationship. But at that moment, as we prepared for our wedding, it was just as God had planned it in the beginning—heaven on earth! Since becoming a pastor, I've had the privilege of officiating at many weddings. Over the years I've grown to love a verse from the Old Testament:

Many waters cannot quench love,
Nor can the floods drown it.
If a man would give for love
All the wealth of his house,
It would be utterly despised.[2]

There is nothing better than the love God gives a man for his wife and a woman for her husband.

At first Nancy and I had planned on a June wedding, but after the Seeds debacle, I wasn't sure I'd be in town in June. To prevent the changing circumstances from keeping us apart, we decided to move the wedding up to

March 4—just two weeks away. The new wedding date wouldn't have worked without the help of the pastor at the Granada Hills Presbyterian Church Nancy had attended since she was a youngster. He came through, and so did Nancy's mother.

There were a lot of arrangements to be made; more than 250 guests attended the ceremony. Nancy's mother took charge of invitations, refreshments, food, the cake, and other logistics. That freed Nancy up to make a dress for herself and her maid of honor. It's amazing that she was able to sew these elaborate and beautiful clothes in such a short amount of time.

Just as incredible was how smoothly everything went. My mom flew out for the wedding, meeting Nancy for the first time. Nancy hadn't realized quite how petite my mom was, so she wore heels to their first get-together. Somehow, though, they still managed to see eye to eye. From the start, they connected.

The wedding itself was great. Nancy's family and childhood friends mixed unexpectedly well with the collection of musicians that attended. Jim Fielder and Steve were there, and Dewey brought along Peter Noone, lead singer of Herman's Hermits, with whom Dewey had become friends. By happenstance, I recently ran into Peter at the airport in Santa Barbara. As I reached out my hand to reintroduce myself, saying, "Peter—Richie Furay," he looked at me with surprise. "It's been forty years," he declared. I was amazed that he remembered.

On that day, however, no one cut a stranger figure than Neil. He'd lately taken to wearing outdoorsy-looking outfits lined with a lot of fringe, which led some people to think he was a Native American. Fearing that he'd show up in full buckskin regalia, I asked him to leave the fringe at home that day. For Neil, who's contrary by nature, that request was an invitation to do something outrageous, and he did. He rented a Confederate army uniform and wore it to the wedding.

Some people in this situation would have gotten angry, but not Nancy and me. One glance at Neil looking so ridiculous put both of us at ease—and his costume added just the right touch of humor to the photos of our big day. Bruce wasn't there, due to his immigration troubles, but the rest of Buffalo Springfield was, and for that day at least, all the ill feelings and conflicts were forgotten.

8

A Legendary Band Self-Destructs

The Impossible Challenge of Keeping Things Together

*T*he Buffalo Springfield didn't fall apart all at once. It was a slow process, drawn out over a year in which the band made a lot of great music together but also suffered through plenty of misunderstandings and mistakes. Decades later it's still hard to figure out how everything could have gone so wrong for such a phenomenal band.

One thing that was right from the beginning was my marriage to Nancy, but we didn't get to ease into our life together with an extended honeymoon. The day after our wedding, the Springfield was scheduled to appear on *Go,* a youth-oriented variety show hosted by actor Ryan O'Neal, who'd become a huge star after the release of the movie *Love Story.* For the taping, Neil wore the same Confederate army uniform he'd worn to my wedding. That's one way to get extra mileage out of a costume rental!

Then it was back to the San Francisco area to play some shows that had been scheduled earlier. Nancy and I stayed in a houseboat in Sausalito, which was extremely romantic. Too bad the rest of the stay was so strange. For one thing, Nancy wasn't allowed to attend our shows at the Longshoreman's Hall, because even though she was married, she was still underage. Then, at the end of the first night, we were warned to get our equipment out of the club because something bad was about to go down. Sure enough, later that night the place was ransacked, for reasons that were rumored to have something to do with the mob. I don't know what actually happened, but I'm glad we weren't in the middle of it.

In March we toured the Pacific Northwest before working our way back to San Francisco. We spent most of April in the Bay Area, with the exception of a second memorable visit to the Hollywood Bowl. For that show we shared the spotlight with the Supremes and the Fifth Dimension, plus another couple of acts that were already part of our story, Johnny Rivers and the Seeds. Being on a bill like that one showed that our fortunes had improved.

After we released "For What It's Worth," Buffalo Springfield was embraced by a lot of publications, especially *TeenSet,* a magazine put out by the late Judy Sims. She absolutely loved the band, and she proved it by the number of features she published about us. I don't know if there was a single issue that didn't spotlight us in some way. The articles weren't in-depth explorations of lyrics and song structure and things like that. Instead, we talked about girls and favorite colors and other superficial topics that people associate today with magazines like *Tiger Beat.* Sure, it was a bit silly, but Judy made it fun. She tried to make us rock-and-roll stars in spite of ourselves, and she probably did more to keep Buffalo Springfield together than most of us in the band actually did.

Neil, in particular, was always throwing us for a loop over the most unlikely things. One of the oddest was his objection to our appearing on *The Tonight Show,* hosted by Johnny Carson. Everyone but Neil was thrilled by the chance to play on the show. For some reason, Neil seemed to think that going on *Tonight* would be selling out. That didn't make much sense to me. After all, he had played with us on several other network TV shows. If doing those shows hadn't compromised us, why would *The Tonight Show* be any different?

It wasn't, really, but Neil was getting more and more involved with producer Jack Nitzsche, and he was looking for any excuse to leave the band. The rest of us paid for Neil's lack of focus. For one thing, *The Tonight Show* offer eventually fell through.

Neil's relationship with Jack wasn't the only thing that undermined the family feeling the group once had. There were plenty of people whispering in Steve's ear too, telling him that he was Buffalo Springfield's real star and he didn't need the other guys dragging him down. With so many outsiders inflating their egos, Steve and Neil were bound to come into conflict, and they did. Nancy recalls a time when they tossed chairs at each other backstage. Yet, for the most part, there weren't many face-to-face confrontations. Instead, Neil would just disappear, leaving the rest of us to wonder when, if ever, he would come back.

Because it was clear that Neil was determined to go solo, we were in a real fix. Bruce remained in Canada, so Jim was filling in on bass. And now we needed to find a guitarist. Because we didn't have a lot of time, we turned to Charlie and Brian for help. They had done as much as anyone to drive a wedge between Steve and Neil, but they had quite a few other bands on their management roster, including the Daily Flash, a group from Seattle. The Flash's guitarist, Doug Hastings, was a big fan of Buffalo Springfield. After Charlie and Brian contacted him, he jumped at the opportunity to step in for Neil.

Doug worked hard to fit in, but once again, it was an impossible situation. Imagine trying to replace any of the original members, especially Neil, Steve, or me. Yet Doug was asked to try. I definitely didn't envy him.

The chemistry among this lineup wasn't great, but one of our first shows with Doug, at a venue called Hal Baby's in Aurora, Colorado, was noteworthy for other reasons—although I didn't realize it at the time. Opening for us on the show was a band called Boenzee Cryque, which happened to include drummer George Grantham and pedal-steel guitarist Rusty Young. I didn't get to meet them that night, but Rusty would play on one Springfield session, and by the summer of 1968, all three of us would be bandmates in Poco.

This was another of those destiny moments. Imagine: I'm playing in the same club as George and Rusty, who would become two of my most important musical collaborators. And our paths first crossed in Colorado, where I'd eventually live, raise my family, and start a church. What are the chances?

But that's not all. Buffalo Springfield would later play shows with Illinois

Speed Press and the Poor, each of which featured future Poco members: Paul Cotton and Randy Meisner, respectively. But odds don't play into it when God is guiding the outcome. He was taking me to the places I needed to be, introducing me to the people I needed to meet, orchestrating His perfect plan long before I had the slightest inkling my life was in His hands. Some people never realize God's greater plan for their lives, while others, like me, only discover the truth as circumstances gradually reveal that something deeper and bigger is going on. It took quite a few more years for my eyes to be opened and my heart to respond to what God had been doing all along.

In the meantime I was still tightly focused on earthly opportunities, and a big one was placed before us. Buffalo Springfield was asked to perform at what would become one of the most famous rock concerts of all time.

The Monterey International Pop Festival

As of 1967, nothing on the scale of the Monterey International Pop Festival, staged at the Monterey County Fairgrounds on a peninsula south of San Francisco, had been attempted. The Beatles had shown that rock acts could fill huge venues, making shows like the ones we played at the Hollywood Bowl possible. However, Monterey stretched over three days, from June 16 to June 18, and attracted hundreds of thousands of young people, setting the stage for Woodstock, which would follow two years later. On top of that, the organizers of Monterey—record-company executive Lou Adler and John Phillips of the Mamas and the Papas—earmarked the profits for a charity, the Monterey International Pop Festival Foundation, and most of the artists agreed to perform without charge.

This concept, which directly influenced events like the Concert for Bangladesh, Live Aid, and Live 8, attracted an unbelievable lineup of talent that spanned all parts of the musical spectrum. R&B and soul were represented by Otis Redding as well as Lou Rawls and Booker T and the MGs. Blues-rock groups included the Butterfield Blues Band, Canned Heat, the Blues Project, and Electric Flag. San Francisco bands like Jefferson Airplane and Big Brother and the Holding Company, starring Janis Joplin, were given prominent slots. And, as if that weren't enough, the Byrds, the Who, and the Jimi Hendrix Experience agreed to participate as well. There were more than thirty acts in all, and nearly all of them were terrific.

For the Buffalo Springfield to be included in that kind of company was nothing short of amazing. And the fact that we were scheduled to perform on the third day of the festival just ahead of the Who, one of the most anticipated groups on the bill, showed that we'd won the respect of our peers. The scene itself was crazy. The flower children were in full bloom, and walking around the grounds, watching people who seemed to be completely out of their minds, was bizarre but memorable. A whole new world was coming to life right before our eyes.

At the same time, Neil's absence made what should have been a triumph into something bittersweet, even a bit of a downer. Bruce had finally gotten permission to return to the States, but he was still heavily into the drug scene. And even if he'd been in prime condition, we hadn't played with him for months, and it showed. We had never jelled with Doug, either, so we asked David Crosby of the Byrds to join us onstage. I'm not sure what, exactly, we thought David would bring to the party. Neil was a lead guitarist, whereas David played rhythm guitar, just like me. And since we didn't have enough time to really incorporate him into our sound, we had to wing it.

That's tough to do with a city's worth of people spread out in front of you, and we didn't manage as well as we would have liked. With Neil missing from the band and with Bruce just then returning after a long absence, the odds were against us pulling off our customary tight, high-energy performance. To make matters worse, I had a really sore throat that turned out to be tonsillitis. We returned to San Francisco after the festival, and only days later I was admitted to a hospital to have my tonsils removed.

The highlight of our performance was probably our version of "Bluebird," which had been released as our latest single. I loved the song—you'll remember that I thought it had a better chance of becoming a hit than "For What It's Worth"—and Steve and the rest of us gave it all we had. The crowd was definitely receptive, but as a single, it became only a medium-sized success across the country. As for the rest of our Monterey Pop performance, it was more than a little rough around the edges.

While I was recovering from surgery, the Springfield played a show in Los Angeles with David once again filling in. To everyone's shock, Neil showed up and joined the band onstage. His appearance seemed like a one-shot, but it didn't turn out that way. We went out on a tour of the Midwest, and by the time we returned that summer, the word was out that Neil wanted to rejoin the band.

Over the years Neil has given different explanations for his change of heart, most having to do with pressure from the record company because his solo career wasn't taking off the way he had hoped. Having seen Neil come and go so many times, I was worried that he still wasn't committed for the long haul, and my concerns proved true. There was also the question of Doug, who had committed to Buffalo Springfield in part because he thought he was being made a permanent member. With Neil back in the picture, there was no place for him. Luckily, Doug was able to catch on with an early supergroup called Rhinoceros, which was put together by producer Paul Rothchild, who worked with the Doors, and Barry Friedman, the future rechristened Frazier Mohawk.

In the end, I supported Neil's return to the band. Holding a grudge and hanging on to bitterness doesn't serve any positive purpose. And refusing to forgive someone actually hurts you more than it does the other person. I also knew that Neil's participation made us a better band, and he'd be a big help when it came to pulling together material for our next record.

BUFFALO SPRINGFIELD AGAIN

For our next LP, we decided that we'd go into the studio for extended stretches with the idea of coming up with songs specifically for the album. In between concert dates we'd pop into various L.A. studios and knock out a song or two, then we'd hit the road again. With Neil back in the fold, we could focus on the task of turning our recorded odds and ends into something that would hang together.

The result of our labors, which we called *Buffalo Springfield Again,* is regarded by many rock-music critics as our best album. I take a lot of pride in that, because I was able to contribute to the overall landscape of the band's sound. It was no longer a two-man show from a writing standpoint, which broadened the spectrum of the group's overall appeal.

People were drawn to Buffalo Springfield because of Steve's and Neil's songs, without a doubt, but they also loved my voice. I had been a big part of our first album, playing rhythm guitar and singing lead or unison parts on a bunch of the tracks. But as the creative tension between Steve and Neil ratcheted up, each of them wanted more of the spotlight. The only way to ensure that I wasn't squeezed out entirely was to write my own songs. Even though I wasn't as prolific as Steve and Neil, I'd been coming up with compositions since the days of the Au Go-Go Singers. Now I was ready to seize the opportunity.

The challenge was creating tunes that stood up to ones written by two of the best rock-and-roll songwriters ever. I guess I must have done all right, because three of my songs made the final cut—the same number as Neil and just one fewer than Steve.

"Sad Memory" was the first song of mine to be recorded by Buffalo Springfield, which is appropriate since it's one of my earliest compositions, written in New York before I moved to California. It's about a girl in college I thought I was in love with, but she didn't have the same feelings for me. The song was recorded during an almost happenstance session. We were supposed to meet at the studio for a group session, but as was often the case, I was the only one who arrived on time. I was waiting for everyone else to get there, and to help the engineers, William Brittan and Bill Lazarus, get a sound level, I started playing "Sad Memory." At that moment Neil walked in, liked what he heard, and decided to add his guitar playing to mine. That's the version on the record—just Neil and me playing as well as we ever had.

I wrote "Good Time Boy" for Dewey, the soul fan, to sing. It was my way of making him a bigger part of the band and emphasizing the family feeling I missed so much. The song had an R&B arrangement, complete with horn charts, that was totally different from everything else on the album. But *Buffalo Springfield Again* was such a diverse album that it worked. We listed Dewey as executive producer on the song just for fun.

The third song of mine included on the album was "A Child's Claim to Fame," which was more serious:

> There goes another day
> And I wonder why
> You and I
> Keep telling lies
> I can't believe what you say
> 'Cause tomorrow's lullaby
> Can't pacify
> My lonesome crying
> Make believe is all you know
> And to make believe is a game
> A child's reign
> You've changed your name
> So sadly I'll watch the show
> As you see what you became
> Truth is the shame
> Too much fame[1]

I was commenting on the interpersonal dynamics within the band. I looked at the childish escapades that were going on among the five of us, with some thinking they were better or more important than the group as a whole, and so I vented my frustrations in a song. This would become a theme for me in my song writing. I'd use the composing process to get things off my chest. But because the music I put to these words was so accessible, none of the other band members seemed to put two and two together, at least back then. Neil, for example, was pleased to add his guitar to the song, and he sings a very distinctive part at the end of it. He might not have been as excited to do that if he had known the lyrics were criticizing some of his behavior. Then again, with Neil, you never know.

Of course, "A Child's Claim to Fame" was a lot more than just words. The music was arguably even more important, considering the influence it has had. The song has been acknowledged as one of the earliest examples of country rock—a sort of blueprint for Poco and dozens of other bands that appeared afterward. I didn't set out to invent a new genre of music when I wrote it; I was just doing what came naturally. Even so, the combination of styles that came together was unique, and the sound has stood the test of time. The people who put together the soundtrack for *Wonder Boys,* a movie released in 2000 starring Michael Douglas, placed "A Child's Claim to Fame" alongside tracks by Bob Dylan, John Lennon, Van Morrison, and even Neil Young. It was nice to be included in their company.

For the song to stand out on *Buffalo Springfield Again* was a real accomplishment, since Neil and Steve were at the top of their games. The album features some of Steve's finest songs—not only "Bluebird" but "Hung Upside Down," "Everydays," and "Rock and Roll Woman," another timeless treasure. Neil countered with "Mr. Soul" and two of the most interesting opuses he made with Jack Nitzsche, "Expecting to Fly" and "Broken Arrow." This last song was engineered by Jimmy Messina, who would soon play a big part in Buffalo Springfield's closing chapter, and an even larger one in the next phase of my musical life.

With so many musical talents contributing to the album, it's no wonder *Again* was so impressive. Nonetheless, the LP's sales didn't match its quality. It was hardly a bust, selling in the hundreds of thousands, but it lost steam after a couple of months and never regained much momentum. Sadly, this underperformance fit the pattern for Buffalo Springfield.

We assigned a lot of the blame for *Again's* fate to Charlie and Brian. While that may not have been totally fair, it certainly reflected our strained relationship. The time had come to move on, and after borrowing money from Atlantic to buy out the management contract, that's what we did. Freedom felt great, but it was a double-edged sword. We were reluctant to sign with another company, so a lot of the management duties fell to Dickie, who didn't have the resources at his disposal to help take Buffalo Springfield to the next level of success.

We got by in the short run on the strength of our reputation, which ensured that bands with bigger names would continue to seek us out as a touring partner. In November 1967, right about the time *Again* was reaching stores, we were asked to open for the Beach Boys. Talk about a thrill. Even though Brian Wilson was no longer traveling with the group, the rest of the original members were on hand, and they sounded great.

The tour was run as efficiently as the best military operation. On a number of occasions, we were slated to play shows in different cities on the same day—and not just neighboring cities but communities with some real distance between them, such as South Orange, New Jersey, and Baltimore, Maryland. That sounds like a recipe for disaster, but it went off without a hitch. We joined the Strawberry Alarm Clock, best known for the song "Incense and Peppermints," and the Box Tops, whose biggest hit was "The Letter," on the tour, and as soon as one band was finished, its members would pack up and head to the airport. There were times when we were on a plane headed to the next concert while the Beach Boys were still playing at the previous one.

On less hectic days we had time to hang out with the stars of the show— and Dennis Wilson was definitely the wild man of the bunch. He was an incredible character and a true prankster. One time we were driving down the highway in a tour bus, and Dennis grabbed a fire extinguisher and started spraying it at passing cars. The other drivers survived their encounter with the craziest Beach Boy—barely.

The rest of us had an even narrower escape when we flew into Boston for a show. The airport may not technically have been closed, but it should have been, because the area was lost in some of the thickest fog I've ever seen. Certainly, thoughts of Buddy Holly and Ritchie Valens went through my mind.

I was reminded of this incident when I saw former rock journalist Cameron Crowe's semi-autobiographical film *Almost Famous*. It contains a very funny scene in which a rock band almost literally goes down in flames. An article about Crowe published by *Rolling Stone* just before *Almost Famous* reached theaters revealed that I was the first musician he interviewed when he was starting out on his writing career. I'm not sure he was even old enough to shave at the time. Obviously, he's come a long way.

THE FINAL NOTE OF THE DEATH KNELL

As 1967 slipped into 1968, I thought Buffalo Springfield was stronger than it had been in quite some time. We had recording sessions lined up for January, not to mention some good concert bookings around Southern California. With the original roster intact once again, there was no reason why we couldn't recapture the magic of those first few weeks at the Whisky.

But I was fooling myself. Steve and Neil were more interested in doing their own music than in collaborating with each other, and Bruce was a mess. His drug use was spiraling out of control, and it would ultimately prove to be his undoing. Police stopped him for speeding and discovered an open liquor bottle and some marijuana in the possession of his underage female companion. He was arrested, and after being released on bail, he was busted again during a raid at the Tropicana Inn Motel, a well-known rock-star hangout in Hollywood. Bruce was subsequently redeported to Canada.

We needed a bass player, but no one wanted to get back in touch with the various people who'd previously filled in for Bruce: Jim Fielder, Ken Koblun, or Love's Ken Forssi. We were so frantic that we reached way back to Mike Scott, who'd played with Steve and me in the Au Go-Go Singers, but the chemistry wasn't right. So we turned to a relatively new prospect, albeit one we'd gotten to know during the recording of our previous album: Jimmy Messina.

This was a great move from my perspective because Jimmy and I had really connected when we'd met before. We discovered that we had compatible personalities. We were both friendly and easygoing, but with a genuine drive to succeed. On top of that, Jimmy encouraged my song writing. With Neil and Steve fighting for supremacy, I probably receded into the background more than I should have. Jimmy took the time to say, "Hey, you've got some really good songs. We ought to record them." That was just the push I needed.

With Jimmy on board, the group should have been able to make another fresh start—about our hundredth. But it wasn't to be. For one thing, our management situation was a mess. Disappointed with the reception the public gave to *Buffalo Springfield Again,* we parted company with Dickie and began using Nick Grillo, the Beach Boys' manager, to help us out on an informal basis. Meanwhile, Neil was restless and disappointed after "Expecting to Fly" was released as a single to little fanfare and poor sales. He reacted by withdrawing from the band again.

Neil's disappearing act was getting old for everyone, and probably him, too. Steve may have been the most fed up, and since he was the Springfield's leader, his opinion represented the bottom line. For all intents and purposes, the band was finished. It just took a couple more months for the final note to sound.

The band's official death notice was delayed thanks to contractual obligations. We were scheduled to play another series of concerts with the Beach Boys, and after some cajoling from, among others, Ahmet Ertegun, Neil agreed to show up for them. I doubt that he knew what he was in for, and neither did the rest of us.

At the time, Mike Love and, to a lesser degree, Brian's brother, Carl Wilson, were followers of Maharishi Mahesh Yogi, the transcendental-meditation guru who'd also caught the Beatles' fancy. We weren't required to become followers of the Maharishi in order to participate in the tour, but the Beach Boys did ask us to go through an initiation ritual intended, I suppose, to improve our karma. What a joke. Certainly none of us was anxious to embrace TM, but we had to take part in what they asked us to do—or at least we *thought* we did. So at our first concert stop in Detroit, we performed a ceremony in front of the Maharishi's photo that involved a handkerchief, a flower, and a piece of fruit.

I know this sounds wacky, but because so many musicians were into TM at the time, we did our best acting job, though quite frankly none of us was buying it. Before one show in a Florida gymnasium, I was hanging out with Jimmy Messina. We were "relaxing" after the sound check—getting loaded— when we began wondering what really would happen if we repeated over and over the "secret word" we were given at the initiation. Before I knew it, we were chanting in a pitch-black locker room. For some reason we paused at the exact same moment, and the room became incredibly quiet. Finally Jimmy asked, "Richie, are you still there?" Rather than answer him, I said, "Let's get out of here," and we did, as quickly as we could. Both of us were completely freaked out. I knew then that, without question, Eastern religion wasn't for me.

LAST TIME AROUND

I was glad Jimmy was in the band, and he turned out to be a tremendous help in pulling together the third Buffalo Springfield album. When it became obvious that the group was on the brink of collapse, Atco representatives demanded that we assemble our last contracted album from the recording sessions we'd staged since completing *Buffalo Springfield Again*. I didn't blame them. Only a few months earlier, they had shelled out big bucks to free us from Charlie and Brian's management contract. It's only natural they wanted to recoup some of their investment.

The problem was, no one wanted to take on the responsibility of putting together an LP. Inevitably, the task fell to Jimmy and me. We flew to New York with the tapes that had been made up until that time, and we did our best to turn them into a cohesive whole. We had two Neil songs, "I Am a Child," a real standout, and "On the Way Home," which I sang. We had five Steve tunes, two of which were up to his previous standards—"Pretty Girl Why" and "Uno Mundo." And we had some curve balls, such as "In the Hour of Not Quite Rain," with lyrics written by an unknown teenager. I kid you not.

In the fall of 1967, Charlie and Brian came up with an idea for a contest on radio station KHJ in Los Angeles. The key part of the ad copy read: "You Write the Words… The Buffalo Springfield Writes the Music… And a Hit Is Born! The winning words are set to music by the Buffalo Springfield and'll be featured in their new album! For $1,000 in KHJ cash plus publishing royalties…get it said!" The winner was Micki Callen, a California teenager who sent in a poem called "In the Hour of Not Quite Rain."

As a promotion, the contest may have seemed like a masterstroke, but it didn't fit the dynamics of the band at all. Steve and Neil would never have considered putting music to someone else's words. If I hadn't tackled the chore, it wouldn't have gotten done.

Surprisingly, the song turned out pretty well. It was heavily orchestrated, and a lot of people considered it to be a success. Yet when Neil was choosing songs for the *Buffalo Springfield Box Set,* he left out "Rain" as well as a Jimmy Messina track, "Carefree Country Day," which we came up with to flesh out the album. Neil's argument was that these weren't truly Buffalo Springfield songs, but I didn't buy that. In a sense, very little on our final collection qualified as Buffalo Springfield songs. Instead, they were solo tracks made by individuals who had been in the same band. By that criteria, "In the Hour of Not Quite Rain" and "Carefree Country Day" had as much right to be included as anything else.

Three of my other songs appeared on the album. I'm listed as a co-writer with Neil on "It's So Hard to Wait," but the two of us didn't sit down and come up with the song as a team. I wrote the lion's share of it, and Neil tossed in a line or two. I received sole writing credit on "Merry-Go-Round," the B-side of the "Uno Mundo" single. And most important was "Kind Woman," which remains one of my best-known songs. It's an unabashedly romantic song, which I wrote for Nancy. Here's how it begins:

I got a good reason for loving you
It's an old-fashioned sign
I kinda get the feelin' like, mmmm, you know when
I fell in love the first time
Kind woman
Won't you love me tonight
The look in your eyes
Kind woman
Don't leave me lonely tonight
Please say it's all right[2]

These words are set to music that shows, even more clearly than "A Child's Claim to Fame" did, what direction the genre that came to be known as country rock would take. In "Kind Woman," the country-music tradition is upheld not only by the style but also by the instrumentation, including pedal steel played by my future Poco mate, Rusty Young, who performed on the session at the recommendation of our roadie, Miles Thomas. With Rusty's help, the song came together as naturally as anyone could have imagined, and it has become popular with listeners and musicians alike. The song has been covered by artists as diverse as rootsy vocalist Chris Smither and R&B belter Percy Sledge.

At the same time, "Kind Woman" has some eccentricities that I corrected when I rerecorded it in recent years. The majority of the song is in waltz time, but here and there I threw in some five-quarter measures. I didn't do it to show off; it was just the way I heard the song in my head. The shifts were more akin to jazz than either country or rock, and they certainly gave the piano player on the session a bear of a time. When I play "Kind Woman" now, I change the time of the five-quarter passages, and the song works as well as it ever did. Now if I can only get George Strait to record it and make it the hit that it should have been.

The title we used for Buffalo Springfield's swan song album, *Last Time*

Around, was certainly straightforward. All of us knew there would be no more comebacks for the band.

AFTER THE SWAN SINGS

It hurt to see the band die, especially considering the potential that existed for rock-and-roll greatness. But some parts of the Buffalo Springfield story I'd just as soon forget, especially a brush with the law that still seems surreal.

In March 1968 Steve was living in a house in Topanga Canyon, where he hosted regular jam sessions that ran into the wee hours of the morning. We thought we were far enough away from civilization that we wouldn't disturb anyone, but we were wrong. One evening the police showed up at the door, told Steve that they'd received some noise complaints, and they politely asked him to quiet down. When Steve agreed, they left. But sure enough, we were back at it again the next night in the company of a famous guest—Eric Clapton, the guitarist from Cream.

Nancy accompanied me to Steve's house that evening, and at one point we left only to return a few seconds later. We came back because I needed to check with Jimmy to see what time he wanted to meet me the next day to go buy a stereo. (Oh, if we'd only had a cell phone.) Those plans were thrown off within minutes when a swarm of L.A.'s finest raided the house, bursting through every door and window to grab anyone within reach. They also searched the premises for illegal substances and found some marijuana.

As all this was happening, Steve managed to slip away to a neighboring house where Dennis Wilson was living. The rest of us were transported to a Malibu police station. From there the men were taken to L.A. County Jail, and the women ended up at the Sybil Brand Institute, a correctional facility for females.

To call this an awful experience would be an understatement. After sitting in a holding cell for hours, I was stripped, forcibly showered and deloused, and taken to my quarters. Of the two bunks there, the bottom one was occupied by a huge mountain of a man who didn't look as if this were his first stay in jail. He pointed to the top bunk and growled, "That one's yours"—and I wasn't going to argue with him. For me, comfort was secondary to leaving the cell in one piece.

The next morning Nick Grillo bailed us out. We emerged into the bright daylight to discover that the entire escapade had been splashed across the pages of the *Los Angeles Times*. I felt especially bad for Nancy, who was the last person in the world who deserved to be behind bars for a night. The headlines embarrassed her, not to mention her mother, who had a co-worker present her with the paper and ask, "Isn't that your daughter?"

Over the course of the next few weeks, I had to testify on behalf of Eric Clapton, who, as an English citizen, could have been in big trouble had he been convicted of a drug violation. Like Bruce, he probably would have been deported. He escaped that fate thanks to good lawyers who managed to get the charges reduced to misdemeanors, such as disturbing the peace. The rest of us received slaps on the wrist.

After our brush with the law, the final Buffalo Springfield concert, on May 5 at the Long Beach Sports Arena with Canned Heat and Country Joe and the Fish, was anticlimactic but somehow appropriate. I felt a mixture of excitement and disappointment during our portion of the show. Our fans, who showed up in big numbers, were dealing with the same emotions, and that give and take resulted in a fiery performance—one of our best in a long time. It was a good ending for a band that had achieved so much in such a brief period of time.

Had I dwelled on how much more we could have accomplished if we'd been able to keep everyone's ego at bay, I would have been saddened. But I was already looking forward to my next project, one I hoped would run much more smoothly than the Springfield.

9

A New Type of Rock Music

Finding Three Other Guys Who Love Country Rock

don't remember either Jimmy or me turning to the other and saying, "Hey, let's start a band." Maybe we did, but if so, the words were unnecessary. We'd gotten along well from our first meeting, and by the second Beach Boys tour, we were spending a lot of time together working on songs. Everyone could tell that Buffalo Springfield was on its last legs, but Jimmy and I were ready to run.

Likewise, there wasn't a lot of discussion about what kind of group we wanted to form. Without even discussing it, we both wanted to blend country and rock. That may seem strange, since the term *country rock* was practically unknown back then. Our music wasn't about labels or categories, though. We were more concerned with what sounded good to us, not what to call it.

In some ways, Jimmy had more of a background in country music than I did. I'd grown up as a fan of rock and roll and folk, but I'd evolved into a big country fan—so much so that one of my main musical influences after the Buffalo Springfield self-destructed was Buck Owens. A lot of people who aren't that familiar with country music dismiss Owens as that goofy guy on the TV series *Hee Haw,* but he was a real musical innovator as a singer, guitarist, and bandleader. He was a genuine inspiration for the country rock sound. Owens and Merle Haggard exemplified a style that came to be known as the

Bakersfield sound because it sprang from the country-music scene in Bakersfield, California. Their approach was harder and edgier than a lot of mainstream country, in part because of instrumentation that wasn't that far from rock. I actually wrote "Just in Case It Happens, Yes Indeed" with the Bakersfield sound in mind.

For example, Don Rich, who led Owens's band, the Buckaroos, until his death in 1974, got a really distinctive sound out of his electric guitar. He was also a terrific high-harmony singer. The combination of his voice and Buck's, not to mention their dueling guitars, really revved up songs like "Act Naturally," which the Beatles covered as a showcase for Ringo Starr, and "I've Got a Tiger by the Tail." Jimmy, who wanted to play lead guitar instead of bass in our new band, was a big Don Rich fan. We were eager to bring some of his flavor to rock music.

Jimmy and I also loved pedal steel guitar. It's a traditional country instrument that is often used in corny or predictable ways, what I call "cry-baby" pedal steel. Yet we knew that a pedal steel didn't have to convey the weepy cliché. On "Kind Woman," Rusty Young came up with a fresh pedal-steel part that transcended all the stereotypes. His playing would be ideal for our next project, we realized, and so would his personality.

This last factor was an important one to me. Buffalo Springfield had been so dysfunctional that I was determined to be very careful about who we invited to join our next band. It may have seemed like the members of the Springfield socialized all the time, but most of our interactions centered on the music we were playing. Otherwise, we were very different people who were into very different things. That may not be what drove us apart, but it certainly didn't keep us together. Understanding that, I wanted everyone in the new group to be compatible personally as well as musically.

Jimmy fit that bill, and so did Rusty. He was a really friendly guy, maybe because he'd grown up in Colorado. (That makes a guy friendly, doesn't it?) I'm sure playing on a Buffalo Springfield record was a big deal for him, but he didn't seem intimidated by any of us. Some people are distant, making it difficult to know what makes them tick, but not Rusty. We clicked right away. As easily as that, our two-person team had expanded to three. Rusty moved to Los Angeles and committed himself fully to our band.

FILLING OUT THE LINEUP

Finding the next piece of the puzzle was a little trickier. Because our concept was so unique, there wasn't a ready supply of players who shared our sensibility. We had to spend time with a variety of musicians to see if they would be a good fit.

Believe it or not, Gregg Allman, who was hanging around Southern California at the time, was considered, but he wasn't exactly what the doctor ordered. There's no question that Gregg is an incredibly gifted guy, and the Allman Brothers Band, which he formed with his brother Duane, would go on to create a genre of its own: Southern rock. But after playing music and hanging out with Gregg for a couple of days, we knew the combination wasn't going to work. For one thing, we were looking for someone who could sing backup vocals, and Gregg, with his strong, throaty voice, was more of a lead singer. On top of that, the blues was a big part of his music. Finally, there was the question of compatibility. Both Jimmy and Gregg were into motorcycles, so they had something in common. But overall, his approach to life and music was just very different from ours, and having gone through that sort of thing with the Springfield, I wasn't ready to do it again. So Gregg went his way, and we went ours, to the benefit of us all.

My old friend Gram Parsons was definitely on our wavelength. He was available too. After the time we had spent together in New York, Gram devoted himself to the International Submarine Band. At first the group was more rock than country, but that began to change over the course of the two years it was together, as is obvious to anyone who's heard the ISB's only album, 1968's *Safe at Home*. However, Gram left the International Submarine Band to join the Byrds before *Safe at Home* was released. This seemed like an ideal

match, since the Byrds had a fascination with country music as well. *Turn!*
Turn! Turn! the album they made in 1965, included "Satisfied Mind," a gospel
song that has been covered by country performers such as Red Foley and Roy
Acuff. Gram loved that tune, which is why it's on *Safe at Home.*

With Gram on board, the Byrds spent the first part of 1968 recording
Sweetheart of the Rodeo, which would become a benchmark in the history of
country rock. Unfortunately, most of Gram's work on the disk wound up
being removed because of a problem with his International Submarine Band
contract. Some of the *Sweetheart* songs on which he sang lead were belatedly
included in the 1990 Byrds box set; a restored *Sweetheart of the Rodeo* was later
released in 1997.

I'm not sure if these circumstances caused Gram to leave the Byrds, but
whatever the case, he and Chris Hillman were trying to form a band at the
same time Jimmy and I were. At one point we discussed combining these projects. That would have been a band that a lot of country rock fans would have
loved to have heard, but things never got past the talking stage because of
other commitments. Gram and Chris wanted a pedal steel guitar in their band
too, and they'd already spoken with Sneaky Pete Kleinow about playing the
instrument with them. This made perfect sense, because Kleinow was an
accomplished musician who had briefly served as a sideman with the Byrds.
But Jimmy and I already had a pedal-steel player: Rusty.

Since we couldn't imagine having two pedal-steel experts in the same band,
our discussions didn't go very far. Before long, Gram, Chris, and Sneaky Pete
formed the Flying Burrito Brothers. Today, interestingly enough, my neighbor
Paige Cofrin manages Sneaky Pete and his new group, Burrito Deluxe.

I doubt that I thought about it at the time, but in retrospect I see my decision to go it alone rather than hook up with Gram as a check on the spirit.
This is not meant to be an insult to Gram, a truly great musician and songwriter whose reputation has only grown in the years since his death. He was
also a keen judge of talent; Emmylou Harris, who sang with Gram on his solo
albums *GP* and *Grievous Angel* is an excellent example of this. Nonetheless,

there was a dark side to Gram's personality that's reflected in his work, and even in the title *Grievous Angel*. It was pretty obvious to me that I needed to form my own band according to the vision that Jimmy and I shared.

My philosophy at the time was reflected in the songs Jimmy and I were working on for our new band. I wanted them to be accessible as well as uplifting—to make people who heard them feel better about themselves and the world around them. I take the same approach today in my ministry. My faith fulfills me, and I want to pass along that feeling to my congregation, just as I use music to infuse fans with the joy that courses through me as I sing and play. I wasn't a Christian when Jimmy, Rusty, and I were forming our new band; still, I had a desire to lift up my fellow man. But now, knowing the truth about Jesus Christ, my efforts mean so much more.

Christianity seemingly held an appeal for Gram, too. Otherwise he wouldn't have covered the song "Satisfied Mind." He might be with us today if he had listened to his heart instead of his demons, of which there were many. He was definitely on my mind when I wrote one of my more popular songs, "Crazy Eyes." Gram had these big, bushy eyebrows, and beneath them his gaze could be ominous and even a little unnerving. The lyrics to "Crazy Eyes" reflect my impressions in lines such as "You thought you saw me. Crazy eyes, blind as you can be…"[1] The song even mentions "Brass Buttons," my favorite of Gram's songs.

With Gregg Allman and Gram out of the picture, Jimmy, Rusty, and I went back to the drawing board. We needed a rhythm section, and finding the right drummer turned out to be a simple matter. George Grantham had kept time in Rusty's previous group, Boenzee Cryque, and Rusty recommended him not only as a drummer but also as a backup vocalist. George, Rusty told us, could sing the type of high harmonies that I associated with Don Rich and the Buckaroos. If he was right, we could kill two birds with one stone.

Taking Rusty's advice, we flew George to California for an audition. Once he arrived, we taught him some of the songs we'd been writing for our new band. We were amazed when we heard how he was able to play intricate drum parts and sing harmony at the same time. George also met our criteria about being a team player. There was no danger that his ego would run amuck, and it didn't take us long to invite him to join us.

That left us in need of a bassist, and once again, Miles Thomas, our roadie with Buffalo Springfield, came to the rescue, just as he had when he recommended that we use Rusty Young on "Kind Woman." Miles knew a lot of L.A. musicians, including members of a band called the Poor. He'd even done some roadie work for the group.

Originally called the Soul Survivors, the Poor, like Boenzee Cryque, had a lot of links to Colorado; Allen Kemp and Pat Shanahan, two of the main players, were from Denver. Also in the lineup was Randy Meisner, a Nebraskan whose playing and singing really impressed Miles.

In a strange coincidence, the Poor signed with our old managers, Charlie Green and Brian Stone, who attracted some interest for the group from a couple of record labels. But the singles they recorded failed to set the sales charts on fire. No wonder Randy was interested when Miles told him about our new project.

Randy wasn't the only candidate for the job of bassist. Also in the running was Timothy B. Schmit. Tim was born in Oakland, California, and raised in Sacramento, where he began playing in clubs while still a teenager. His band went through a series of names before settling on Glad, which eventually put out an album called *Feelin' Glad* on the ABC label. Apparently, he thought a group featuring two former members of Buffalo Springfield had a greater chance of success than his combo. Like Randy, he, too, wanted to try out for us.

We were in a very fortunate position. Randy and Tim were extremely talented, as is shown by the success they've had over the course of their careers, and both of them aced their auditions. It was obvious to me that from a musical standpoint, we couldn't go wrong with either guy. Still, we had to choose. So, in keeping with my desire to achieve a family feeling within the band, we looked at whose personality seemed to mesh best with the rest of us. That's when Rusty spoke up in Randy's favor. For some reason, Tim rubbed Rusty the wrong way. Jimmy and I didn't have strong feelings either way, and since we wanted Rusty to be happy, Randy got the nod.

The odd thing about this decision was that in trying to recruit a bassist who would mesh with the rest of us, we came to find out that Randy didn't fit in with the other four of us nearly as well as we would have liked. It wasn't that he was a bad guy. While he may have wanted more of a say in the band than he felt he was getting, he didn't start arguments over the issue. He was just a little off-center in relation to the rest of us and seemed to come from a slightly different place. This disconnect probably explains why Randy had such a short tenure with the group.

Not that Randy's personality entirely disrupted the family feeling I was seeking. From the beginning, the camaraderie we achieved in the new band was much more comfortable than it had been in the Springfield. To make a group work, and work well, everyone's ego has to be in check. Otherwise, competition will kill the creativity you can generate as a team.

I sometimes think of a rock band as if it's a family, where each member looks out for the others and you operate in a way that helps *everyone* succeed— not just one or two members. The Bible describes it this way: "Let nothing be done through selfish ambition or conceit, but in lowliness of mind let each esteem others better than himself. Let each of you look out not only for his own interests, but also for the interests of others"[2] In the Old Testament, the concept is stated even more simply: "Can two walk together, unless they are agreed?"[3]

Jimmy, Rusty, and I were looking for special qualities that would make the five of us one. George certainly fit the family concept, but for some intangible reason, Randy wasn't there in quite the same way.

By this time Nancy and I had set up housekeeping at a little rental in Laurel Canyon, about a mile down the road from Mark Volman's place. At $150 a month, we got what we paid for. The house was old and fairly small, with a foundation that had become so saturated with water over the years that the house always felt a bit moist inside. And as an unpleasant bonus, the bathroom seemed to be slowly sinking into the soil.

But the warmth of our feelings for each other made it more than livable. We stayed there for the better part of two years, and as the band was getting started, it became our rendezvous spot—a place where everyone was comfortable dropping by. I can still picture Jimmy riding up on his motorcycle, his dog Jasper on the back. Most of the time he didn't come on band business, but simply because we all enjoyed each other's company. That feeling endures to this day. Although Jimmy and I have had our problems over the years, we've never lost our love and admiration for each other. We're like brothers in that way. We might say unkind things to each other from time to time, but we'd never let anyone else get away with it. If they tried, they'd have to answer to one of us.

THE COUNTRY ROCK SOUND

The band rehearsed in the Laurel Canyon house, and musically things heated up very quickly. Jimmy's guitar playing was terrific, George and Randy formed a tight rhythm section, Rusty's pedal steel added just the right amount of country authenticity, and the singing was beyond our wildest expectations. George's high harmonies were a big part of that, but so were Randy's vocal contributions, which helped create a wonderful, round tone.

With our sound coming together, word began to circulate among members of the L.A. music community about the great new project Jimmy and I had assembled. Fellow musicians often dropped by to hear our rehearsals, and a frequent visitor was a young singer from Detroit, Glenn Frey, who was part of a duo called Longbranch Pennywhistle. My future bandmate J. D. Souther was the other part of the duo. As Glenn sat on the floor, listening closely to every note we played, he was learning lessons that would serve him well in his next band, the Eagles.

Our band was definitely a key influence on Glenn, as the Eagles' subsequent hiring of Randy and Tim makes clear. Years later, during one of the Eagles' reunion concerts, Glenn publicly gave a nod to one of his influences. I was at the show during a stop in the Denver area, and after pointing me out in the crowd, he made reference to the influence Buffalo Springfield had on his musical journey. It was a nice compliment, but I wondered why he mentioned the Springfield rather than talking about all the times he watched Poco in my living room. I guess, in his eyes, mentioning the Springfield seemed hipper. Either way, it was nice that he acknowledged one of the things my life's been about—inspiring others. If I can have an influence on them for eternity, too, then everything's been worthwhile.

Our new band was jelling, as was our sound, so we needed to find a manager and a place to play. Plus, we needed something to call ourselves. Dickie Davis wound up helping us on all three counts.

Dickie had stayed in touch even after the Springfield had severed its management ties with him in favor of the Beach Boys' manager Nick Grillo. It might seem odd that we'd reach out again to Dickie after we'd become frustrated with his limited ability to promote us during our time with the Buffalo Springfield. Even so, I put a high value on friendship, sometimes to my professional detriment. The thought that we could turn to someone we knew, rather than having to go through a long and arduous search for management, was very attractive. Dickie didn't have the tools to get the job done, but we were too busy to deal with such things ourselves.

Besides, Dickie had remained a pretty big player in the L.A. music community, with a commanding presence and plenty of connections to area venues. He was tied in closely with the Troubadour, and when he told us we could use the club as our personal rehearsal hall, we were excited. My house had been a great place to woodshed at first, but with so many people, like Glenn Frey, trooping to our door to check us out, it was no longer ideal. The Troubadour, on the other hand, would allow us to work on a real stage and hone our dynamics to a fine edge. So we signed up with Dickie and made the Troubadour our home away from home.

THE PUBLIC MEETS POGO

By October we were ready to make our public debut, but we needed something to put on the marquee. A number of handles were batted around, but the one Dickie liked best was Pogo, the name of a hat-wearing possum in a popular comic strip of the same name by artist Walt Kelly. Even though *Pogo* debuted back in the 1940s, it experienced a surge of popularity among young people in the 1960s because of Kelly's way of working politics into stories about a potpourri of talkative swamp creatures. Dickie thought associating ourselves with Pogo would immediately let people know that we were cool and smart, with a country edge.

Not being a big comics reader in recent years, I wasn't all that wild about the idea, but neither was I dead-set against it. For our first public appearance at the Troubadour, as one of several bands playing a Monday night hoot-enanny, we called ourselves Pogo. That changed for the next two shows, one at the Troubadour and the other a benefit concert at the University of Southern California, where we joined Three Dog Night, Hoyt Axton, and other groups. Those nights we performed as R.F.D. The name was probably inspired by *Mayberry R.F.D.,* a television series that had aired its first episode in September; it was a spin-off from *The Andy Griffith Show.* In that context, R.F.D. meant "Rural Free Delivery." The letters were also Dickie's initials—Richard Franklin Davis—but that didn't stop some people from thinking it stood for "Richie Furay's Dream." In some ways, this last theory was appropriate because the band was the fulfillment of the dream I'd had after the Buffalo Springfield ended. However, by mid-November when we began a two-week run at the Troubadour, we were back to being Pogo.

Under either name, we were an immediate hit. After the collapse of Buffalo Springfield, critics and fans were watching closely to see what the members of the band would do next, and our reviews were mostly raves. They not only equaled the best ones Buffalo Springfield received, but many of them were better. The fans who saw us during those shows, which paired us with singer-songwriter Biff Rose (probably the only person in the world to have had his compositions covered by both David Bowie and Tiny Tim), were just as enthusiastic. We'd thought we were on the right track, and the audiences' reactions proved it.

Just as had happened with the Springfield, record-company executives began swarming around us. Talent scouts were eager to see if we would live up to our reputation, and when we did, their bosses didn't wait long to start making offers. The label that showed the most interest was Columbia, headed by Clive Davis, who's gone on to have a career that rivals Ahmet Ertegun's at Atlantic. His background was as a lawyer, but he had a great instinct for identifying talent. Prior to 1967 Columbia hadn't signed many rock acts, concentrating instead on pop and folk artists. That changed after the Monterey International Pop Festival, when Clive reached out to several of the artists who'd made the event so special, including Janis Joplin and Santana. By the next year, everyone knew that Columbia wanted to record the freshest contemporary groups, and Pogo certainly qualified.

So why didn't we sign a contract and get on with things? Because I was still under contract with Atlantic Records through the Springfield, and Ahmet wasn't going to let a competitor like Davis take one of his assets without compensation. Clive, for his part, had leverage over Ertegun in a different situation. Steve Stills had recently formed a musical partnership with ex-Byrd David Crosby, who had sat in with the Springfield on several occasions, and Graham Nash, a member of the Hollies, a band that had hit with "Carrie Anne" and several other catchy, radio-friendly tunes. Ahmet wanted to sign the trio, but Nash was still contractually obligated to Columbia, the Hollies label. Ahmet and Clive were both stuck.

The solution to this problem came courtesy of another major figure in music history, and in my career. His name was David Geffen, and he'd go on to become a record-label owner, a movie mogul, an entertainment tycoon, and a multimillionaire.

David wasn't a legend in 1968. He was a rising star still in his twenties. Hailing from Brooklyn, he had an unbelievable drive to succeed, and his ambition landed him at William Morris, the talent agency that handled the Springfield's affairs. (He later moved to another talent company, CMA.) Clive was familiar with David, having signed one of his clients, singer-songwriter Laura Nyro.

Given this background, David was uniquely positioned to broker an accord with all parties, and that's exactly what he did. He proposed that Clive exchange my rights for Nash's. That way, Epic, a Columbia subsidiary, could sign Pogo, and Atlantic could hook up with Crosby, Stills, and Nash. Realizing that this idea was like a baseball trade that benefited both teams, Ahmet and Clive agreed. David would demonstrate the sort of creative thinking that led to this agreement again and again in the decades that followed. He's a controversial figure and isn't well liked by everyone whose paths he has crossed, but my experiences with him were mainly positive. Even after he had become one of the foremost moviemakers in America, within a week he personally answered a note I wrote to him. That's one reason why he's earned my respect over the long haul.

BACK IN THE STUDIO

With our contractual complications behind us, all systems were go, and we soon began recording our first album. At first everything went well because we had a bunch of songs ready. Some dated to the waning days of Buffalo Springfield, like "What a Day," which had been recorded as a demo with Steve Stills doing the vocals. He had never taken the lead on a song I'd written, so I'm glad it was recorded. (It's included in the *Buffalo Springfield Box Set.*) The Springfield also took a swing at "Nobody's Fool" and "Can't Keep Me Down," which was later renamed "Do You Feel It, Too." The latter tune wound up on our *From the Inside* album and was covered by the Nitty Gritty Dirt Band.

Also in the hopper was "Grand Junction," an instrumental by Rusty, and "Make Me a Smile," which I wrote with Jimmy. I also collaborated with Skip Goodwin, who wrote the lyrics for a trio of compositions: "Calico Lady," "Tomorrow," and "Consequently So Long."

More personal for me were the songs whose words I wrote, including "My Kind of Love," another Springfield-era song that was released as a single around the time of *Pickin' Up the Pieces* but didn't find a place on an album until a 1990 compilation titled *The Forgotten Trail*. The song could be interpreted as a sad ballad about love and loss, but it was really another reflection of my feelings about the end of the Springfield. I don't mind that people interpret it differently. In fact, that's one of the great things about music. A given listener may think a song is about something totally removed from what the composer intended, but if the person can relate it to his or her life in a meaningful way, the writer has done the job.

Our mission, meanwhile, was to capture our songs in the studio. We played as a unit, not five separate musicians with independent agendas, which is why the songs give off such a warm glow. But there was trouble brewing that I didn't recognize at the time, and it came to a head while we were mixing the album.

As Randy remembers it, he had asked if he could come down to the studio to hear the mixes that I was working on with Jimmy, who, as someone with an engineering and technical background, was doing most of the physical work. When I supposedly told Randy no, he felt my refusal meant that he wasn't an equal member of the band, and he reacted by quitting.

My recollection of this incident is fuzzy, so I don't want to contradict Randy. I do know that mixing recordings is a long, tedious, and laborious process, and when you're in the middle of a difficult stretch, the last thing you want is to be interrupted; you have to stay focused. We were also dealing with union engineers, and we weren't allowed to touch the studio console. Mixing is as much a "feel" process as anything else, and it's hard to communicate exactly what you want. Overall, there were a lot of variables that complicated the situation.

Maybe Randy caught us at a moment when we weren't as patient or understanding as we should have been. But it still seems strange that an incident as seemingly minor as this would have caused him to leave the band. As I've pointed out, he was a bit aloof compared to the rest of us and didn't fit into the Pogo family as well as we would have liked. If he felt the same way, he might have been looking for a way out.

At any rate, Randy's abrupt departure left us in a fix. For one thing, we had shows to do, and rather than cancel them, we played them as a four-piece, with Jimmy taking on bass duties. This was never going to be a good long-term solution, because Pogo had been designed so that Jimmy could play lead guitar. Then there was the album itself. We had to take Randy's bass parts off the songs we'd cut, and his vocals, too. Even more awkward, we already had final cover art—an illustration of the five of us, Randy included. We wound up commissioning the artist to draw in Jimmy's dog, Jasper, in the place that had been occupied by Randy. I don't think we intended to slight Randy by doing that, but I'm sure he took it as a not-so-subtle message about what we might have thought of him.

Randy and I didn't see each other again until he appeared about ten years later on *I Still Have Dreams,* one of my solo albums. And it was another decade before we reteamed for a Poco reunion. The reunion project was difficult from the start, but Randy and I did our best to smooth things out between us. I have no hard feelings, and I hope he doesn't either.

As if these complications weren't enough, we'd soon be faced with another obstacle. In the spring of 1969, right before we were slated to take the stage at the University of California in Santa Barbara, we were served with a stack of documents from none other than Walt Kelly. The papers contained thousands of words that added up to one big threat: If we continued performing as Pogo, he would sue us.

Today such a reaction would be entirely predictable. Just like companies, artists zealously protect their trademarks and copyrights. We were shocked, though. Representatives of the Buffalo Springfield Roller Company had actually sent us a letter supporting our use of their firm's name. The last thing we expected was for Kelly, who had such a hip, liberal reputation, to take the opposite course. We weren't doing anything to discredit him or his characters. To the contrary, we probably had brought him extra publicity, giving him even more credibility with the youthful readership that he had cultivated late in his life.

Since Kelly didn't see things that way, we were left with few options. We could go to court and ask for legal permission to use the name, but since Kelly had been using it for decades before we'd taken it as our own, we had little hope that a judge would rule in our favor. (No one would have believed we'd named the band after a pogo stick.) Or we could give ourselves a very different name, potentially undoing all the work we'd done over the preceding months to establish it in the minds of the public.

Eventually we came up with an inspired compromise. We'd change the name to something so close to "Pogo" that it wouldn't confuse the fans. By changing the *g* in Pogo to a *c,* we became Poco. From the start I liked the new name better than the old one.

Of course, this situation wasn't the only bump in the road. The band would be shaken in the months and years to come, and the challenges that would confront me in my personal life would be even greater, shaking me to the very depths of my soul. Having not yet found my way to the Lord, I felt that I was facing every crisis alone. I'm thrilled to know that I was dead wrong. God was there all along.

10

The Bottom Keeps Falling Out

Fleeting Success and the Damage of Sexual Sin

When Poco's first album, *Pickin' Up the Pieces,* was released in mid-1969, I prepared myself for a rocket ride to stardom, but the album barely got off the ground. Today it's regarded as a lost classic because its sales were so modest.

In many ways the mediocre performance of the LP didn't hurt us too badly. Our fellow musicians continued to respect what we were doing, and we were much sought after by bookers and concert promoters. Shortly after we became Poco, we put on some great shows at the Boston Tea Party in Boston and the Bitter End in New York City, and as the weather warmed, we landed on some terrific multiband bills. We joined Chuck Berry and Santana at the Northern California Folk Rock Festival in May, appeared with the Who at the Hollywood Palladium in June, and shared the stage with the Doors at the Vancouver Pop Festival at the end of August. We also flew to Colorado in late June for the Denver Pop Festival, which featured Johnny Winter and Creedence Clearwater Revival. We were scheduled to perform at the Troubadour in L.A. the day after our Denver appearance, but the flight was late, forcing a young comedian and banjo player named Steve Martin to vamp until we arrived. He wasn't very happy with us, but I'm sure he developed a lot of good material—maybe even his arrow-through-the-head routine—while he filled the extra time.

THE GARGOYLE HOUSE

Whenever I was home in Los Angeles, I had a new place to hang my hat; Nancy and I were living in a rental property on Beverly Glen that's as odd a place as I've ever lived. The house had several disturbing decorative features, including gargoyles and a pentagram, and our landlord shared stories with us about a ghost that supposedly haunted the building. According to him, one group of visitors had reported seeing a Chinese servant in one of the bedrooms, only to be told by the residents that they didn't have a servant. The ghost turned up often enough that he was given a name: Noodles.

We didn't take these tales seriously until one day just before we formally moved in. Nancy was downstairs using the vacuum, when suddenly she heard a moan and felt as if she'd hit something, even though nothing was there. She was so freaked out by the experience that she huddled under a staircase that was over the furnace register, terrified of what she'd encountered.

We weren't Christians at that time, and Nancy never saw or heard any other ghosts at the house. But in hindsight she feels that the Lord was looking out for us and protecting us, waiting for the day when we would finally give our lives to Him.

In the meantime I was concerned with more immediate problems, such as finding a bass player for Poco. Jimmy had been filling in on bass guitar ever since Randy left, and although he'd done a great job, he was restless. He thought he'd have to play bass only for a brief time, as a stopgap to get us past the next shows on our schedule. Instead, his temporary commitment had stretched into several months, and he was getting more and more frustrated. All along he had wanted to play lead guitar in Poco, and he wasn't getting the chance to do it.

The longer the situation dragged on, the more likely it was to cause a rift in the band. Given what I'd just lived through with Buffalo Springfield, that sort of drama was the last thing I wanted. We needed to find a bassist quickly, and I felt we already had an excellent candidate: Timothy B. Schmit. He'd had a great audition back when we were first putting the group together. Of course, Randy had too, and we wound up choosing him because we initially thought he'd be a better fit for the band. As Randy's sudden departure shows, we were wrong. It made me think that maybe we should have selected Timothy in the first place.

Timothy had moved on with his life after we invited Randy to join the band, and it was unrealistic to think that he would simply drop everything to hook up with us. Pride was a factor as well. We'd rejected him, and just because we'd had a change of heart, it didn't mean the hurt had gone away. Finally, there was the matter of Rusty's feelings toward Timothy. Randy had gotten the nod because Rusty hadn't warmed up to Timothy, and nothing had changed. Truth be told, Rusty questioned Timothy's musicianship, which I couldn't understand. In my opinion, Timothy was an extremely competent bass player and a very good, if stylized, harmony and lead singer. For whatever reason, Rusty thought otherwise.

In the end, though, Rusty wanted what was best for the band, and when he saw how the rest of us felt about Timothy, he agreed to go along with whatever we decided. Now we had to convince Timothy to come onboard.

Timothy had returned to Sacramento, where he was majoring in psychology at Sacramento State College and playing with his old band, Glad. Dickie and I found out that Glad had a show there, and we decided to drop by. We figured our best chance was to catch him off guard, ask him to join Poco, and then keep our fingers crossed. This plan seemed doomed to failure, but sometimes even doomed plans work out. I was straightforward with Timothy about where Poco was at and why we wanted him to join the band. Apparently, that was the right approach. Even though he was close to completing his degree, he said, "Sure. I'd like to get involved."

I was thrilled with his decision, but getting him quickly up to speed proved to be tricky. Rusty may have said he'd go along with making Timothy a member of the band, but that didn't mean he was pleased about it. When we brought Timothy to the Troubadour so he could start learning our songs and get a feel for the band's dynamic, Rusty was very chilly toward him. In fact, the tension was thick enough to slice. For example, if there was only one chair available at a table, but it was next to Timothy, Rusty wouldn't sit in it.

I suppose I could have taken Timothy aside and explained that things just weren't going to work out, but I had made up my mind. We needed to move forward, and I was certain Timothy was the guy who would help us do it. That put Timothy and Rusty in the position of having to maintain a professional relationship for the good of the group, and to their credit, they managed to do it. I don't think anyone looking at the band from the outside would have sensed the strain in their relationship. Nevertheless, the strain took its toll on Rusty, in particular.

THE SILENCE OF AM RADIO

The slow sales of our debut album increased everyone's anxiety level. None of us could figure out why the critical acclaim lavished on *Pickin' Up the Pieces,* not to mention the enthusiasm we generated in concert, failed to translate into legions of record-buying fans. We concluded that the problem was a lack of airplay on Top 40 radio. Underground FM stations, which were multiplying in big cities and college towns, gave us quite a few spins, but in that era, AM radio still drove record sales. Rock-and-roll D.J.s and programmers thought we were too country to play on pop radio, whereas country jocks considered us to be too pop to fit in on country radio. Of course, when you listen to country music today, it doesn't take a rocket scientist to recognize the influence our music had way back then. But at the time we couldn't find acceptance in either radio format.

The one thing that might have broken the logjam would have been a big push from our record company, but none was forthcoming. After having gone to great lengths to free me from Atlantic Records, Clive Davis lost interest in Poco for reasons that had nothing to do with our music. He was irritated by Randy's departure, mainly because it cost Columbia a great deal of money for extra studio fees and the redesign of the album cover, and Walt Kelly's threatened legal action only made matters worse. In addition, Clive didn't get along well with our manager. We never knew precisely why, but it likely had to do with Dickie's manner. He's a tough, sometimes abrasive person who would push and push until he got what he wanted. His approach might have left Clive, a refined and fairly soft-spoken person, with a bad taste in his mouth.

Dickie's temperament didn't upset us because we knew he was only trying to do the best he could for the band. On the other hand, some of his decisions did absolutely nothing to help us achieve significant commercial success. For instance, Poco was asked to perform at a festival near the upstate New York community of Bethel in August 1969, but as Rusty remembers it, Dickie turned down the invitation because he had something better in mind. The festival turned out to be Woodstock, the biggest concert of the 1960s, which drew a crowd of four hundred thousand, spawning record albums, a major feature film, and a mythos that still survives today. Woodstock also launched the careers of many who might not have been remembered had it not been for that event. And the other show that was supposedly so much better? Neither Rusty nor I can remember what it was, which tells me everything I need to know.

Things got so bad between the two Davises, Clive and Dickie, that when it came time for us to start making our second album, Clive wouldn't sign off on studio time. Despite having a nine-album deal with Epic (can you believe that?), we were frozen out. The most logical person to turn to was Dickie, who may have been the reason we were in trouble in the first place. So it's fortunate that someone else was in our corner. Enter David Geffen again.

At that point David was focusing most of his energies on Crosby, Stills, and Nash. During a New York City visit, David took several of us to his apartment to hear CSN's self-titled first LP, which would be released in May 1969. He played the entire album, which features Steve's "Suite: Judy Blue Eyes" and Graham's "Marrakesh Express," both of which would soon turn the recording into a blockbuster. As much as I wanted to like it—and I did—it was hard to hear, because I saw what was on the horizon. CSN would have the thrust of

Ahmet Ertegun, Atlantic Records, and David Geffen behind them, moving the album forward, while we were left to wade in the quicksand with Clive, Epic, and our manager, Dickie Davis.

My instincts turned out to be extremely accurate, with CSN going through the roof after they performed at Woodstock. (Luckily for them, they didn't have Dickie telling them to skip the festival.) They garnered massive publicity from their performance, which they subsequently celebrated with their cover of Joni Mitchell's song "Woodstock." They received even more attention when they added an unlikely new member to the group: Neil Young.

In many ways it made no sense for Neil to join Crosby, Stills, and Nash. Neil and Steve spent much of their time during the Buffalo Springfield years fighting for leadership of the band, and going solo had allowed Neil to be the unquestioned person in charge of his music. Yet the two of them thrived on the competition, with each one pushing the other to do better. Add the creative connection between them, and it becomes more obvious why they couldn't say good-bye once and for all. That's why Steve and Neil have one of the great love-hate relationships in rock-music history.

THAWING THE STUDIO FREEZE-OUT

Crosby, Stills, Nash, and Young aside, David Geffen was extremely fond of Poco, too, and in our time of need, he rose to the challenge. I remember sitting in his office while he called Clive to talk about our predicament, and I was completely astonished by the conversation—although "conversation" is probably too polite a word for what actually happened. I don't know whether David acted as he did for my benefit, but there was yelling and screaming going on that made Dickie look like a rank amateur. This is the same type of behavior that seemed to have turned Clive against us in the first place, but David was so forceful, so relentless, so unstoppable, that even this legendary music executive couldn't resist his will for long. By the next week the lockout was over, and we were back in the studio to record our second album.

We decided to give the LP the simplest title imaginable: *Poco*. After *Pickin' Up the Pieces* came and went so quietly, we felt that we were basically starting at square one. We needed to introduce ourselves to the country's music buyers, and what better way to do it than to make our name the only word on the record jacket.

We definitely approached *Poco* differently from our debut album. The marketing people at Epic Records had been completely confused by *Pieces,* and we didn't want them to stay that way. That meant either tilting our music more toward country or more toward rock, and we wound up choosing the latter. Back then the traditional country genre was slow to accept artists who didn't dress conservatively, wear their hair short, and come up through the Nashville-based industry ranks. Since we looked more like rockers than country-and-western musicians and came from a background that was more rock-oriented, we figured we'd have a better chance with rock-music fans, even if there were parts of our sound that might strike them as unusual.

Had the music critics known we were thinking along these lines, they would have taken us to task. A lot of reviewers believe that performers shouldn't make musical changes in response to market conditions. Instead, the purists argue for letting your music evolve naturally, and if there's no audience for it, that's tough. But in the real world, musicians want to reach as many people as possible, and sometimes making changes—even small ones—can help them achieve that goal. It's entirely possible to broaden your appeal without tarnishing your art or minimizing your creativity.

Taking such factors into account, I think Poco's second album holds up pretty well. Sure, it's a bit of a compromise, but it's one that held on to our original flavor even as it allowed us to explore new areas of sound.

The biggest curve ball on the album is the last cut, "Nobody's Fool/El Tonto de Nadie, Regresa," a nearly twenty-minute-long opus on which Rusty and Jimmy played their hearts out. Back then, lengthy jams were hot, with such groups as the Grateful Dead becoming famous for stretching out onstage and going where no band had gone before. We wanted to prove that we could do the same, and I think we succeeded. The track may not be what most folks anticipated, but it's good to shake people up now and then. And when we played it live during the early seventies, the crowds went wild.

Other songs on the album bridged country and rock, including "You Better Think Twice," which Jimmy wrote, and one of my songs, "Anyway Bye Bye," which runs longer than seven minutes and features a great pedal-steel solo by Rusty. (At some spots in the song, Rusty's instrument doesn't sound like a pedal steel. By running it through a Leslie cabinet, he was able to emulate a Hammond B3 organ.) "Keep on Believin'," which I also wrote, extends the country rock vision that I had in mind when Jimmy and I were starting the band. As for our decision to include "Honky Tonk Downstairs," a cover of the twangy hit written by Dallas Frazier and performed by George Jones, it was our way of saying that we had no intention of abandoning country entirely. In fact, we thought that by bringing more of a rock edge to other tunes, we'd draw in the sort of people who never thought they'd like country music and convince them otherwise.

If only it had worked. When *Poco* came out in May 1970, our record label put very little effort into promoting the album. David's yelling had gotten us into the studio, but it hadn't convinced Clive to make the sort of investment in us that might have allowed us to turn the corner. Whereas *Pickin' Up the Pieces* has been rediscovered by aficionados of country rock music, *Poco* remains one of our more obscure recordings, although George Strait told me he learned "Honky Tonk Downstairs" from the album. It may not have been our best, but it contains a lot of great music that was never heard as widely as it should have been.

Poco's slow sales led to grumbling within the group from an unexpected party: Jimmy. He began saying that I was hogging the spotlight and not giving him enough room to shine. I was blindsided by this claim. Jimmy and I had worked shoulder to shoulder from the time when Poco was little more than a vague idea, and I thought I'd gone out of my way to keep him happy. For instance, I'd insisted that we bring Timothy into the band over Rusty's objections so that Jimmy could get back to playing lead guitar. Yet Jimmy felt stifled, and before long he informed us that he wanted out. He said he'd stick around through the recording of a live album that would follow *Poco,* but after that he was gone.

This was a blow, both for the band and for me personally. After Buffalo Springfield, I'd handpicked a group that I was sure would be together for the long haul, but in just over a year, one member had left and another—my partner, cofounder, and friend—wanted out.

Was I responsible? I didn't think so, but I couldn't completely rule out the possibility. I considered myself to be easygoing, the sort of person who wants to make everyone around him feel comfortable and wanted. But with Jimmy ready to leave and Randy already gone, I wondered if I had been deluding myself. Reflections like these took me to a dark place where I began to feel empty and filled with self-doubt.

LEADING A DOUBLE LIFE

What happened next is among the oldest and most tragic stories in the world: I got involved with another woman. This led to the first major crisis in my marriage, and I have only one person to blame: me. A tragedy is doubled when you bring it on yourself.

Today, more than three decades removed from this disastrous time, I'm astonished that I was so susceptible to temptation, especially since Nancy had just given birth to our first child, a daughter we named Timmie Sue. She was the first Poco baby, but just barely. She was born on September 7, 1970, one day before Timothy B. and his girlfriend had a baby of their own.

I was overjoyed about starting a family and made sure that I was home as the big day neared. We arranged for Nancy to go to the first hospital in the Los Angeles area that allowed men in the delivery room. To put it mildly, this was a novel experience for me, and when Timmie's head began to emerge from her mother's body, I apparently began to babble. Nancy remembers me saying,

"She's so beautiful! She looks just like me!" My comments were so funny to her that she literally laughed her way through the rest of the delivery.

From that first instant, I loved Timmie with every ounce of my being, and I felt the same way about Nancy. It would have been terrific if I could have stayed with them longer, but business called me away. With our two record albums barely selling, the only way I could make money was by touring. Poco was known as a great live act, and people came to our shows whether or not radio stations played our songs. With a growing family, I needed every dollar I could make, so just four days after Timmie came into my life, I was onstage in San Diego, and a week after that I was in Massachusetts to kick off a series of dates that would keep us on the road and far from home for months.

The scene around these concerts was nothing nearly as crazy as the accounts in books such as *Hammer of the Gods,* about Led Zeppelin, a band that attracted groupies in droves. But the early seventies was an age of sexual liberation, and there were always women around who wanted to take their love of music one step further. Rock musicians commonly took advantage of these situations, embracing the philosophy Steve Stills sang about in a solo piece released that same year: "If you can't be with the one you love, love the one you're with."[1]

Though that was the mind-set of the day, it turned out to be a sad testimony for so many musicians, leaving a trail of heartbreak, broken homes, and shattered lives—and for what? When there's no commitment in a relationship, there's no relationship at all. Without committed love between two people, there might be episodes of sexual pleasure, but not the trust and deep intimacy that come with a committed marriage. The Bible doesn't put limits on sex to spoil our fun; it sets boundaries to contribute to our happiness and well-being. Some of the best wisdom in this regard is found in the book of Proverbs:

Drink water from your own cistern,
And running water from your own well.
Should your fountains be dispersed abroad,
Streams of water in the streets?

Let them be only your own,

And not for strangers with you.

Let your fountain be blessed,

And rejoice with the wife of your youth.[2]

I was not a rock musician who slept around on the road. I had always been faithful to Nancy until the heavy touring schedule and the ongoing struggles within Poco wore me down. These are only excuses, but they got the best of me. That's when I fell for someone on the fringes of the music business: a secretary who worked for an executive at Columbia Records. She was a musician, a piano player with real talent. The time we spent together was innocent at first. We'd talk when we saw each other, and maybe flirt a little. Nothing out of the ordinary, and nothing dangerous—or so I thought. But my mind was playing tricks on me, and before I realized it, I got in too deep. Subconsciously I began to think that, because of her musical abilities, she understood me better than Nancy did, and I wondered if Nancy was still as interested in me now that she had Timmie in her life.

Had I been thinking clearly, the answers to these questions would have been obvious: Nancy loved me and was committed to me; the other woman was an interesting person and should never have been anything more than a friend. But at that point my judgment was clouded. In my state of emotional turmoil, I leaped to the conclusion that someone other than my wife was the woman meant for me.

By early 1971, shortly after *Deliverin'*, our in-concert album, hit stores, I was living a double life. When Nancy and my mom flew to New York to see Poco play a concert at Carnegie Hall, I told them they couldn't come back to the hotel with me after the show because the room was too crowded. In truth, I hadn't booked a room at the hotel since I was staying at the secretary's apartment.

Something had to give, and finally it did. I was talking with Nancy on the phone, and she could tell from my tone of voice that something was terribly wrong. She asked if I was messing around, and I confessed. Next she demanded to know how many other women there had been. Rather than being reassured to learn that there was only one, she was even more concerned. Since I was involved with only one woman, Nancy realized I wasn't just out for pleasure. I was in a romantic relationship.

Talking to Nancy that day was like being doused with cold water. I immediately made plans to fly back to Los Angeles, and during the flight I sat beside Rusty's wife. As I tried to explain why I was with another woman in New York, I kept complimenting Nancy. That should have told me something. Even so, I still wasn't ready to make any final decisions. When I got back home, I suggested to Nancy that we separate for a while, to give both of us time to think. But she made it clear that we didn't need a separation; she wanted a divorce.

Nancy moved out of our house and back with her mother. Her mom had recently broken her wrist and was home from work, so she was able to watch Timmie while Nancy went job hunting. Nancy found a position within days, and she quickly hired a lawyer and made plans to start divvying up our belongings. Nancy was obviously ready to move on with her life without me.

Confused and upset, I went back on tour with Poco, taking the secretary with me. We were in Texas when the scales fell from my eyes. In a moment I realized I was making the worst mistake of my life. I was terrified and felt sick inside. I had no explanation then for the way this feeling came over me, but I know now that it was the Holy Spirit stepping into my life.

I could have ignored this sensation, but I was so ashamed and overwhelmed by a sense of guilt that I couldn't. I literally felt as if I was about to vomit from the fear that Nancy would reject my change of heart and would refuse to have any part of me. But I had to try to get through to her, so I sent the secretary home to New York and returned to Los Angeles, determined to win back my wife.

HOPING FOR RECONCILIATION

After having told my wife that I wasn't sure I wanted to remain committed to her and choosing to take another woman on the road with me, the process of trying to win Nancy back was humbling. (Even thinking about it now and having to put this part of my life out there for all to see makes my stomach churn.) I had to call Nancy's mom to ask her to get in touch with Nancy for me. She told me she wasn't sure if Nancy would ever talk to me again. I didn't want to hear that, but I understood.

As it turned out, though, swallowing my pride paid off. Nancy and I got together to talk, and we were able to look at what we'd be losing if we split up. After many hours and a lot of tears, we agreed to give our marriage another try.

Our reconciliation didn't magically heal every wound. For one, I had destroyed the trust we had shared as husband and wife. To help ensure that my fidelity wouldn't slip, I decided to have Nancy travel with me. In my enthusiasm for this plan, I paid to fly the wives of everyone else in the group to Boston as a surprise—not the smartest thing for me to do, as my bandmates would soon let me know. Even worse, I wasn't in Boston when Nancy and the other wives arrived. I had dashed off to New York to completely break things off with the secretary, and I didn't make it back in time to meet Nancy at the airport. She was extremely angry, and when I arrived in Boston, it took me what seemed like ages to calm her down and reassure her that I wasn't in New York fooling around with the other woman or having second thoughts about our getting back together. Returning to the point where our love was as natural and unselfconscious as it had once been took what seemed like an eternity.

These memories are painful to relive, but relating them here serves a purpose. While Nancy and I weren't yet Christians, the Lord was already involved in our lives, and He wanted us to stay together. By guiding us through this fire and allowing us to emerge with our marriage intact, He gave us wisdom that we're now able to use in counseling other couples who are going through similar experiences. One of the greatest blessings of being a pastor comes when I can say to people, "I know what you're going through." I can reassure struggling couples that there's hope through the Gospel of Jesus Christ and a life surrendered to Him. Our own story is proof that no marriage is damaged so much that it's beyond God's "grace to help in time of need."[3] Yes, by the grace of His love and the power of the Holy Spirit, a marriage threatened, even as ours was, can grow stronger.

Our marriage was strengthened because of our struggles. And thank God it was, because it would be tested again, even more severely than before. By then, however, we would have something else to help us face the challenge—*faith*.

11

Will Deliverin' Really Deliver?

Leaving Poco to Form the First Country Rock Supergroup

The crisis in my marriage made it more difficult than ever to focus on what had previously been my overriding goal: to achieve a commercial breakthrough with Poco.

Deliverin', culled from shows at the Boston Music Hall and the New York Felt Forum before Jimmy's departure, was the biggest-selling recording we'd made to date, climbing to number twenty-six on the *Billboard* album charts. (Our first two albums topped out at numbers sixty-three and fifty-eight, respectively.) The LP resonated with a lot of people because it provided a real sense of what Poco was like in concert, where we were at our peak. The great songs on the album didn't hurt, either. We put our stamp on a couple of my Buffalo Springfield tunes—"A Child's Claim to Fame," which we performed as a medley with Timothy's "Hard Luck," as well as "Kind Woman"—and offered definitive versions of some earlier tracks, including Jimmy's "You Better Think Twice."

I was pleased by the vitality and excitement of *Deliverin'* and wanted to keep the momentum going. We took the first step by choosing Paul Cotton to replace Jimmy, who would go on to achieve great success by teaming with Kenny Loggins.

Paul had been part of a group called the Illinois Speed Press, which put out two albums on Columbia, the parent company of Epic. We'd played with the Speed Press in the past—the first time way back in August 1969—and found Paul to be a talented singer, guitarist, and songwriter. His previous band may have been a bit more rock and roll than Poco, but we shared enough in common to make Paul's entry into our group a fairly smooth one, and he proved to be a perfect addition. A lot of people feel that the lineup circa *Pickin' Up the Pieces,* with Jimmy and Randy, was Poco's finest, and I certainly look back on it fondly. Still, I think the edition featuring Timothy and Paul was the best Poco lineup. When they joined Rusty, George, and me, the band really hit its stride.

MUSIC FROM THE INSIDE

With the band reconfigured, we now needed the right producer for our next album. Since Jimmy had left, we had the luxury of looking outside the group for someone with new ideas and, hopefully, the ability to translate our live sound to the studio. Steve Cropper, who produced our next album *From the Inside,* seemed like a promising candidate, which is undoubtedly why the record company suggested him. As a guitarist and founding member of Booker T and the MG's, he played on some of the greatest soul records of the 1960s, including ones by Sam and Dave, and he co-wrote a couple of absolutely classic singles: "In the Midnight Hour," which teamed him with Wilson Pickett, and "(Sittin' On) The Dock of the Bay," the last and biggest hit by the late Otis Redding.

Although Cropper served as a producer on some of those sides, he'd only recently begun to focus on album-length projects. He oversaw 1970's *Them Changes* by Buddy Miles, the drummer and sometime Jimi Hendrix sideman who'd so impressed Steve Stills a few years earlier. Epic was sure that Cropper was just what Poco needed to give us the sound we were looking for, and after meeting him, we decided to give it a try.

Unfortunately, what should have worked didn't, and I chalk that up to a lack of chemistry and differing musical tastes. Cropper was an extremely nice guy and a terrific guitar player. We got along well, and years later, when I recorded my first solo album *I've Got a Reason,* I asked him to contribute. But his Southern R&B approach didn't blend well with Poco's style, which became more rock-oriented with Paul's addition but remained in touch with our early country influences. Cropper was also a bit too laid back when it came to structuring arrangements. Thanks to him, the record has a good, rocking sound, but he didn't do much to shape any of the songs for AM radio, which we desperately needed.

The recording sessions went smoothly, with one huge exception. We cut the album in Memphis, Steve's home base, and the secretary with whom I'd had my dalliance months earlier kept phoning me. Even though Nancy had joined me in Memphis so we could continue to work on our relationship, I kept taking the calls. Of course this upset Nancy, and she expressed her displeasure by hopping on the next plane to Los Angeles. It was another reminder that while on the surface everything seemed better between us, the pain inflicted by infidelity still lingered.

To this day I have a difficult time performing, or even hearing, some of my songs on *From the Inside* because they remind me of things that were happening at the time I was carrying on the affair. Songs such as "What If I Should Say I Love You" and "Just for Me and You" were started and finished before anything happened between me and the secretary, but I added what I thought were clever little alterations during the recordings, and they still haunt me.

Though it has been more than thirty years, I'm still reminded of what I almost lost to selfishness. I recently wrote a song titled "In the Still of the Night" that has helped me cherish Nancy, the bride the Lord has given me. It says:

I'll be yours 'til the end, however long that may be
And that's a promise that I plan to keep
When I say that I love you, I mean what I say
And Baby, those words don't come cheap.

We've had our moments, those crazy moments
When the storms of life came down strong
Hurtin' each other,
Thinkin' another could be the one, but somehow we held on, and
In the still of the night, there's a song in my heart for you
In the still of the night, there's a light that will shine for you
In the still of the night[1]

Other cuts on *From the Inside* spur much fonder recollections. We picked "From the Inside," which Timothy wrote, as the album's title song because it spoke to our way of making music. To us, it came from the heart. Making this choice also let Timothy know that we saw him as a full member, not a side-man or a Johnny-come-lately with lesser status than the rest of us. It was another example of my eagerness to make every member of the band feel like family.

On his first Poco album, Paul also excelled, providing us with three first-rate numbers: "Railroad Days," "Ol' Forgiver," and "Bad Weather." The last of these showcases my first guitar solo on record. I came up with it while I was doodling on an acoustic twelve-string. When I played it for Paul, he liked it, so I played it on the recording. Paul's an underrated songwriter, and "Bad Weather" is one of my favorites among his tunes.

Yet despite so many good ingredients, *From the Inside* never came together as I had hoped. With two relatively new members in the band, we were still getting a feel for one another, and the lack of a strong production hand prevented some of the songs from being all they could have been. Epic, meanwhile, continued to give us far less support than we needed. "Just for Me and You" was issued as a single, but when it didn't receive a significant push from the label, it faded away, just like the 45s before it.

Poco had a number of supporters within the hierarchy of Columbia Records, including Don Ellis. At the time, however, nothing happened at the company unless Clive wanted it to happen. In that respect, he was a lot like Ahmet—a dominating presence and personality who determined to a large degree who would make it and who wouldn't. And for whatever reason, Clive never made Poco a priority.

Things got worse after *From the Inside* failed to bring in the returns. The album sold fewer copies than *Deliverin',* stalling at about the same place our first two records had. This response made us more determined than ever to find a compatible producer who knew how to get us on AM radio, and we quickly zeroed in on someone I feel to this day was the right man: Richie Podolor. He was one of the hottest producers in rock music at the time, with a surefire hit-making touch proven by his work with such bands as Steppenwolf and Three Dog Night.

A Poco fan, Richie eagerly joined us in the studio, where we cut "C'mon" and "A Man Like Me," a pair of guaranteed crowd pleasers that we'd included on *Deliverin'.* Poco never sounded better or more exciting in the studio than we did on those recordings, so good that I couldn't believe D.J.s would be able to resist playing the record. But we never got the chance to find out. We brought the finished product to Columbia's New York headquarters and played the songs for a roomful of executives in suits and ties. But these men with supposedly well-trained ears rejected the songs almost as if word had come from the top. I guess it sounds a bit like a conspiracy theory, but the power some of these guys held was unreal. If they liked you or had a personal stake in the group, they could always get the job done. Let me repeat that: They could *always* get the job done.

Richie Podolor had produced enough hit records that our new single should have been given serious attention. But Columbia refused to release the songs to radio and wouldn't authorize us to record additional material with Richie. We were dumbfounded. It was almost as if they wanted us to fail. It was also an insult to Richie and the band.

TIME TO LEAVE L.A.

I had been burned by New York record executives, and I also had become disillusioned with Los Angeles. I'd never been much of a glad-hander or partygoer, nor did I care about being seen at trendy events. I kept a low profile then, just as I do today. I also had become more interested in providing a better home environment for Nancy and Timmie, who'd just celebrated her first birthday. Looking at my personal life, I decided that Nancy and I needed a change of scenery, where we could make a fresh start without tripping over reminders of the recent traumas we'd endured. An article Nancy read in the *Los Angeles Times* about the horribly polluted air in the region brought all of these feelings to the surface. Both of us knew it was time to leave.

The other members of the band were sick of Los Angeles too, and for a while all of us considered moving to San Francisco. In fact, George got a place there, anticipating that we'd be hot on his heels. But at the last minute, Nancy and I realized that the hustle and bustle of the Bay Area would be just as frantic as life in L.A. So we started looking for alternatives and soon settled on Colorado. I had loved the state ever since visiting it in my teen years, and because George and Rusty were from there, we figured they would be enthusiastic as well. Even though it was quite a distance from L.A. and New York, the two main power centers of the music industry, we weren't concerned. All we needed was an airport.

Heading to the mountains was done practically on a whim. We moved within a week or so, but not before traveling to San Francisco to break the news to George. I can see him now, standing on a ladder painting his brand-new apartment as I told him, "Guess what? We're all moving to Colorado." Luckily, George is pretty low-key, or I might have been wearing that paint myself! I know he was upset and disappointed, but the appeal of moving to Colorado helped to ease any frustration he was feeling.

Back then, a lot of musicians and hippies were settling in a community called Nederland, not far from Boulder, Colorado. The influx stirred up tensions between the new crowd and the old-timers who had been there for years. We were warned to stay away from the area, but we ended up getting a house on Sugarloaf Road, only four or five miles from Nederland, and we never had any problems. The rest of the band put down roots closer to Boulder, where the University of Colorado is based. We were half an hour or less from everyone in

Poco, which was fairly comparable to the distances that separated us in L.A.—except that in Colorado the drive was a lot more pleasant. Moving to Colorado was absolutely the right choice, which is why we're still here more than three decades later. It's certainly one of God's most beautiful places on earth.

The Colorado air cleared my head, reenergizing me for the uphill battle that I knew awaited me with Poco. I remained convinced that we had the talent and the songs to make all our dreams come true, but we had two significant obstacles to overcome: the laziness of our record company and the disinterest of radio programmers. (You have to blame somebody, right?) To succeed, we needed to release an album so good, so strong, so undeniable that even the doubters and the naysayers would have to give us our due. I thought Richie Podolor was the ideal person to help us, but Clive and Epic disagreed, and a reunion with Steve Cropper was out of the question. That meant that once again we had to find a new producer.

Our search led us to Jack Richardson, another guy with impressive rock credentials. He produced a string of smash albums for the Guess Who and also worked with Alice Cooper. His partner, Jim Mason, was an added bonus. Jim eventually moved to Colorado and worked with me on *Dance a Little Light,* my 1978 solo album, as well as producing platinum albums for another of the state's country rock exports, Firefall.

LAYING DOWN A GOOD FEELIN'

Following a major European tour that saw us perform in England, France, Germany, Belgium, Holland, and beyond, we began prepping for what would become *A Good Feelin' to Know,* rehearsing at the Skunk Creek Inn, a nondescript place in a southeast Boulder shopping center. Jack flew out to get a preview of our new songs before the whole gang headed to Chicago to record. Unlike Steve Cropper, who let us do our thing without a lot of guidance, Jack and Jim had tons of ideas. I like the collaborative process because give-and-take between artists can generate something more satisfying than any of them can create individually. I treated the band the same way. I wanted everyone to contribute, which is why the song-writing credits on *Good Feelin'* are so evenly distributed: three for me, three for Paul, two for Timothy.

The album began and ended with my compositions. "And Settlin' Down" was a natural opener, since we kicked off many of our concerts with it. The song has a really upbeat feeling that audiences loved. The closer, "Sweet Lovin'," was completely different, an adventurous piece written to celebrate Timmie's birth. (She was originally named Timothy Suzanne, but as a teenager she got tired of receiving letters addressed to Mr. Timothy Furay, so we went to court and had her name legally changed to Timmie Sue.) The song featured background vocals that recalled a choir and left plenty of room for Rusty's amped-up pedal steel. In between was the album's title song, a musical celebration that was one of our hardest rocking songs, thanks largely to Paul's tremendous guitar playing. And just for fun, we threw in a cover of Steve Stills's "Go and Say Goodbye," a song I've loved ever since the first time I heard it, sitting in the little apartment we shared on Fountain Avenue in Los Angeles. I enjoyed the original Buffalo Springfield rendition, but Poco lifted it to another level.

With Timothy's "I Can See Everything" and Paul's "Ride the Country" in the mix as well, *A Good Feelin' to Know* felt like our most commercial record to date. "A Good Feelin' to Know," which had been chosen as the lead single, had all the characteristics we associated with radio smashes. We returned to the road around the time the song was sent to stations, confident that we'd be hearing it on the radio very soon. I really believed we had all the ingredients for success: a proven producer, a great song, and a dynamic band. Once again I was confident we had done our part. Now it was out of our control. Still, I had hope and high expectations. I was sure we finally had our radio song.

RADIO SILENCE

Well, I was wrong. I vividly recall punching the radio buttons as we traveled through Connecticut on the way to a gig, searching for "A Good Feelin' to Know." What a shock when we heard "Take It Easy" by the Eagles coming through the speakers. The song's lead singer was Glenn Frey, who not long before had sat on the floor of my living room watching Poco and wishing he could be in our shoes. Now the tables had turned. With the help of none other than David Geffen, who had signed the Eagles to Asylum Records, his own label, Frey and erstwhile Poco member Randy Meisner had the AM radio hit that continued to elude us.

I suppose I could have viewed "Take It Easy" as a good sign—proof that D.J.s who'd scorned country rock were now willing to give it a try. Instead, I was devastated. Somehow, I knew that the stardom the Eagles would soon be experiencing would never be ours.

My disappointment was profound, but rather than sharing it with my bandmates or even Nancy, I internalized it. On the surface everything seemed fine. At every performance I continued to give every ounce of my energy and passion, just as I always had. I was and am a professional and would never compromise that integrity in my life. But in my private moments, my mind began to play tricks with my heart. Poco was the musical dream and passion of my life, but all of a sudden I saw it as a dead end. I needed to figure out what to do next.

The person I went to for counsel was David. If anyone could point me in the right direction, it was he. So during a visit to Los Angeles, I arranged to meet with him at his home.

David's place during those years wasn't a mansion by Hollywood standards, but it was beautiful. Even though the place exuded prosperity and achievement, David remained as approachable as ever, and he immediately put me at ease. Within minutes I had unburdened myself, telling him that my time with Poco had run its course. He listened attentively before presenting me with an option I hadn't known existed. David had relationships with J. D. Souther and Chris Hillman, two prominent musicians whom I knew from the L.A. music scene. J. D. and Chris were between projects, and David said that if we got together, we would represent a first of its kind—a country rock supergroup. "You'll be as big as Crosby, Stills, and Nash," he said.

In a matter of moments, I was swept up in David's exuberance for the plan, which he presented as a can't-miss proposition. J. D. had been a member of Longbranch Pennywhistle with Glenn Frey, and even after Glenn moved on to the Eagles, their musical alliance continued. The two of them would co-write several of the Eagles' biggest sellers, including "Best of My Love." Chris, meanwhile, had been a core member of the Byrds before moving on to the Flying Burrito Brothers with Gram Parsons, and he'd also hooked up with Steve Stills in a side project called Manassas. Adding in my experience with Buffalo Springfield and Poco, the three of us had impeccable country rock credentials. Just as important, we'd have the full backing of David, who seemed to have the golden touch.

David assured me that creating a country rock supergroup would be easy, and I assumed he knew what he was talking about. But that turned out to be one of his least accurate predictions. Still, with me looking for a way out of Poco, David had what looked to be the perfect solution. We sealed the deal with a handshake, and I knew that David would keep his word. Some people tell horror stories about David, but he always played straight with me.

BREAKING THE NEWS

With a new band in my future, I was left with a dilemma: how and when to break the news to my comrades in Poco. The whole group had recently moved to Colorado in a display of loyalty to the band. But now the person who'd placed the biggest emphasis on unity—me—wanted to split. Evaluating that decision today, I can see that it was a selfish move. But as the case has been throughout my life, a greater plan was being set in motion. The providence of God, and the way He orchestrates every movement of life's symphony, is a pretty amazing thing.

After much thought, I decided that the blow would be eased if I took a page from Jimmy Messina's book. I would participate in a final Poco album before exiting the band. We were already in the planning stages for what would become *Crazy Eyes,* and once again we decided to work with Jack Richardson. Everyone was in high spirits, and I matched their mood, making the album an appropriate last hurrah for this particular phase of Poco.

The recording sessions were loose and featured more guest performers than in the past. One of them, ironically, was Chris Hillman, who played some first-rate mandolin. We had less luck with George Frayne, piano player and leader of Commander Cody and the Lost Planet Airmen. The group's biggest hit was a revved-up cover of the old Johnny Bond chestnut "Hot Rod Lincoln." The Commander was recording in the studio next-door to the L.A. facility where we were working, and he stopped by to contribute. His part called for him to play an F-sharp chord at a certain point, but when the time came, he was silent. Once the tape stopped rolling, we asked him about it, and he said, "That's a really good steel-guitar chord, so I laid out." That didn't make a lot of sense to us, but he had his mind made up; on each take he refused to play the chord. Ultimately, we couldn't use him on the album.

Fiddler Billy Graham's contributions do show up on *Crazy Eyes,* although not his most memorable one. We were cutting "Fool's Gold," a real hoedown of a song written by Rusty, and as the rest of us watched from the control booth, Graham raised his bow and started sawing away in the totally wrong key. In response, everyone broke up laughing. To this day I feel sorry for the guy. Still, our silly outburst shows how much fun we were having.

In spite of this atmosphere, I held myself at a bit of a distance from everyone else, creatively speaking. I knew I would be needing tracks for my next group, so I didn't write a lot of material for *Crazy Eyes*—just two songs, my lowest output on any Poco album. The LP ended with "Let's Dance Tonight," one of the two songs from my history that I always wanted to record again; the other, as I mentioned earlier, is "Kind Woman," which I have taken another shot at for my 2006 *Heartbeat of Love* CD. A lot of people enjoy "Let's Dance Tonight," but to me it's an exciting rock-and-roll song that for some reason didn't get charged up to the degree it should have.

My other contribution was "Crazy Eyes," my reflection on the time I spent with Gram Parsons, which we paired with our rendition of what's arguably his most gorgeous composition, "Brass Buttons." "Crazy Eyes" is extremely ambitious—an epic, really—that benefits enormously from the additions made to it by Bob Ezrin, Jack Richardson's associate in Canada. (They had collaborated on some of Alice Cooper's albums.) We recorded the song in a stark, bare-bones style before shipping it to Bob, who layered it with strings and other orchestration that made it sound absolutely huge. All of us were knocked out when we heard it. Since then, Bob's had an impressive career, working for the likes of Aerosmith, Peter Gabriel, Rod Stewart, Lou Reed, and Pink Floyd.

We filled out *Crazy Eyes* with two of Paul's songs, "Blue Water" and "A Right Along," and Timothy's "Here We Go Again," as well as a cover of J. J. Cale's "Magnolia." I considered it to be another good record, on par with *A Good Feelin' to Know*, but I wasn't a bundle of nerves wondering whether it would go gold. Mentally, I'd already moved on. Now it was a matter of formalizing everything.

After the album was finished, David made the announcement for me at a band meeting in his office. The rest of the guys were caught off guard and were none too pleased by my decision. I understood their reaction, but my focus was elsewhere. I was driven to make it big, and back then I was willing to do whatever it took—even bidding farewell to the musical family I'd so painstakingly assembled. I'm sure I've heard some thoughts about my decision expressed on subsequent Poco albums. That's a typical way songwriters express frustration.

All that was left after that was to fulfill my touring responsibilities. We spent much of 1973 opening for bands such as Yes, Frampton's Camel (guitarist Peter Frampton's band before he went solo), and even the Beach Boys. The latter was a flashback of sorts, since the Buffalo Springfield had shared the bill many times with the Beach Boys. Finally, on September 4, around the time *Crazy Eyes* was released to critical praise and typically lackluster sales, I played what I thought would be my last show ever with Poco, at the Worcester Polytechnic Institute in Worchester, Massachusetts. In truth, I wasn't actually done with Poco, and I never could have guessed all that would transpire before the band came back into my life.

SOUTHER, HILLMAN, AND FURAY

Once I'd completed my commitments to Poco, I was able to pay closer attention to my new group, which had been named the Souther-Hillman-Furay Band, a moniker that recalled Crosby, Stills, and Nash. Chris was charged with putting the band together, and he drew from a pool of musicians who were familiar to him.

On drums, Chris chose Jim Gordon, who had been a member of Derek and the Dominos, a group that teamed Eric Clapton with Duane Allman, brother of my old acquaintance Gregg Allman. Jim received a co-writing credit on "Layla," a rock landmark. He was an eccentric person, but none of us could ever have guessed the tragic turn his life would take. For pianist, Chris picked Paul Harris, a busy studio expert who'd played alongside him in Manassas. Al Perkins, the pedal-steel player Chris wanted, had been in Manassas too, not to mention the Flying Burrito Brothers. He was a great talent and I knew it, but I was dead-set against his being in the band. My opposition to Al had nothing to do with his personality or his musicianship. I just didn't want to be around him because he played a guitar with a fish on it—a symbol of his Christian faith. Inside the symbol were the words "Jesus lives."

At the time I was blind to everything other than my personal quest for success. And for some reason I was convinced that Al's presence and his Christian faith would drag us down. He could have been into any other religion, from Buddhism to Islam; he could have been an alcoholic or a drug addict; he could have been a womanizer; he could have been anything other than what he was, and I wouldn't have objected. I was hung up on appearances, and because Al was an outspoken Christian, I feared that he might turn off the music fans that I wanted to attract.

Here's the irony. Al was living the type of life I ended up embracing. His life echoed these words from the New Testament: "For I am not ashamed of the gospel of Christ, for it is the power of God to salvation for everyone who believes, for the Jew first and also for the Greek."[2] This is what a Christian testimony is all about, and it's what Al lived. His example remains a part of my life. Thanks, Al.

But I'm saying this in hindsight. At the time I resisted the love of Jesus with all my being, even trying to reject Al just because he was a Christian. But the Lord was at work anyway. And unbeknown to me, He was beginning to mold my life in a new and amazing way.

12

On the Brink of Commercial Success

How "Super" Could This Group Become?

When I finally gave in to Chris Hillman's choice of Al Perkins, I thought I was simply trying to avoid conflict with Chris, with whom I hoped to finally achieve enough fame and fortune to fill my soul. In retrospect, I realize that God brought Al and me together. But the road I took to finding faith in Jesus was far from a smooth one. In the coming year I would go through trials that could accurately be described as emotional hell on earth.

During the first part of 1974 I was focused on stardom, and I was heartened by the amount of attention David Geffen was paying to my new project. On one occasion he made a special trip to Colorado. I picked him up in my boxy '72 Toyota Land Cruiser, and we actually ran out of gas on the way home. When we finally arrived at the house, David pulled out three albums by Laura Nyro, the singer-songwriter whose success had launched his career. He played the albums for me back to back, just so I could hear her music. A lot of people think of David only as a multimillionaire businessman, but on that night I got to see the other side of him: a passionate guy who loved music just as much as I did.

Because I wanted members of the Souther-Hillman-Furay Band to connect in this way too, I arranged for Chris, J. D. Souther, Paul Harris, and Al Perkins to get together at my house and work out some tunes. (Jim Gordon couldn't make it, probably because of previous studio commitments.) This was the same approach that had worked so well with Poco, but lightning didn't strike twice. We staged the sessions in my garage, making this supposed supergroup a literal garage band for a few days. Everyone was completely professional, putting as much effort into songs written by other band members as we did into our own tunes. Unfortunately, magic moments were few and far between.

Plenty of factors contributed to the lack of creative chemistry. For one thing, I was a bit apprehensive about playing with a new group. Poco had been like a family. We were friends who had been making music together for a long time. We knew one another. We knew when to push one another. We knew when to lay back. When everything was clicking, the affection we felt for one another came through in every note. That wasn't the case with SHF, and as we were feeling each other out, I sensed that I was treading on troubled waters. We didn't know one another very well, and I wasn't able to connect with my new partners on a deeper level, either personally or creatively. From my perspective, no one really let his guard down. I know that things take time in any relationship, but there remained a distance between us—a sense that we were just going through the motions.

I've gotten to know Chris better since the SHF days, and our relationship is strong. We shared the same concert bill recently, and I had him play on my latest CD; we get along quite well. Back then, however, we couldn't get past being overly polite with each other. The same was true of J. D. He struck me as a man of many contradictions. He was very confident in his abilities as a songwriter, as well he should have been. His name is on some of the Eagles' biggest hits, including "New Kid in Town" and "Heartache Tonight." But he seemed beset by insecurities. His personality was difficult to penetrate, and I never managed to do so. In a strange way, he seemed like the odd man out. He had a mystery about him that's not far removed from the title of one song that wound up on our debut record: "Deep, Dark and Dreamless."

Frankly, "Deep, Dark and Dreamless" didn't make a big impression on me, and I wasn't knocked out by many of the other songs we'd assembled, either. I contributed three tunes—"Fallin' in Love," "Believe Me," and a more reflective effort, "The Flight of the Dove"—and I felt that all of them had commercial potential. As for the songs that Chris and J. D. had brought, they were nice enough, but they didn't have that intangible but essential quality, the special combination of melody and lyrics that quickened my heart rate and got me excited.

In addition to the songs we had chosen for the album was the matter of our voices. All three of us individually had good singing voices, but when we harmonized, there wasn't a spark, as there had been in Buffalo Springfield and Poco, or the Byrds or the Burritos for that matter. Some voices combine in unique and memorable ways, and some don't. Ours didn't. At least that's my take.

With all of these concerns weighing on me, it's no wonder that the rehearsals felt awkward. But with David so confident that we were destined for a commercial breakthrough, I tried to put my reservations aside. After all, he had some of the best instincts in the music business. Maybe he saw something in us that I was missing. But the truth is, some things that might look good on paper don't always play out that way in real life.

The After-Dinner Sermon

As I was wrestling with my doubts, I asked Al and his wife, Debbie, to join Nancy and me for dinner one evening. Al asked if he could bring some tapes to play after dinner. I said fine, thinking he would be bringing music, much as David had done.

I was wrong. Following a very pleasant meal, we headed to the living room, where Al put on a tape of Pastor Chuck Smith from Calvary Chapel in Costa Mesa, California, teaching from the Bible. To put it mildly, I was taken aback. I felt Al had tricked me into listening to a sermon that went on for over half an hour. I hadn't attended church in years, and suddenly I was having a church service in my own home.

Even so, I didn't make a scene. I just sat back and listened, and I was surprised when I actually got interested in the tape. In the recording, titled "The More Sure Word," Chuck talked about the many biblical prophecies regarding the Messiah, prophesies that were given hundreds of years before Jesus was born. Chuck pointed out the overwhelming odds against a single individual fulfilling these prophesies. Accomplishing just eight of them would be the equivalent of a blindfolded man having one chance to find a particular silver dollar in Texas if the entire state were covered with identical-sized coins piled two feet deep. Yet the Bible lists more than three hundred prophecies that Jesus fulfilled!

This was a lot of information to digest, and while I was doing so, Al put on another of Chuck's sermon tapes. In all, Nancy and I sat there for almost an hour and a half. By the end of it, I was frustrated with Al, at least on the surface. I couldn't take in any more information. Underneath I was thinking about what Chuck had to say about Jesus. Al had planted a seed.

The evening had a strong effect on Nancy, too. Without my knowing about it, Debbie began telling Nancy about her own experience of committing her life to Jesus. A book Debbie passed along—*Satan Is Alive and Well on Planet Earth* by Hal Lindsey—really struck a chord with Nancy.

Soon Nancy was looking at the world in an entirely new way. She was swept up in the love of Christ—she was truly born again. But rather than sharing her good news with me, she mostly kept it to herself, for reasons that I'd discover all too soon.

BACK INTO THE STUDIO

While Nancy was entering into her new life of faith, I headed to the Los Angeles area with the rest of the SHF crew to begin recording our first album. We would be working with Richie Podolor, the producer I'd most wanted to be in the studio with.

Richie had cut the two songs with Poco that everyone in the band loved, but which our record label, Epic, rejected. When it came time to pick someone to oversee my latest project, I immediately thought he would bring something special to the undertaking, and my instincts proved to be correct. The album we recorded, titled *The Souther-Hillman-Furay Band,* may not be the finest album in my discography, but it's very listenable. And Richie, who cut it at American Recorders in Studio City, California, with help from his longtime partner, Bill Cooper, deserves a lot of the credit. He was a master of the radio-friendly pop song, as he proved time and again, and he was a good musician, too. "Ride, Captain, Ride" by Blues Image still gets airplay today largely because of its clever guitar part, and Richie is the man behind it.

My song "Fallin' in Love" also benefited from Richie's gifts. We couldn't come up with the right introductory hook for the song, and after letting us play around with it for a while, he said in his trademark high-pitched voice, "Hey, guys, I've got an idea." I remember Richie being very polite. He knew he had a great idea, but he also understood the egos of musicians and simply asked. If we had said no, I don't think he would have pushed us. But when you're making a record, the producer, the band, the engineer, everyone becomes a part of the team, contributing to the final outcome. A few seconds later, Richie was in the studio, reeling out the opening lick of the song, which helped make it as identifiable as it is.

We made steady progress with the recording, and before I knew it, we'd completed most of the basic tracks. Still, I wanted to tinker with my songs a bit more, and one Saturday afternoon I left the rental house where Nancy, Timmie, and I were staying—they had joined me there a few days earlier. I headed to American Recorders accompanied by my trusty 1962 Martin D28 acoustic guitar—the one I had used to write practically every song I'd recorded. But as I parked my Porsche 911 in the studio lot, I hesitated about bringing the instrument inside. Our main focus that day was to put vocals on one of Chris's songs, and I didn't want him to think I was more interested in getting around to my song rather than his. So without giving it too much thought, I left my guitar in the car—thinking I'd get it after we'd polished off the vocal.

What a mistake. The "few minutes" I expected to spend working with

Chris stretched into hours, and I didn't get back to my car until well after midnight. As I approached the Porsche, I saw that the windshield was shattered. But that's not all. The key turn for the ignition had been ripped out and, worse, my precious guitar was gone. Apparently, the thieves had intended to steal the car, and when something prevented them from doing so, they grabbed whatever they could get.

Some people in this situation would have counted their blessings. But while the guitar cost a lot less than the Porsche, it had infinitely more sentimental value. That Martin was an extension of my creativity. I'd cradled it in my arms during high moments, low moments, and everything in between, and with its help I'd become a well-known singer and songwriter. I couldn't imagine living without it.

I was upset, but I didn't have long to nurse my wounds. Nancy, Timmie, and I were scheduled to fly to Hawaii for a month-long vacation prior to the release of the first SHF album and the beginning of SHF's inaugural tour. We jetted to the islands and set up housekeeping in Haleiwa, on the north shore of Oahu, in a house that we rented from Chip Douglas, a producer for the Monkees and Turtles. Chip co-owned the house with David Cassidy, then a teen idol from his starring role in TV's *The Partridge Family*. The place was beautiful, but it had one eerie aspect: a library filled with occult books that made me feel that spiritual warfare was lurking in the shadows. That might have been one of the reasons why I was so preoccupied, even though the scenery around us was gorgeous. Whatever the case, I was thinking not just about the guitar but also about my new musical venture and how it would be received.

THE CALM BEFORE THE NEXT STORM

While we were in Hawaii, Nancy spent a lot of time reading the Bible, which she'd never really done before. This would become a lifelong practice for her. In fact, she's probably better at carving out a portion of her day to have quiet time with the Lord than I am. Her devotion to reading the Bible on our vacation should have made me wonder what was going on, but I didn't quiz her about it. My lack of curiosity shows how obsessed I was with my career and how little attention I was paying to my wife. If I had been more observant, I might have realized that she was pulling away from me.

Upon our return to Los Angeles, I discovered that my business manager had left a message about my Martin D28. He told me the police had discovered an instrument that matched the description of the guitar, right down to the serial number, at a pawnshop in Pacoima, a community on the eastern edge of the San Fernando Valley. Nancy and I drove there together, and on the way she said she'd been praying for my guitar to be found. Had she said something like that a few months earlier, I probably would have shrugged it off as the sort of cliché people mouth all the time. But her recent fascination with the Bible, not to mention the intensity with which she shared this revelation, caught me off guard. I replied that if my guitar was actually there, I would seriously think about changing my ways, and I suggested that she might be on to something with her faith.

But seconds after finding out that my guitar was indeed in the pawnshop, and in amazingly good shape considering everything it had been through, I forgot all about what I'd said to Nancy. I wasn't ready to become a Christian. On the other hand, my off-the-cuff vow, flippant as it was, had some significance. That seed of Al's was starting to take root, whether I knew it or not.

For Nancy, the process was already complete. When she realized there was a hunger inside her that could only be satisfied by God's grace in Jesus Christ, she accepted the Lord with open arms. But unlike Al and Debbie, she didn't seem to care if I followed her lead. The growing distance between us was becoming obvious. I asked her to accompany me to Aspen, where David Geffen had booked a two-week run for the SHF Band at a venue called the Gallery—the idea being that the shows would get us ready for a tour in support of our new album. To my surprise, Nancy turned me down, saying she'd rather stay in Boulder with Timmie. Nothing I said could change her mind.

I was confused and upset by her decision, but I didn't dwell on it because our string of shows was looming. News of the dates had leaked out, and quite a few Poco fans had traveled cross-country to see SHF for the first time. The crowds were large and boisterous, helping to quiet some of my reservations about the group.

A FRESH ENCOUNTER WITH FAITH

After one of the SHF shows in Aspen, two young women whom I had known previously as "Poconuts"—the name given to Poco's most loyal fans—came up to say hello. After complimenting me on our set, one of them said, "We've been talking with Al and Debbie Perkins, and we've just accepted Jesus Christ as our Lord and Savior."

What could I say to that? "That's good for you," I answered as casually as I could. "But I've got a whole lot more to do in my life before I make a decision like that."

Even as these words were coming out of my mouth, part of me knew that I wasn't being entirely honest. I'd been exposed to many kinds of trendy Eastern and mystic religions, but none of them had ever appealed to me. Subconsciously, I understood that there was something different about Christianity. That's why I had reacted so negatively about bringing Al into the band, and yet I had listened as he played me tapes that demonstrated why he believed as he did. I was still struggling with the mistaken notion that people have to give up who they are when they become a Christian. The truth is that while God changes certain things about you, becoming a Christian only makes you the person God created you to be. You gain more than you can ever measure—not just a new perspective *about* life, but a *new* life. As it says in the New Testament: "Therefore, if anyone is in Christ, he is a new creation; old things have passed away; behold, all things have become new."[1]

The next morning Al called me and asked if I wanted to join him and Debbie for dinner that evening. By then I recognized Al's routine. He would lure me in with some of Debbie's wonderful cooking, and then he'd ask me if he could share the Gospel with me. Outwardly that was the last thing I wanted, but inside something else was going on. As Al spoke to me, the melody of "Will You Still Love Me Tomorrow," an old Shirelles' song, went through my mind. But instead of hearing the song's actual lyric, "Tonight you're mine,"[2] I heard "Tonight's the night." Without really meaning to, I accepted Al's dinner invitation.

That evening things went pretty much as I had expected. Following the meal, Al began talking about his faith. He told me that God loved me, in spite of my cynicism, and that His arms of love were open to receive me if I'd just open my heart to receive the grace, love, and forgiveness He offered me in the sacrificial death of His Son, Jesus. Then Al asked, "Do you want to pray? Do you want to receive God's free gift of salvation in Christ and surrender your life to Him as your personal Lord and Savior?"

Al had already put these questions to me several times over the months I'd been keeping company with him, and I told him no each time. It had been easy. But suddenly everything was different. The words just came from my lips. "I want to pray with you tonight," I said.

There were no fireworks going off when I joined Al and Debbie in prayer, no big emotional trip. The feeling was more of a readiness to take this step, to learn firsthand about what Al, Debbie, and Nancy had discovered. The powerful Scripture in John 3:16 that defines the Gospel—"For God so loved the world that He gave His only begotten Son, that whoever believes in Him should not perish but have everlasting life"—had finally become real to me. From that moment on, I would realize that love isn't simply an emotion; it's an action.

In retrospect, I believe that at that moment in Aspen, I was born again. But afterward I couldn't comprehend everything that had taken place. As I have grown in faith, I've learned that salvation is not only a specific moment in time, but it is also a daily process that continues in our lives.

When we were finished at Al's house, we went to play another night of music at the Gallery, and the performance was fairly typical. The music flowed through me as it always had—nothing was dramatically different. The explanation, of course, is that the Holy Spirit had always been with me; I just hadn't known it. The difference was that now He was dwelling *inside* me too.

By the time the set concluded and the club had cleared out, the hour was far too late to call Nancy, but I eagerly phoned her the next morning to share what had happened to me at Al's house. I knew she had embraced Christianity, and I was certain that she would now be overjoyed at the prospect of the two of us embarking side by side on the new adventure of a life in Christ. So imagine my surprise when, after telling her that I had become a Christian, all I heard on the other end of the line was dead silence.

A NEW MARITAL CRISIS

I had overlooked earlier clues that there were problems between Nancy and me. After coming through the fire I'd set with my sexual infidelity, I had committed another of the biggest errors anyone can make: I took our relationship for granted. People looking at Nancy and me from afar always thought we were the perfect couple, but they weren't looking deeper, and neither was I. For me, all that had mattered was my career, and by concentrating on that to the exclusion of everything else, I had sent Nancy the message that she wasn't important to me. She wanted me to be her husband—a loving, caring, nurturing partner—and I had failed her.

A day or two later, Nancy came to Aspen to give me a ride home after the SHF shows, and her mood was just as chilly in person as it had been on the phone. I tried everything I could to engage her in conversation, but nothing I said seemed to reach her. It was the longest and most uncomfortable car ride I've ever experienced.

At home Nancy still didn't want to talk, at least to me. When a good friend of hers called, the tone of Nancy's voice changed entirely. Her face lit up, and the Nancy I knew and loved emerged. At the end of their brief chat, she told her friend that she loved her. The remark was the kind of thing all of us say to people who are close to us, and it would have been thoroughly unremarkable at any other time. But on this night Nancy showed more affection for her friend during a five-minute conversation than she'd directed toward me in a month.

After Nancy hung up the phone, I asked about what was going on between us, and she leveled with me. She told me that our marriage was over. She wanted out.

I was blindsided. I hadn't thought we had any problems, at least not until very recently. We had just returned from a month-long vacation in a Hawaiian paradise, and as far as I could tell, Nancy had enjoyed herself. Just about the only evidence of something being amiss was her decision not to join me in Aspen, and I wouldn't have thought in a million years that she had made this choice because she no longer wanted to be with me.

I tried everything I could to break through her resolve, but nothing moved her. Her mind was made up. Totally devastated, I phoned Al, who was already in California preparing for the start of the SHF tour. I was crying so hard that I could barely speak. It's amazing that he could figure out what I was saying. After listening to the emotions pour from me, he said, "Why don't you get on an airplane and come out here?"

At that point I didn't know what else to do. Nancy didn't want me in Boulder, and the concert tour was about to get underway. David was putting the muscle of his record company, Asylum, behind our new album. If we didn't get out on the road and support it, this new venture might suffer the same fate the previous ones had: critical acclaim but modest record sales. I had to go.

As I jetted to California, I had no idea that I was on the cusp of a seven-month-long odyssey that would push me to the limits of my emotional and physical endurance. The only thing that kept me going was love. Love for Nancy and Timmie. Love for the Lord. And most important, His love for me and my family. Jesus' closest disciple, the apostle John, wrote these words: "There is no fear in love; but perfect love casts out fear." One verse later, he added, "We love Him because He first loved us."[3] I've come to learn in the years since that we wouldn't even know what love is were it not for God demonstrating it to us through Christ's death.

If love crowds out fear, then what I needed more than anything just then was the reassuring comfort of Christ's love. Because at that moment I was more afraid than I'd ever been before. I was afraid that the relationship Nancy and I had managed to salvage several years earlier was now lost forever. I was about to embark on a concert tour with a new band that promised to deliver the big commercial breakthrough I'd been working for and dreaming of for years. But as I considered my life, all I could think was that my future looked darker than ever.

13

A New Life of Faith

Traveling the Long Road Back Home

Throughout the painful struggle that followed my separation from Nancy, my connection with the Lord was at its most powerful. In the end, He not only saved a marriage; He literally saved a life. And He did so against the unlikeliest of backdrops: a rock-and-roll tour.

Some of the most memorable tales from SHF's travels revolve around Jim Gordon. I was amazed that a drummer with such an astounding list of credits would agree to join our band. For the most part, this large man—he is well over six feet tall—seemed like a real teddy bear. Still, he had a temperamental side that I first saw at American Recorders while we were making our first album. He was so good at what he did that he'd generally put down the perfect rhythm in one or two takes. When the rest of us, who weren't nearly as proficient on our instruments as he was, would require ten or even fifteen run-throughs of a song to get everything just right, he'd become frustrated. But even when he was fuming, he would get the job done.

Granted, Jim's professionalism sometimes slipped while we were on tour, especially after he'd put some alcohol into his system. One of our early dates was in Fort Wayne, Indiana, where we played alongside the Eagles and Joe Walsh, who would soon become an Eagle himself. We got back to our hotel too late to order room service, which infuriated Jim. We were on the upper floor of a two-story hotel, which had open balconies and walkways that led to each room. Jim, wearing only a bathrobe, tiptoed from doorway to doorway, and whenever he found a room-service tray that had been left out for the hotel's staff to collect, he examined it for leftovers. When he came across plates that weren't to his liking, he pitched them over the railing to the parking lot below. If SHF had returned to Fort Wayne, I know of at least one hotel where we wouldn't have been allowed to stay!

On another occasion we were driving in a caravan of a few vans from Pennsylvania to Ohio, and Jim asked us to stop so he could answer nature's call. We pulled over on the side of Interstate 80, one of the busiest thoroughfares in the country. We waited for Jim—and waited and waited. And just when we wondered if we should send out a search party, we spotted him on the side of the highway. He was in a sprinter's stance, and after a semi roared past, he took off as if he thought they were in a race.

Today these antics would be a lot easier to laugh about if it weren't for Jim's actions many years after we'd lost contact. In 1984 he was sentenced to a prison term of sixteen years to life for murdering his mother.[1] We knew that Jim had something of a Jekyll and Hyde personality, and because of his size, his mood swings and eccentric behavior gave me pause every so often. But none of us in SHF could ever have guessed that he had such violence in him. It's a tragedy on every level.

PRACTICING A NEW LIFE OF FAITH

One of the reasons I didn't get to know Jim very well was because of a shift in my lifestyle, inspired by my newfound faith in Jesus. Up until I was born again, I continued to use illegal drugs, mainly marijuana and hashish, along with various kinds of pills. But after becoming a Christian, I tossed out my drug paraphernalia and flushed all the substances I had with me down the toilet. I also stopped drinking alcohol. No one told me to do these things; it was a choice I made because I didn't want anything distorting my thoughts or getting between me and the Lord.

Going through so many sudden lifestyle changes would have been even more difficult had I not been blessed with a terrific support team. On tour I really leaned on Steve Giglio, whose nickname is Bugs. He was SHF's road manager, and he held the same job when I embarked on a solo career. Along the way we became great friends. Bugs, who was also a Christian, was always there encouraging me when I was in a fragile emotional state. Just as important were new Christian acquaintances who could speak to me in the language of true believers. Al and Debbie Perkins headed this list, and they introduced me to many others who had connections to Calvary Chapel, the church in Southern California that was the incubator of the Jesus movement in the early seventies.

Keith Ritter, a counselor who worked through Calvary Chapel in Costa Mesa, California, evolved into something of a spiritual father for me, and I also grew close to Greg Laurie, a dynamic pastor, Bible teacher, and evangelist, and his wife, Cathe. Over the years that followed, he would have great influence in my life. In addition, I got to know several fellow musicians who had found the Lord, including John Mehler and Tom Stipe, who went on to become the senior pastor at Crossroads Church of Denver. Both John and Tom would be part of my next musical incarnation, the one that would follow the Souther-Hillman-Furay Band. These people and many others were prayer warriors for me, and every one of them gave my spirit a much-needed boost.

In the meantime I became a devoted Bible reader. Al and the rest of my bandmates let me have a lot of space during this period, and I tried to reward their kindness and understanding by giving my all during our performances. For me, the stage was a sanctuary of sorts—the one place where I could get my mind off my troubles with Nancy and lose myself in music. Yet no matter how hard I tried, SHF never clicked with audiences on the same level that Buffalo Springfield and Poco had.

One possible reason was a lack of material. Poco had six albums' worth of songs toward the end of my run with the band, and whenever we tired of one particular tune, we could dip into our catalog and find one that charged us up. In contrast, SHF had made just one LP at that point, and it wasn't as ripe with possibilities as it needed to be. The lack of chemistry between Chris, J. D., and me didn't help matters either. No wonder our audiences were generally more subdued than the ones that had always flocked to Poco shows.

In many ways I was relieved when we completed our first batch of concerts. Yet the end of the tour brought me face to face with the unpleasant reality of my personal life. I pleaded with Nancy to let me come home to Boulder, but she wouldn't bend, basically leaving me homeless.

A LONG STRETCH OF HEARTACHE

I wound up staying for extended stretches with Al and Debbie; John and his wife, Lynda; and Tom and his new bride, Mary Ellen. I also spent a lot of time with Keith, whose counseling probably kept thoughts of suicide from taking root in my mind. I was so emotionally fragile that I spent many of my days walking around in a fog. Without the hospitality, fellowship, and sincere friendship I received, I don't know what I would have done. That's why today I put such a premium on providing comfort to members of my congregation who are experiencing crisis. As God said through his prophet Isaiah: " 'Comfort, yes, comfort My people!' says your God."[2]

In the same way, I realize that the Lord never left my side even in the midst of heartache, and although He didn't address me in literal words, He did speak to my heart in a very direct way. One day I decided to visit a Christian bookstore I'd discovered, and as I was heading north on the 605 freeway to get there, a tremendous storm broke out. It was raining so hard that no one in his right mind should have been driving (and just then, I wasn't in my right mind). As the heavens above me opened up, I started crying so hard that I couldn't see. My chest was convulsing with heartache. I pulled onto the shoulder of the road, and once my car stopped, I called out to the Lord, begging Him to reunite me with my family. In the midst of my torment, a voice—a still, small voice that would become louder as I grew in faith—resounded within me. "That's how much I want you to want Me," it said.

There was so much meaning in that statement that it took me a moment to process it. God was telling me to refocus my priorities. I wanted Nancy and Timmie back with every fiber of my being, yet I needed God even more. He had to be first in my life; everything else was secondary. Only He could relieve the agony and the hurt that coursed through my body. Once I came to grips with that, I would be prepared for reconciliation with my wife and daughter.

With a new focus on the Lord as my first priority, I continued to do what I could to break down Nancy's defenses. Like many a husband trying to woo back his wife, I kept phoning her to see if her attitude toward me had softened. Although she would usually take my calls, she would barely speak to me. In retrospect, I suspect that Nancy was torn between her dissatisfaction with our marriage and the wisdom found in the book of Malachi in the Old Testament, in which the Lord says plainly that He hates divorce.[3] She wanted out, but did God see things the same way?

The sad truth is that the divorce rate among Christian couples is pretty much the same as it is for the rest of the population, even though believers have the tools, as well as the power of the risen Lord, to make their marriages rich and rewarding. In the first century, the religious leaders questioned Jesus about divorce. He responded by explaining that divorce is the result of the hardness of people's hearts.[4] And, unfortunately, everyone is vulnerable to that condition.

Nancy seemed to believe that if she had left me before I became a Christian, she wouldn't be violating God's prohibition of divorce. And, in fact, she had been preparing to do just that when I came to the Lord. So my decision presented her with a spiritual dilemma. She didn't want to reconcile the teachings of the Bible and her faith in the Lord with her loss of love for me and her frustration over my neglect of her. She remained at a distance and wasn't going to allow herself to let our relationship go on. Since her mind was made up, she would just deal with the biblical teachings later.

Desperate to break through Nancy's wall of silence, I asked Debbie Perkins to write her a letter on my behalf, encouraging her to join me in trying to solve our problems. Debbie agreed, and after she sent these thoughts to Nancy, I checked the mailbox every day for a reply. When a letter to Debbie finally arrived, I waited while she and Al silently read Nancy's response. I could tell from their expressions that the news wasn't good, but I was still eager to learn what Nancy had to say.

I never got the chance. Rather than passing the letter to me, Al and Debbie tore it into tiny bits, saying, "You don't want to read this." My insides felt as if they were being ripped apart too, despite the fact that they gave me only the most general sense of what Nancy had written. According to them, she was moving forward with her life. And because she didn't want it to include me, divorce would be among the first things on her agenda.

Later, when Al and Debbie left for the grocery store, I raced to the trash can to retrieve the shredded letter. I tried my best to piece it back together, but they'd done too thorough a job of tearing it to shreds. To this day I don't know exactly what Nancy wrote. I believe some things are better left in the past, so I never asked her. Besides, Al and Debbie's decision to destroy the letter before I could read it tells me everything I need to know.

As my personal life spiraled into even greater turmoil, my career was on the upswing. Thanks to David Geffen, *The Souther-Hillman-Furay Band* album came out of the box faster than any of my previous albums, and "Fallin' in Love," the first single from the album—which I wrote and sang lead vocals on—became a modest Top 40 hit. We needed to get back on the road in order to capitalize on this strong beginning. To that end, our management booked dates throughout most of the fall.

Under other circumstances I would have been on top of the world. But this time around, I couldn't have cared less if the record soared to platinum status or sank like a stone. With Nancy wanting our marriage to be over, success in the music world no longer mattered to me. It's amazing how a crisis can put the events of life in such a different perspective. I was obligated to participate in the concerts, though they meant very little to me. What did matter was the Lord and my family, in that order.

God Shows Up

One of the last gigs on the schedule took place in St. Petersburg, Florida. Al and I took a stroll on the beach one night, and as we were walking and praying, the Lord spoke to my heart again. "You made a commitment to Me," He said. "Now it's time we talk about it."

I didn't say anything to Al about this, but I couldn't stop thinking about those words. When I went back to my room that night, I was putty in the Lord's hands. I went to sleep and then awoke in the middle of the night. It's hard to describe what I saw glowing in front of me other than to say that it was the brightest light I'd ever seen. Almost anyone seeing this might have panicked, but for some reason I experienced nothing but the deepest sense of calm. I sat in bed and looked at the light, and I don't know whether it lasted ten seconds or ten minutes. What I can say for certain is that I didn't hear a voice and I didn't see a figure. I just sensed the Lord's presence. He was in that room, and He reassured me about everything in my life. I interpreted the serenity that washed over me as a message that somehow, some way, everything was going to work out. Nancy and I would reconcile, and our marriage would be restored.

The next morning I woke up feeling invigorated. A passage from the Bible helps explain why:

> There are many who say,
> "Who will show us any good?"
> Lord, lift up the light of Your countenance upon us.
> You have put gladness in my heart,
> More than in the season that their grain and wine increased.
> I will both lie down in peace, and sleep;
> For You alone, O Lord, make me dwell in safety.[5]

This was the message of hope I needed just then. Maybe some of you are going through a difficult time and need hope in your situation. I encourage you to open your heart to Jesus no matter what's going on and no matter how difficult a time you're going through. He will be faithful to meet you right where you're at.

This day marked the beginning of a dynamic relationship with my Lord, the type of relationship He wants to have with all His children. It was then that I began to learn to trust Him, even though my life was full of pain and confusion. Trusting God means, in part, that you believe that He loves you even when your circumstances would indicate just the opposite. Trust doesn't happen all at once; it's an ongoing process learned through time spent dealing with life's challenges and circumstances.

I really felt as if my life was starting over, and with this fresh beginning, all things were possible. I was positive that Nancy would call and say she wanted me to come home. But the phone never rang, and things actually got worse. It was the darkness before the dawn.

The Life-and-Death Crisis

The tour ended in late September, and I returned to Los Angeles, where I was staying with Al and Debbie. By then the Santa Ana winds were blowing, and the city was dry and almost unbearably hot. Seeking relief, I went to the balcony of their apartment and began to pray—and a few minutes later something unexpected happened. Despite the blazing heat, an incredible chill ran through my body. I couldn't have been colder if I'd been in Antarctica.

Baffled, I went back inside with the idea of continuing my prayers in the bedroom, and the voice inside me just kept growing louder and stronger. It spoke with a directness that shook me to my bones. "Go home," it said.

Go home? I would have loved to go home. I'd been yearning to go home for what seemed like ages. But I could tell the voice wasn't just a manifestation of my wishful thinking. There was an urgency to the words, as if disaster was lurking and only quick action could avert it. With my head still spinning from the impact of this command, I called Keith and asked him what I should do.

"You should go home," he said.

I told Al and Debbie that I had to get back to Colorado. They'd felt something ominous in the atmosphere too, and they dropped everything and drove me to the airport the next morning. After we arrived, I prayed with Al and Debbie, said my good-byes to them, and then raced across the terminal to the nearest counter. I was standing in line to purchase my ticket when I felt a huge presence behind me. Turning, I saw a large man, well over six feet tall. When I offered him a polite smile, he started singing "Pickin' Up the Pieces."

Looking back, I realize that the man's presence in line behind me was a clear sign that I was doing the right thing. Even his choice to sing "Pickin' Up the Pieces" was significant, because I was trying to pick up the pieces of my life at that time. But I was so full of anxiety about getting home that I tried to ignore the man. I got my tickets and headed toward the gate. I was almost there when I heard the man again, and as he crooned the line, "There's just a little bit of magic in the country...,"[6] I knew he wouldn't be satisfied until I talked to him. In the end I was lucky I did.

The man was John Lee, and after we got the introductions out of the way, I shared my situation with him. The Denver airport where I'd be landing was the better part of an hour's drive to my Boulder home, and since Nancy didn't know I was coming, no one would be at the airport to meet me. I figured I'd have to catch a cab, but John said he could help. He was getting a lift from a friend whom I happened to know: Kenny Weissberg, a writer for Boulder's newspaper the *Daily Camera*. Kenny also was a D.J. for KBCO, a local FM radio station that would bloom into one of the country's most famous and influential rock outlets. I'd done an interview with Kenny about six weeks earlier, proof that it really is a small world. John said that Kenny would give me a lift, and he did. Years later he lifted me again; he became a concert promoter for Humphrey's by the Bay in San Diego and has booked me for many concerts there in recent years.

After we landed in Denver, Kenny and John drove me right to my door, but Nancy had left to pick up Timmie from her preschool. I didn't have a key, so I got out a credit card and slid it along the latch. I'd seen characters do this on television, but it's not as easy as it looks. Failing to break into my own house, I sat down and waited. The delay gave me time to think about what I was going to say and how Nancy might react to my arrival. I feared that she wouldn't be overjoyed to see me, and I was right.

When Nancy got home, her first question was, "What are you doing here?" She was really agitated, and after we went inside and began to talk, I found out why. She was pregnant, but she didn't want to have another of my children. She was scheduled to have an abortion the next day.

Suddenly I understood why the voice I'd heard only hours earlier had been so insistent. Had I delayed for even one more day, Nancy would have gone through with the abortion, and I would never have known the joy that Katie, our second daughter, would bring into my life. Neither would I have gotten to know Parker Lily, Katie's daughter. The Lord's intervention prevented a terrible mistake from being made.

The conversation that followed was serious and often painful, but at the end of it, Nancy backed away from her earlier decision. The abortion was canceled, and she agreed to come back to California so we could see if there was a way to save our marriage. In a movie this would have been Nancy's and my happy ending, but real life is never that simple. Nothing illustrates the obstacles we had to overcome more than comments Nancy made during a counseling session that Keith arranged: "I don't love him, I never loved him, and I'll never love him again."

Each of these statements hit me like a hammer blow. Our marriage certainly wasn't perfect, but had we really been living a lie all this time? Was there not a moment of true love when we looked in each other's eyes? It's no wonder that my world collapsed when Nancy announced that she was going home to Colorado without me to think about what to do next. I couldn't see any way that our marriage could be restored. All I could do was ask myself: *Had I really heard the Lord's voice? Hadn't He spoken to me just days before when He said I should go home? And what about the light that appeared in the motel room?*

With things looking darker and darker, I realized that this was the wrong time to give up. The Lord had saved my unborn daughter. If He could do that,

He could do anything. As the angel Gabriel told Mary, the mother of Jesus, in the New Testament: "For with God nothing will be impossible."[7]

A Contractual Obligation

I would have gladly put the Souther-Hillman-Furay Band on the back burner permanently. The group hadn't hit the supergroup heights that David predicted, and none of us was as committed to the project as we needed to be. Even so, we owed Asylum another album. At the time one of the hottest studios in the country was Caribou Ranch, a state-of-the-art recording facility owned by Jim Guercio that happened to be only a few miles from my house in Colorado. By recording the album there, I'd have an excuse to be close to Nancy and Timmie for more than a month. I hoped our proximity might bring us closer.

I didn't have a lot of material ready for the second SHF album. Some artists become incredibly productive when they're in crisis, but I was so overwhelmed by the way my world was crashing around me that I couldn't concentrate on song writing. I had only two compositions ready to go: "On the Line" and "For Someone I Love." But the latter song turned out to be one of my most important tunes.

A lot of people think "For Someone I Love" was written after my conversion to Christianity, but it came together long before that life-changing night in Aspen, and prior to my separation from Nancy. As I contemplated the lyrics, I interpreted them as a song that not only anticipated my new life in Christ but also predicted my eventual reconciliation with Nancy. The crucial lines are: "Maybe just a little more time, when the winter snows melt and it's spring and who knows. I hope the sun is a shinin' and you ain't a pinin' for someone you love."[8]

As producer for the new record, we went with another big name: Tom Dowd. He spent years on the staff at Atlantic Records, overseeing some of the label's greatest jazz artists, including John Coltrane and Charles Mingus. On the rock side, he worked with the Allman Brothers, Black Oak Arkansas, Eric Clapton, and many other notables. Unfortunately, he didn't seem especially attuned to our project. Perhaps the music just didn't connect with him personally. Or maybe he could tell that we were suffering from a type of malaise. In any event, he was more of an engineer on my songs, in particular, than a hands-on producer.

"On the Line" provides a good example. It was very difficult for me to sing, because it required me to pitch my voice so high. Looking back, the song would have worked better if we had altered the arrangement and maybe worked in a different key. With all his years of experience, Tom should have suggested a key change, but he didn't. He just recorded it the way it was.

I'm sure I didn't put up much of a fight since my mind was elsewhere. The entire recording process, which took place during the early months of 1975, was a blur. I have no recollection of helping J. D. and Chris with their tracks. In fact, I can barely recall their songs at all. I was there physically, but not emotionally. This is one of the only times in my career that I may have compromised the professionalism I've always prided myself on. Humans are frail, and at that point in my life, I couldn't find the strength I always had before. My apologies to J. D. and Chris.

They may have shared some of my lack of enthusiasm for the SHF Band, because the three of us agreed that the album would be our swan song. We wouldn't embark on another tour after the album was completed. Once the last note was put on tape, the Souther-Hillman-Furay Band would be finished.

Reaching this agreement allowed me to focus more of my energies on Nancy, not that it seemed to be doing much good. Just before I returned to Colorado, Nancy briefly moved out of our house. She didn't have to because of me; I was staying in a cabin on the Caribou Ranch property. Nevertheless, she set up temporary housekeeping at the Foot of the Mountain, a motel in Boulder. Once when I was driving by the place, I saw her walking Timmie and stopped to talk, but she wouldn't give me the time of day. I got much the same treatment when I phoned her. She'd take the calls but wouldn't talk for long.

During one of these brief conversations, Nancy asked me to move all of my belongings out of our house. When I couldn't bring myself to empty my house of my own possessions, an SHF road manager, Ronald Perfit, who went by the nickname "Fly," volunteered to put my things in storage. That was a horrible day. Mutual friends told me Nancy was hurting as badly as I was, but that was really hard to believe.

A Gradual Thaw

At long last a ray of hope appeared. As we were getting close to wrapping up the second SHF album, *Trouble in Paradise,* Nancy called and said Timmie would like to see me. I was thrilled, if not shocked. And I wondered if this was the moment I'd been waiting for.

Our first get-together was followed by a second, and that time Nancy agreed to spend the night with me. But she wasn't ready for me to move back in. Just as quickly as things seemed to be moving forward, they came to a screeching halt, and I wound up going back to California.

As much as I didn't want to head west without Nancy and Timmie, it was the right thing to do, because I learned even more lessons about my faith. Just because I was a born-again believer didn't mean that my life was going to be all blue skies, green lights, and tops-down weather. I began to see that the Lord doesn't always deliver us from crisis situations, but He does promise to get us through them. We live with limited sight, but God is not limited. He knows the end from the beginning, and He is always at our side. In the Old Testament, the prophet Isaiah said it best: "God's ways are not our ways."[9] But God's way is perfect, His plan for us is perfect, and He is working all things "together for good to those who love [Him], to those who are the called according to His purpose."[10]

As the lyrics to "For Someone I Love" predicted, the breakthrough came in early spring, when Nancy said she was ready for me to move back to Colorado. My heart leaped, and I immediately made plans. I even traded in my beloved Porsche 911, which wasn't a very practical car for winter driving, in favor of a 1975 Chevrolet pickup. This exchange seemed like a bad bargain at the time, but I still have that truck all these years later.

What happened next shows how difficult and trying the process can be when one is learning to trust and to let the Lord work. By the time I called Nancy to say I was on my way, she'd gotten cold feet. She told me to stay in California, but my mind was made up. I hopped in the truck with Bugs, my road manager and friend, and we drove to Colorado.

As could be predicted, I wasn't greeted with open arms. Since Nancy was well along in her pregnancy, she would have been emotional anyway—and the circumstances only added to her uneasiness. We walked on eggshells around each other for weeks, and my attempts to improve the situation met with only limited success. During one late-night discussion, Nancy said that her heart still held no love for me. I suggested that she ask Jesus to give her that love, believing that He would be faithful to answer her request.

Obviously, I was learning some things as well. The Lord was giving me on-the-job training and teaching me about my role as a husband. He wanted me to take the initiative in leading my wife in our marriage, just as Jesus does with His bride, the church. Husbands are to love their wives with a self-sacrificing love.[11]

Still, reconciliation isn't like flipping on a light switch. For us, it was a challenging process. Even after Katie was born, Nancy was planning to leave me, but the Lord prevailed, and she never did. Little by little the love returned, and it has continued to grow and deepen ever since. We personally committed ourselves to the Lord and collectively did the same with our marriage, which God restored. And He blessed us with a new daughter too. For that and for so much more, I am eternally grateful.

14

A Christian Making Music

Striking Out in Another New Direction

Long before the general public knew that the Souther-Hillman-Furay Band had run its course, I was already working on the songs that would form the foundation of my first solo recording *I've Got a Reason*. I had high hopes for this material, but now my ambitions were focused in a different way: I wanted to put together *the* rock-and-roll band for God. I thought that if God was involved in the project, I couldn't miss, but I was wrong.

Instead of chart-topping success, I faced additional years of struggle and disappointment. Even more interesting, I came to know what it feels like to be a victim of prejudice for doing nothing more than loving the Lord. Only in retrospect did I understand that the challenges I confronted were all part of God's plan for me—a plan I'd been following, in one way or another, since the day I was born.

As my latest musical collaborators, I chose drummer John Mehler, keyboardist Tom Stipe, and a bass player named Jay Truax. They were gifted, highly skilled performers who just happened to be Christians. This last quality was important. I wanted a team of people whose lifestyle was in synch with mine and who could identify with my new direction because they'd made their own choice for Christ. That way, we would all be working toward a common goal. All of these guys were part of the emerging contemporary Christian music scene.

A NEW TYPE OF MUSIC

With the Richie Furay Band, I wanted to make music that would do more than simply proselytize. As a singer-songwriter, I'd always seen it as my job to talk about my life. My personal experiences were a creative wellspring, and they differentiated me from every other songwriter. The messages in my songs were unique because I was the only person who had lived my life. And as many artists find, the more personal my lyrics were, the more the average listener could identify with them.

The events that had so recently changed the course of my life naturally found their way into the songs I was writing. It was a completely organic process, and I never thought for an instant that Christianity should be off-limits. My spiritual rebirth had taken place, and I wanted to share the joy it produced with music lovers, just as I'd shared so many other feelings in the past. I tried to do it in a way that didn't come off as preachy, since I wasn't making records directed to the church. This was uncharted territory, but I wanted to share my love relationship with Christ with a new audience.

Since my compositions reflect real-life experiences, many of the songs I wrote for *I've Got a Reason* were colored by my marital tribulations. "Mighty Maker" was a prayer to the Lord to restore our marriage, while "You're the One I Love" was a declaration of affection for Nancy that was written from the viewpoint of a Christian believer.

As for "Gettin' Through," one of four songs I co-wrote with Tom, and "We'll See," they were attempts to explain my faith to musician friends who didn't know the Lord. A lot of these people had spent ages searching for meaning in their lives, and most of them still are, although their successes have kept them satisfied in the short run. These quests led them to dabble in everything from drugs to Eastern religions. I wanted to tell them that Christianity wasn't a fad, but something real, substantial, and made to last forever. Like "I've Got a Reason" itself, these songs never mentioned the name Jesus Christ, but they are suffused with His Spirit. He's all over this record.

Finally, "Still Rolling Stones" expressed my frustration with being typecast because of my newfound religion. The title intentionally alluded to *Rolling Stone* magazine, which had started looking at my music differently ever since word of my Christian conversion began circulating. Many other publications followed suit to the point where my faith, not my music, was being reviewed. That sort of bias made no sense to me back then, and it still doesn't.

Of course, even my supporters were having a tough time coming to grips with what my conversion might mean to my career. At one point, before I completed *I've Got a Reason,* David Geffen said to me, "You aren't going to give me any of that Jesus music, are you?" I didn't take this comment as an indication that David was anti-Christian, and in the years that followed, he proved me right. For instance, he worked with and stood by Donna Summer after she came to the Lord. His question merely reflected the standard music-industry view that Christianity created a big marketing problem. Money was and is the bottom line, and that's on both the Christian and the secular sides of the record-industry fence.

In the sixties and seventies, artists would occasionally mention Christian concepts in songs, using words and phrases you wouldn't normally hear on the radio. And several of these songs became pop hits. Examples include Norman Greenbaum's "Spirit in the Sky," Ocean's "Put Your Hand in the Hand," and the Doobie Brothers' cover of "Jesus Is Just Alright," a song that I never really embraced, since Jesus is a lot more than just "all right." But as far as I know, most of these performers were not talking about their life-changing experience with Christ; they were just singing a song. Worse, many musicians who had become popular in the secular realm were shunned after they embraced Christianity. Singer-songwriter Barry McGuire is a case in point. His work with the New Christy Minstrels and his solo hit "Eve of Destruction" made him a huge star, but when he gave his life to the Lord, he disappeared abruptly from the secular arena. In order to keep recording, he had to move to a Christian record label. That may have been by choice, but probably not his.

I didn't want to make this choice, since the Christian music industry wasn't nearly as well developed then as it is today. More important, I was still just as talented an entertainer as I'd been in the past. The only thing that had changed was my faith, which, in my opinion, made me even better. As a result, the idea that I could no longer perform as I had been doing seemed not only ridiculous but offensive.

This attitude only supported my pioneering efforts. I was among the first born-again performers to speak about my convictions in secular settings rather than retreating to the friendlier confines of a Christian record company. My determination to do so made me a target, and I took plenty of hits. But none of them knocked me off course.

I'VE GOT A REASON

When it came time to put my new songs on tape, I reached out to Michael Omartian and Bill Schnee, a pair of proven and talented producers who were also Christians. In the years that followed, Michael worked on a range of Christian and secular projects, producing Grammy-winning tracks for singer Christopher Cross and collaborating with the likes of Rod Stewart. I also benefited from the contributions of friends and acquaintances from years gone by. For instance, Steve Cropper and Al Perkins both played guitar on the album. Al had previously asked me to join Mason Proffit, a rock band he had joined that was moving into the Christian arena. Even though I declined his invitation so I could concentrate on my own songs, we remained close friends.

Despite these cameos, Tom Stipe, John Mehler, and Jay Truax formed the backbone of the Richie Furay Band, underpinning Michael and Bill's stellar production. As I saw it, the songs were professional, commercial, and enjoyable from a purely musical standpoint, but they also provided additional layers of meaning to anyone who would look deeper into the message.

Because the songs were so personal, I knew the album needed attention and tender, loving care from the record company. Too bad things didn't work out that way. By 1976, when *I've Got a Reason* was released, David Geffen was no longer at Asylum. He'd left the previous year to become vice chairman of the film division at Warner Brothers. His replacement, Joe Smith, was a very talented person, and if his legend never reached the heights scaled by David, Clive, and Ahmet, it came close. For me, though, his arrival spelled bad news. David, a longtime champion of my work, may have been worried about how to sell an album that was perceived as Christian, but I suspect he would have done everything he could to get it a wide hearing. Joe, on the other hand, didn't know me, and he showed no interest in making my album a priority.

When new executives take charge at record companies, they often pour their energy into their own projects and give short shrift to ones associated with their predecessors. That's exactly what happened with *I've Got a Reason*. Asylum was contractually obligated to put out the album, but the label offered little promotion beyond sending copies to music critics, most of whom seemed unable to set aside their personal biases and preconceptions while listening to it. Likewise, we received no tour support, forcing me to buy a van to squire us around while we were on the road. We worked hard to overcome these obstacles, touring from August until November 1976 with the likes of Janis Ian, the Beach Boys, and Jimmy Buffett, but we were fighting a losing battle. With no support, the project quickly faltered and never recovered.

Response to the album was another in a long line of musical and personal disappointments for me, but one thing that didn't falter was my faith. I'd gone through too much to let a professional disappointment get between me and the Lord. Besides, things were getting better between me and Nancy. For one, Katie was a wonderful blessing to our family, as well as a symbol of the Lord's love.

I also understood that the commitment I had made to God was a serious one. I was determined, having put my hand to the plow, to maintain my focus, as Jesus talks about in the gospel of Luke.[1] I had given my life to the Lord, and I wouldn't be distracted by a lack of support from my record company. There was no turning back.

My resolve carried over into my work. There was a dividing line in the music industry, and I wanted to bridge the gap, creating music that Christians and non-Christians alike would find enjoyable and valuable. No one had ever pulled off this feat on a large scale, and I wanted to be the first. While I was mulling over how to accomplish this goal, I took some time off to be with my family. The more time I spent around Nancy, Timmie, and Katie, the closer I grew to them and to the Lord, Who soon saw fit to bestow another blessing upon us. In 1977 Nancy gave birth to our third daughter, Polly. The happiness she brought to our hearts and home would be reflected in my next album.

DANCE A LITTLE LIGHT

On the surface, the songs that would appear on *Dance a Little Light,* my second solo album, seem less overtly spiritual than my previous recording. Even so, many of them were just as permeated with my faith as anything I'd recorded since my conversion. Take "Someone Who Cares." It could be interpreted as being about a friend or a spouse, but it also worked as a tribute to the Lord. "Ooh Dreamer" was a reflective song that gave listeners a sense of my aspirations on every level. Even my cover version of the rock oldie "This Magic Moment" echoes with my conviction. After all, there's no more "magical" a moment than when a person has accepted the Lord and is walking with Him on a daily basis.

Other songs touched on universal thoughts and emotions. "Bittersweet Love" is as simple and direct as its title, and "Yesterday's Gone" resembles the country hits that would come along two or three decades later. But "Stand Your Guard" dealt very specifically with what I was going through at the time. In it, I asked why some listeners were so put off by my faith. Many of them seemed almost wary of it, which perplexed me, since there's nothing to be frightened of. In the lyrics I try to examine this irrational fear, even as I remind myself not to waver but to stand my guard.

My producer this time around was Jim Mason, who has become a lifelong friend. Helping him was engineer Eric Prestidge, who's worked on a lot of great rock and country records over the years. I also called upon a wealth of talent to help out on the album. My Poco friends Rusty Young, Timothy B. Schmit, and George Grantham appeared on the album, as did Jimmy Messina. Al Perkins and Chris Hillman from the Souther-Hillman-Furay Band also kicked in, as did Virgil Beckham, a performer I'd met not long before, who co-wrote three songs with me that made the final cut. And *Partridge Family* graduate David Cassidy, whose house Nancy and I had used in Hawaii just before our marital crisis, contributed some vocals.

The recording sessions, held at a small studio in North Hollywood, were upbeat and a lot of fun. Everyone got along well, and the music sounded great, fueling my optimism. I may get dragged down at times, but not for very long. I tend to look on the bright side of situations, and with the Lord in my life, there's always a ray of sunshine breaking through the clouds. The finished version of *Dance a Little Light* seemed more broadly accessible than *I've Got a Reason* had proved to be, and I felt that if people were exposed to it, they'd like what they heard.

But once again, few got the chance to decide for themselves, because Asylum expended little effort promoting the album. The label poured precious few dollars into touring or promotion, and as far as I could tell, the staff hardly lifted a finger to get the songs on the radio. As Yogi Berra is credited with saying, it was déjà vu all over again.

With airplay so difficult to come by, and Asylum offering little help in other respects, I realized that the only way to let folks know that I had a new album was to tour as much as I could. I hated to leave my growing family, but I wanted *Dance* to become my breakthrough, and I wouldn't accept Asylum's lack of effort as a reason for failure.

I hit the road alongside the rest of the Richie Furay Band in March 1978 and kept traveling, with only intermittent breaks, until mid-August. During that span I began playing shows at Christian colleges and other venues where I could expect to find people who were open to the songs I was writing. I found such concerts to be relaxing and fulfilling, because I felt more free to talk from the stage about being born again. What was disappointing, though, was that I was preaching to the choir, which wasn't part of my original plan.

In the meantime we were also performing at clubs and theaters on the secular-rock circuit. For those dates I did relatively little expounding on my faith, preferring to let the music speak for itself. I played songs from every stage of my career, touching upon Buffalo Springfield, Poco, and the Souther-Hillman-Furay Band tunes as well as my solo material. I saw no need to abandon my earlier work. They formed my musical foundation, and none of them contradicted my Christian beliefs.

As has been the case for most of my career, audiences at Christian and secular concerts alike were enthusiastic about our performances. But their reactions weren't enough to move *Dance a Little Light* off the starting line. Album sales remained slow no matter what we did or how hard we worked, and after a couple of months, the optimism I'd felt during the recording process began to ebb. I had given Asylum what I felt was a very commercial album, and the label had let it die. I wondered if it was time to change directions again—a thought that gave me an empty feeling. I continually asked myself, *How could I have been so wrong? How did I miscalculate so badly?* I didn't have the answers, but I knew something had to give.

BACK TO THE SUNSET STRIP

Executives from Asylum Records were scheduled to attend a mid-May Richie Furay Band show booked at the Roxy on the Sunset Strip, and I found myself hoping that they'd come up afterward and tell me they were dropping my contract. I still owed Asylum one more album, but considering what had happened with the first two, I figured they'd want to cut their losses. The thought of signing with a Christian record label was becoming more attractive with each passing day.

For all I know, when the Asylum executives arrived at the Roxy, they were as eager to be rid of me as I was to be rid of them. But if so, the Richie Furay

Band unwittingly changed their minds, because our performance blew them away.

Having appeared at so many gigs over such a long period of time, the band was extremely tight, and we ripped through a set that included solo material like "This Magic Moment" as well as Poco favorites such as "C'mon." The performance was outstanding, and as a result, I believe, the Asylum representatives saw what they'd be losing if I were to leave the label. Backstage they gushed about the concert and urged me to get back into the studio and record a new album as quickly as possible. I could only ask myself, *Why? Why should I?* I'd poured my heart and soul into a project without any record-company support, and now they were asking me to do it all over again.

Compliments aren't supposed to make hearts sink, but this one did. Despite having done nothing to make *Dance a Little Light* a hit, Asylum wasn't about to let me go. On the plus side, the executives who saw our show at the Roxy had seemed sincere. Maybe this time, I thought, they would put their money where their mouths were. And in at least one respect, they did.

I STILL HAVE DREAMS

I didn't have a lot of time to write new material for the next album, but I had a couple of strong tunes I'd penned on my own, "Headin' South" and "Island Love," and four others that I co-wrote. Of the latter, the most passionate songs were "Satisfied" and "What's the Matter, Please?" which addressed the shifts in the way some music critics perceived me after I became a Christian. I added three compositions by bass player Billy Batstone—most prominently "I Still Have Dreams," which gave the record its title—and a cover of the Rascals' "Lonely Too Long." It was a strong collection, especially considering the little time I had to prepare.

Armed with this material, I rushed to Caribou Ranch and recorded the album in short order. But the finished product wasn't all I wanted it to be. During my previous tour I'd grown fond of the sound of a live band. In contrast, the

Caribou sessions seemed far too studio bound. The songs lacked the spontaneity and vibrancy I wanted them to have.

Luckily for me, I had Charlie Reardon in my corner. Charlie worked the Rocky Mountain region for Asylum, and he had become my biggest supporter in the company. In fact, he even took on some managerial responsibilities for me, albeit without a formal contract. When I told Charlie about my concerns, he didn't lecture me about the amount of money Asylum had already poured into the Caribou sessions. Without hesitation he went to his bosses at the label and gained their permission for me to record the entire album again. More than that, they agreed to let me start over in Los Angeles and made it possible for a highly regarded support crew to help.

First on the list was Val Garay, who'd either produced or engineered albums by Linda Ronstadt, James Taylor, and other stars of what was known as the L.A. sound. When I played him the songs that made up *I Still Have Dreams,* he loved them but agreed that they could be improved. And he knew just the people who could do the trick. Val had worked with a group of session musicians known collectively as the Section: guitarists Waddy Wachtel and Dan Dugmore, drummer Russ Kunkel, keyboardist Craig Doerge, and bassist Leland Sklar. They were the most in-demand collection of studio musicians in the business. Getting them to work with me was a real coup.

As usual, I also called in some friends for help, including J. D. Souther and the first two Poco bassists, Timothy B. Schmit and Randy Meisner. Having both Timothy and Randy on the disk might have raised a few eyebrows, since Randy had left the Eagles a couple of years earlier and was replaced by Timothy. But the politics of the situation didn't bother me. Randy, whom I hadn't been in close contact with for several years, and Timothy were both excellent singers, and that was what mattered most.

Because of the skills of the Section, I was able to give *I Still Have Dreams* the in-concert, you-are-there feel I wanted, and 90 percent of my vocals were recorded live as the tracks were being cut. It was one of my most memorable moments in the studio. The songs seemed to jump out of the grooves.

I was convinced that the record had several hits on it, and for the first time in my solo career, someone at Asylum—Charlie Reardon—agreed with me. Charlie tirelessly promoted the release, which hit stores in 1979, and it's due to his hard work that the album's title song, "I Still Have Dreams," inched into the Top 40, topping out at thirty-nine. Nonetheless, the momentum that seemed to be building ebbed, and the album faded away.

The reasons for the sad fate of *I Still Have Dreams* are complicated. Although Asylum didn't move heaven and earth on behalf of the album, the efforts of Charlie, who unfortunately died in an automobile accident during the early 1980s, were impressive. Still, he was fighting against changing trends. Disco had turned the music world upside down a couple of years earlier, becoming so popular that even such veteran acts as the Rolling Stones started adding heavy beats to their tunes. (I gave "Oooh Child," a song from *Dreams,* that kind of a feel too.) Then, after the disco backlash, styles like new wave and corporate rock rushed in to fill the vacuum. These developments put country rock, the genre I helped to launch, in a precarious position. The biggest groups, such as the Eagles, continued to flourish, but many others found airplay harder and harder to come by. And without airplay, album sales suffer.

When *I Still Have Dreams* didn't take off, I chose not to embark on another extended tour. Spending half a year trying to pump life into *Dance a Little Light* had exhausted me. Besides, I had another incentive to stay close to home. In 1979 Jesse, my fourth daughter and the final addition to our family, was born. Counting Nancy, that meant I had five beautiful girls in my life, and I didn't want to leave them for long. Family and the Lord took precedence over another run at success. Soon thereafter, I parted company with Asylum.

My decision doesn't mean I intended to retire from music—not yet, anyway. I still needed to support Nancy and the kids, and the best way to do so, I thought, was through performing. But I also wanted to spread the Word, and after my bitter experience at Asylum, I came to the conclusion that the Christian music industry was worth a try. My heart was still torn, but after a few conversations with Buddy Huey, who at the time was the head of Myrrh

Records, one of the largest Christian labels, I agreed to sign on and give it a try. Not only did he offer me a contract, but he leased the masters of *I've Got a Reason* from Asylum in order to rerelease the album on the Myrrh label. His idea was to get the disk, which he loved, into the Christian market shortly before my Myrrh debut as a way of introducing me to an audience that would be receptive to my message. More than two decades later, in 2003, *Reason* was released a third time. An independent label, Wounded Bird, made it and my other solo material available again. I was gratified by this action, since relatively few people got a chance to hear the albums when they were new.

SEASONS OF CHANGE

I had a great time writing and recording the songs for my first album to be released on a Christian record label. On *Seasons of Change* I worked closely with a good friend, David Diggs, who had contributed to my last two albums on Asylum, and together we came up with material that expressed my faith in a straightforward way. Being able to do so without worry was a great relief, even though I knew that this direction was going to limit whatever audience was out there. No longer did I have to put my love of the Lord into a sort of code that wouldn't raise a red flag for secular music executives.

Some of the songs dealt with difficult topics from a Christian perspective, including "Endless Flight," which explored the marital problems that Al and Debbie Perkins were experiencing at the time. Other songs simply gloried in the greatness of the Lord. From their titles to their lyrics, "Hallelujah," "My Lord and My God," "Home to My Lord," and the rest made no apologies for being songs of praise and worship.

Nonetheless, *Seasons of Change*, which reached stores in 1982, didn't become a Christian-music phenomenon, and its middling sales performance left me searching for answers again. The words of the apostle Paul, "Lord, what do You want me to do?"[2] were ringing in my ears. It seemed as though I was fighting against everything imaginable, and I certainly didn't want to be fighting against God. But for the moment, my first instinct was to pin the blame on Myrrh, which I felt was too focused on two of its other artists: B. J. Thomas and the very young, very talented Amy Grant. It was obvious that corporate muscle was behind them and not my album. Then again, I know I presented the label with a difficult challenge. In the same way that Poco had been too rock for many country fans and too country for plenty of rock listeners, I may have seemed too Christian for a mainstream audience and too mainstream for those who preferred Christian music. On top of that, I refused to remodel my sound with an eye to the eighties. The album may have been called *Seasons of Change,* but musically I still wanted to sound like myself. From a commercial standpoint, this decision stranded me in no man's land.

Another factor was my unwillingness to put together a big show band and tour for extended periods. I told my booking agent at the time that I would only play dates for a few days here and there with my acoustic guitar, which Myrrh may have interpreted as a lack of commitment. But I didn't have the money to underwrite a band, and Myrrh wasn't going to help with such an endeavor. Besides, I wanted to put my family first. When I had spent months at a time away from Nancy during the Poco days, I'd nearly destroyed my marriage, and I wasn't about to put my marriage at risk again.

I was at a crossroads, and I prayed for the Lord to put me on the right path. The words of a psalm encouraged me:

Wait on the LORD;
Be of good courage,
And He shall strengthen your heart;
Wait, I say, on the LORD! [3]

So I waited! This time around, however, God didn't speak to me in the way He had during my separation from Nancy. I believe that because my knowledge of Him was now much stronger and more deeply rooted, there were more lessons of faith and trust that He wanted me learn.

15

Finding a New Calling

Who Would've Guessed That I'd Become a Pastor?

The journey that resulted in my becoming a pastor began on the road, but it ended up leading me back home.

My friend Greg Laurie was a key to this transition. The early part of his life was tough (he had seven fathers during his childhood), but his story is a dramatic testimony of what can happen when you give yourself completely to the Lord. Greg was saved through the ministry of Pastor Chuck Smith, the founder of Calvary Chapel. After answering the call of God upon his life during the early seventies, Greg formed a Calvary Chapel in Riverside, California. Greg is both a dynamic Bible teacher and a charismatic evangelist whom the Lord has used in a fresh and powerful way to communicate the Gospel.

Greg subsequently launched a radio ministry, and during the period before and after the release of my *Seasons of Change* album, I often traveled with him to cities where a local radio station was picking up his program. I'd share my music at appearances where Greg was introducing himself to the radio audience. We visited some pretty exotic locations, such as Hawaii and Alaska, as well as Washington DC, New York City, and many other cities.

Watching Greg connect with crowds was a revelation for me. His audiences consisted mainly of Christians who brought their unbelieving friends with them to hear Greg's evangelistic messages. There wasn't a direct correlation between what he was doing and what I aspired to do musically, but I realized that we had a lot in common.

Like Greg, I've always wanted to help people gain a positive outlook on life. When I first became nationally known, the United States was in the midst of the Vietnam War, and because the war was so unpopular, negativity was the order of the day. People needed to see that despite the chaos, there was still hope—and I used my music to spread that message. Greg, for his part, came out of the Jesus movement of the seventies. He had a gift for communicating God's Word in a dynamic but simple way, and when he did, he reached many of the same audiences I had been focusing on. That was still true when we were traveling together in the eighties, and even though I'm older than Greg, I looked up to him as a mature, spiritual man—a mentor. I am so thankful that the Lord brought men like Greg into my life, since his uncompromising stand for Christ continues to be an inspiration to me. Together, the two of us used our individual talents for a common goal: to tell people about Jesus.

In retrospect, I'm sure these trips sowed the seeds for my next career shift, but I didn't realize it at the time. Back then I was still uncertain which way to turn. It took an unlikely meeting to point me in the right direction.

GETTING DIRECTION ON A DIRT ROAD

One day as I was walking on the dirt road that led to the mailboxes about three-quarters of a mile from my house, I was stopped by Jack Blease, a man who was fairly new to the neighborhood. He told me he'd been chatting with another neighbor who had mentioned that I was a Christian. He told me he was a Christian too, and he suggested that Nancy and I get together with him and his wife, Cathy, for a Bible study.

During my time in California, I had often attended Bible studies at the home of my friend Keith Ritter, and I'd found them to be a unique way of growing spiritually. Because they're interactive, they help people deepen their relationship with the Lord by sharing life experiences together. So Jack and I decided we would hold an evening study at his house.

Nancy and I were looking forward to the study, but it didn't live up to our expectations. We opened the Bible and discussed a few things, but we never really probed as deeply into the Scriptures as we had at Keith's home fellowship in California. I found out later that Jack had a background as a preacher, but in our small meeting he never took charge, and I didn't either. For the most part we sat around engaging in idle talk.

At the end of the evening, we made plans for another get-together the following week. But to make sure it went better than the first meeting, I decided to visit a Christian bookstore in Boulder, where I purchased some commentaries on the book of John that I used to prepare a study on the first chapter. Along with these, I used some Chuck Smith teaching tapes to get me started. To this day I continue to use the techniques I developed back then. I listened to the tapes, read the commentaries, and then let the Lord speak to me about the passages. I didn't know if this would work, but on the big night, everyone seemed to be making progress. As a result, our second Bible study was much more meaningful for all concerned.

I wasn't around Jack for long. Shortly after our second Bible study, Nancy and I began to sense that something was wrong in Jack and Cathy's relationship, and before long they split up. We're still in touch with Cathy, who is now happily married, but we lost contact with Jack. Nevertheless, he played a substantial part in my life. If he had conducted the Bible study more forcefully, I might have been content to sit back and let him take the lead, which was not what the Lord had in mind. Because I had to step up to the plate, I discovered that I had a gift I hadn't previously recognized.

God's Spirit was prompting me to embrace a leadership role, and in doing so, I took the next step toward fulfilling the destiny He had planned for me all along. Looking back I can see that the Lord never takes anything away that He doesn't replace with something that's far greater. I had thought that music was what it was all about for me, but I was quickly learning that for life to have real meaning, Jesus has to be the foundation; everything else must be built on Him!

Just because Jack and Cathy were no longer attending the Bible study didn't mean the meetings needed to end. The Bible talks about the need for

Christian fellowship,[1] and since I'd experienced the benefits of such gatherings in California, I reached out to another couple we knew: Doug and Pat Gibney. The Gibney's daughter, Dee, was a friend of Timmie, our oldest daughter. In fact, I'm proud to say that I had an influence on Doug's subsequent conversion. He was one of the first people for whom my life would have a powerful impact for Christ.

Doug had been a New York City police officer in the same precinct where Frank Serpico had previously worked, but after moving to Colorado, he wound up on the opposite side of the law, and drugs were eating away at his life. When I met him, he was living in nearby Nederland, where he worked as a custodian at the town's high school. He was very close to the end of his rope. His marriage was in trouble, and he had no idea know how to fix it.

I didn't pressure Doug into accepting Christ. Instead, I simply shared my testimony, and it touched him. The idea that someone from the world of popular music had gone through many of the same struggles he had seemed to make a real impact on him, and he was impressed by the life-changing effect Christianity had on me.

Doug gave his life to Christ, and he's currently the pastor at the Calvary Chapel of Nederland, Colorado. Fortunately, the Calvary Chapel movement isn't biased against people whose lives are on the edge of disaster or who lack standard theological training. Take Mike MacIntosh. Although Mike had eaten so much acid in his youth that he feared he'd permanently blown his mind, Chuck Smith took him under his wing. Mike now pastors Horizon Christian Fellowship, one of the largest churches in San Diego. As for Steve Mays, he was once a gun-toting drug dealer, but after accepting the Lord, he became the pastor of Calvary Chapel South Bay in Gardena, California.

Rather than shunning troubled people, Chuck has always encouraged them, and Mike, Steve, and Greg are living proof of how such compassion can pay off. In a different way, so am I. Rock and roll might not seem to be the best training for a pastor, but in my case, it was ideal, and the people of Calvary Chapel were open-minded enough to let me prove it.

For the Bible studies I led, I followed the format of the ones I'd attended in California, which had been inspired by what Chuck developed when he founded Calvary Chapel in 1965. He started with the philosophy that the best way to teach the Bible is book by book, verse by verse. That way, people can learn the whole Bible, not just sections of it. Using this approach, none of the hard issues can be avoided, and no minor topics can be overemphasized. Chuck was also determined to make sure his congregation was the best taught and best loved.

This idea is so simple that it translates easily to Bible studies. I was a novice, but by taking things slowly and deliberately, I was able to lead everyone through well-known and obscure passages alike, deepening and broadening our knowledge with every line of Scripture—"precept upon precept, line upon line."[2] This method worked wonderfully, and with Doug and Pat aboard, our Bible studies slowly gathered steam. We didn't advertise our meetings, which usually took place on Wednesday evenings, but somehow word got around, and more and more people began to attend.

I don't think my celebrity had anything to do with the popularity of the studies. Certainly, many of those who attended were familiar with my background, and since music was usually part of the structure, they got a chance to hear me sing and play guitar. Even so, Jesus, the object of our faith and devotion, was the subject that interested all of us, and we kept the focus firmly on the Bible.

Before long, about fifteen people were consistently attending the studies, and that was more bodies than could fit comfortably in our little home. In fact, the house was too small for just our family, and we'd already begun building a roomier one a bit closer to Boulder. In the meantime, we knew we had to come up with a bigger space for our gatherings, and Doug came through. He had access to the Nederland High School building, and he arranged for us to use it for Bible studies on Wednesday nights. We met there for about two months, and things went so well that when our house was completed and ready for us to move in, we decided to split the study in two. The people closest to Nederland would continue to attend at the high school under the guidance of Johnny Smith, a pastor from Texas who'd become one of our regulars, while folks who lived nearer Boulder would come to the studies I led at our new home.

I thought the new arrangement was ideal until we were hit by a major snowstorm during one of our first studies. After several people had a difficult time getting off the mountain, I realized we needed a place in Boulder that would be more accessible for all of us. Steve and Marie Jorgenson, a young couple with a lot of contacts in the college community, decided to make their home available. With their help, the study not only survived but prospered.

We were doing so well that during the first part of 1983, one of the people from the study asked me when we were going to start having Sunday-morning services. She felt our study was large enough to justify this step, but I didn't want us to do anything prematurely. So I told her we'd begin meeting for Sunday services when the Lord opened the door.

That response didn't sit well with some who were ready to take this step, so they took it upon themselves to stage Sunday-morning services. They continued coming to studies on Wednesdays, but they didn't mention what they were doing on Sundays. It wasn't long before I found out, though, that, for whatever reason, their Sunday worship services fell apart after only a few weeks. Still, the incident was a reminder to me that politics aren't unique to the music industry. They can come into play with any group, and more often than not, the effect is negative.

Politics, secrets, hidden agendas, and competition are examples of spiritual warfare that can divide people in Christian circles. Satan is not going to sit back and let his territory be invaded without a fight, and he uses whatever means he can—even sincere Christians—to accomplish his purpose of dividing and conquering. The Bible-study members found it necessary to regroup. To move forward I had to make sure that we made use of all the equipment the Lord gives us to go into spiritual battle. In the New Testament, the apostle Paul exhorts Christians to "be strong in the Lord and in the power of His might. Put on the whole armor of God, that you may be able to stand against the wiles of the devil."[3] And likewise, "The weapons of our warfare are not carnal but mighty in God for pulling down strongholds."[4] We were in a spiritual battle where the enemy of God and His church was trying to destroy the Bible study before we could become a church.

A Bible Study Grows into a Church

In our case, the mini-mutiny didn't lead to disaster. The best way to heal the split, I felt, was to find a neutral location for the study group to meet—one that couldn't be associated with either faction. I found one at the Seventh Day Baptist Church in downtown Boulder, and the space worked so well that I soon felt the Lord urging me to branch out to Sundays. Our first service was held on Easter Sunday in 1983, and everyone was so pleased by it that, beginning on Mother's Day, we made Sundays a permanent part of our worship calendar.

Over the next two years, the Rocky Mountain Christian Fellowship, as we called ourselves, continued to develop. We still held our Wednesday-night Bible studies, and on Sundays we convened for morning services, returning to the building that evening for a worship-and-prayer meeting. It was a full day, but an exciting one, and after a couple of years, positive word of mouth had caused our congregation to swell beyond the capacity of the church sanctuary. That meant looking for another new space, and we found what we needed at Boulder Junior Academy. Bethel Fellowship, pastored by James Ryle, had been using the school's gymnasium for services, but thanks to a donation of land, they were constructing a home of their own. (The congregation was renamed Vine Life Christian Fellowship, and James has since gone on to other ministries.) When they moved out of the gym, we moved in.

At the time, I saw Boulder Junior Academy as a steppingstone to an even larger headquarters for our church. We'd built a strong track record by then, and with so much more space, I assumed that the Lord intended our membership total to shoot up—but it didn't. Our congregation plateaued at a couple hundred people. We wound up staying at the school for eighteen years.

A lot of factors contributed to this situation. For one thing, the school-gym setting proved to be both a blessing and a curse. The gym provided plenty of room, but it made us seem as if we weren't as firmly established as other churches that had their own buildings. I'm not sure that was what kept attendance down and prevented us from creating the sort of infrastructure that attracts families. But we couldn't support as many programs and ministries for as many different groups as bigger churches could. This motivated some of our people to go elsewhere.

But a more definitive reason was that the city of Boulder proved to be an extremely difficult place to build a congregation. Our church appealed to college students who tended to leave the area after graduation, as well as to other young people who frequently left the city after a few years because of the high cost of living or other matters. Plus, many of those who did stay on in Boulder were wealthy, white-collar people who enjoyed the outdoors lifestyle and didn't want to be bothered about going to church on weekends. A lot of the residents who did attend church, meanwhile, seemed to feel more comfortable in traditional, denominational churches. So it was a tough beginning.

Since I'm not the kind of person to shy away from a challenge, we pressed on—but there were many times of deep discouragement. One year during the month leading up to Christmas, the building was packed, and I was convinced that we'd finally turned the corner and were growing. The week after Christmas, though, the turnout dropped considerably because so many people had gone home for the holiday. That took me by surprise, and as I drove toward home, I opened up my heart to the Lord, pleading with Him to tell me what I should do—and He did. In a strong voice, He asked, "If only two come, will you still minister?" I didn't have to think about my reply. "Yes," I told Him. In the future I would learn the lesson that the church is not mine but His, and He adds to the body of Christ whomever He wills.

This moment helped me put things into perspective, and so did a conversation with Greg Laurie. His congregation was huge, but he understood that numbers were secondary in importance to keeping focus on the Lord and helping people in need one at a time. The apostle Paul wrote to the Christians living in ancient Corinth: "It is required in stewards that one be found faithful."[5] And David said, "I have set the LORD always before me; because He is at my right hand I shall not be moved."[6] Greg simply reminded me, "You minister to the people who come." And that's what I did. Even as the Old Testament prophet Zechariah encouraged, "Do not despise the days of small things."[7]

The people who stuck with us did so in part because of the great worship team I rounded up. The first recruit was Scott Sellen, an acquaintance of mine from Calvary Chapel in Denver. Scott began coming to Boulder with his wife, Carolyn. He's a highly accomplished guitarist and banjo player, and he eventually became my song-writing partner and friend—a relationship that continues to this day. I would play guitar alongside Scott and a fine fiddle player, George Wargo, who became our third instrumentalist. Our sound had a bluegrass feel that made our songs of praise feel warm and inviting.

Playing with Scott and George helped ease my transition from full-time musician to pastor. I still had a booking agent, and I occasionally played shows at Christian colleges and similar venues, but I did so as a folk singer—one voice and one guitar—rather than traveling with a band. Because the Lord in His graciousness made sure that music was still in my life, I never felt a void when my career as a performer diminished. Neither was I consumed with jealousy when I saw musicians with whom I'd played achieve secular stardom. For instance, Poco had great sales success in the years after I went solo. With a new lineup fronted by Rusty Young and Paul Cotton, Poco topped the adult-contemporary charts in 1979 with the song "Crazy Love." But I never resented their success or wondered why it hadn't happened when I was in the band. That was all behind me. At that time it was most important for me to do as the Bible teaches in Philippians 3:14—to "press toward the goal for the prize of the upward call of God in Christ Jesus." So I was sincerely pleased for them and wished them nothing but the best.

I was too busy focusing on the Lord to have time for envy or for thinking about what might have been. I had made my decisions earlier, and I'd moved on. The Lord had given me back my marriage and my family, and He had found me worthy to lead a ministry, so I had no regrets. The familiar verse from the Psalms—"The LORD is my shepherd; I shall not want"[8]—speaks volumes. When Christ is truly the center of your life, nothing is lacking.

Still, musical opportunities would occasionally come my way, and I didn't turn my back on them. I realized that the Lord gave me the talent for singing and performing, and whenever I used these skills, I felt that I was honoring Him. It was on such an occasion that I met Mark Ferjulian, who would become my friend and manager for over two decades.

During the mideighties, Greg Laurie expanded his mission to the Philippines, and he asked me to accompany him to minister in three major outreaches at a large amphitheater in Manila. Then on Sunday, worship teams would fan out and preach at several local or home churches. Mark, a friend of Greg's who owned a chain of record stores in Los Angeles called Moby Disc, helped organize travel plans for the participants. I got a good vibe from him when he phoned me about airplane tickets and other travel details. Traveling alone to this part of the world made me a bit apprehensive, but I would soon make another friend for life.

My first stop was Hong Kong, and after I landed, I was taken to the Hilton hotel to get acclimated to the climate and time difference. Mark was waiting in the lobby for me, and we hit it off right away. As it turned out, he had worked with some big names in the entertainment world, among them Sly Stone. Mark was also a fan of Buffalo Springfield and Poco. As our conversations opened up, he guessed that I was receiving substantial royalties from the Springfield's records, which had continued to sell steadily in his stores over the years. That wasn't the case, I told him. Actually, I hadn't seen any Springfield royalties for a long time. He volunteered to check and see if there was some kind of bottleneck, and there was. A sizable amount of money had piled up over time, but it hadn't been forwarded to me because the music company "didn't have a current address for me"—yeah, right. By finding these funds, Mark not only provided me with something of a windfall, but he proved himself to be a good businessman and a good friend. But most important, he was a brother in the Lord, so our relationship just naturally took off.

BUFFALO SPRINGFIELD AGAIN?

After I got back to the States, Mark and I formalized our business arrangement, and in 1986 a surprising turn of events made it seem as if a manager would come in handy. I got a call from Steve Stills about a possible Buffalo Springfield reunion.

Every once in a while, there'd be a buzz about reassembling the original Springfield players: Steve, Neil, Bruce, Dewey, and me. Back in 1973 when I was with Poco, the idea came close enough to reality that it even spawned an item in *Rolling Stone*. The magazine quoted me as saying, "It's all up to Neil right now," which it usually was. To no one's surprise, the whole thing fell through. But for our next reunion try, more than ten years later, Steve assured me that Neil was on board. He wanted the five of us to meet at his place in Encino for rehearsals that would hopefully lead to a tour, and maybe even a new recording.

I hadn't given any thought to getting back into the world of rock and roll. Mentally and emotionally I'd put aside the ambitions that had driven me for so long. Yet I couldn't help but be intrigued by the notion of playing with these friends again. The Springfield was a terrific band, and I knew it would be cool to play again with the original lineup. On top of that, I figured that with the passage of time, there'd be no more head games of the sort that had caused us to break up long before our time. We'd simply be old friends making music together after too many years apart.

My church congregation might benefit as well, I hoped. The publicity generated by the Springfield reunion would bring attention to our church and provide us with the opportunity to share the Gospel of Jesus Christ with those who might visit us. So I told Steve he could count on me.

That summer I flew to California and headed to Steve's house, where he'd set up a beautiful rehearsal area. Shortly after I arrived I realized that the more things change, the more they stay the same. Steve, Dewey, and Bruce were there, as were photographers and journalists who wanted to be on hand for this historic moment. The only one missing, as usual, was Neil. But in the end his tardiness turned out to be a good thing, because it allowed us to break the ice, and it gave me time to let everyone know about the amazing life changes I'd gone through since we'd last played together.

I was in the kitchen when Steve came around the corner. We exchanged hugs and greetings, and then, out of the clear blue sky, he said, "I hear what you're doing, and I think that's really neat—but you don't believe in that rapture stuff, do you?"

Steve hadn't intended to put me on the spot, and I didn't take it that way. By this time I was incredibly comfortable talking about my relationship with the Lord and even controversial subjects, such as "the Rapture." For the next forty-five minutes, as we waited for Neil to make his appearance, I shared my testimony, and far from making the others uncomfortable, the conversation drew everyone toward me. One reason these rock and rollers weren't uneasy about the subject matter was that I'd gone out of my way to make everyone feel relaxed. I didn't show up in a white collar and black suit; I don't wear that anyway, because we're casual, man! Instead, I wore shorts, a T-shirt, and flip-flops, just like everyone else, and talked in a casual way. I didn't want any barriers to come between us as we sat down to make music together. But when the moment arrives, you have to seize it. Truthfully, though, it goes with the territory.

As I spoke, everyone listened politely, and afterward Steve's mom, who was also there, made a point of saying how special she thought the dialogue had been. I definitely agreed with her. I wanted my bandmates to know that I was still Richie, but I was a Christian, too, and my faith was very important to me.

I see this moment as being set up for me by the Lord, because the eternal destiny of my friends is never far from my heart. But convincing people who have seen you at your worst that you're different now because of a personal relationship with God through faith in Christ, though intimidating, is a way of introducing His work into their lives. In fact, reaching those closest to you with the Gospel is one of the hardest things Christians are called to do, but it's what being born again is all about. God makes radical changes in a person's life from the inside out.

Of course, the people we don't know may listen at times when our nearest and dearest friends simply shut us out. As Jesus said, "A prophet is not without honor except in his own country and in his own house."[9] But understanding that didn't make me reluctant to talk to Steve and the others. It inspired me even more.

Our conversation was just ending when Neil arrived, and he seemed upbeat about our being together again. That evening we plugged in and played, and from the first note, everything clicked. The sound was a bit ragged by our old standards, but that was to be expected. The potential was obvious to everyone, and it didn't dim over the course of the next several days. After making plans to gather in a month or so to rehearse again, I returned to Colorado surprisingly confident that the reunion would actually happen.

Things didn't work out that way. During our next set of rehearsals, the spark that had flared the first time around wasn't there. It's hard to pinpoint exactly what was different, but overall, people weren't as focused and intent as they'd been before. That had an impact on the music, which didn't flow. We left knowing that it would take more work than we'd anticipated to prepare us to play in front of huge crowds again. The question was whether everyone would be willing to hunker down and put in the necessary effort.

Our answer came prior to the next set of rehearsals, which were slated to take place a month or more afterward. Steve, Bruce, Dewey, and I showed up at the appointed time, but Neil, once again, was nowhere to be found. After waiting for a while, we were able to track him down at a studio where he was mixing a solo record. Typically, he hadn't told anyone he had this task on his schedule, and when he gave us no indication that he was willing to set it aside for a while, I knew it was over. I flew back to Colorado the next day, thinking my rock-and-roll days were behind me once and for all.

Today I believe that our attempt to reunite the Buffalo Springfield was a test to see if I was ready to engage in such an endeavor—and sure enough, another musical reunion was in my future. This one would not only test me further, but it would shake our little church to its foundation.

The Challenges of a Poco Reunion

At First It Seemed Like Such a Great Idea

*I*n 1989 when I got a phone call about plans for yet another musical reunion, it had a familiar sound. This time around, though, the person named Young in the band was Rusty, not Neil, and the group wasn't Buffalo Springfield but Poco.

I hadn't been holding my breath waiting for something like this to happen. After the attempt to put the Springfield back together had fallen apart, I focused all my energy on the church. I didn't dwell on my rock-and-roll past because I was content and fulfilled spending time with my family, the church, and everything else the Lord had set before me. However, I had to admit that I was interested in Rusty's proposal.

To celebrate the twentieth anniversary of Poco's debut album, he said, we would record and tour with the original lineup: Rusty, George Grantham, Randy Meisner, Jimmy Messina, and me. In many ways this would be a first for the band.

The five of us had made *Pickin' Up the Pieces* in 1969, but Randy left before the album came out, and his bass parts were removed from the final released version. Likewise, he had played live with us for about six months. As a result, only the people who saw our great shows at the Troubadour in

Los Angeles, and those who caught a handful of other dates in California, got to see Poco as Jimmy and I had initially envisioned it. A reunion, then, would give our fans something old and something new.

As a bonus, the project had a couple of powerful supporters: singer-songwriter Richard Marx, who was then at the height of his popularity, and Marx's manager, Allen Kovac, who would go on to handle the career of the Bee Gees. Kovac had already secured a contract with one of the biggest labels in the country, RCA Records, and was ready to make us Marx's opening act for a nationwide tour. The only thing that was still needed to put all these plans into motion was for me to come aboard.

Considering what had happened with the failed Buffalo Springfield reunion, I took a cautious approach to Rusty's proposal. I wanted to make sure everything was on firm footing before signing up. After a series of phone conversations and meetings, I came to the conclusion that this reunion had real possibilities. It would be fun to spend time making music with good friends from times gone by. I was still in fairly close contact with Rusty and probably communicated with George once or twice a year, but I hadn't seen or spoken with Jimmy for quite a while. As for Randy, our last contact had been around the time of my solo career, over a decade earlier. The thought of reaching back through the years was exciting.

Just as important, I thought the reunion could have a positive influence from the standpoint of my faith. In a way I saw it as a missionary outreach, though I knew I wouldn't be able to share my testimony from the stage. But the attention we would attract was likely to carry my story to a lot of people via newspaper and magazine articles and media interviews. That would certainly draw attention to the direction my life had taken, and people who heard about it might then open themselves up to the Lord. On top of that, I welcomed the opportunity to tell the other members of the band firsthand about what had happened to me. The New Testament reminds us, "Always be ready to give a defense to everyone who asks you a reason for the hope that is in you."[1]

TALKING TO THE CONGREGATION

Once I'd committed to the reunion, I decided to inform my congregation. The governing structure of our church didn't require me to do so, but the congregation was fairly small, and it seemed only fair to let everyone know what was happening. Besides, I would need their prayers and full support—and unlike the attempted reunion with the Buffalo Springfield, this time I would be spending an extended stretch in California, where we planned to record the album, and another six weeks away for the first leg of the Poco reunion tour. I wanted people to know about these circumstances in advance and to have a chance to ask questions and voice any concerns they might have.

It seemed that no one had any complaints or major concerns about my participation, at least not on the Sunday when I announced the news. Most of the people in the church seemed to believe, as I did, that the Poco reunion would have a positive influence and would provide plenty of opportunities to give a good witness. But in spite of the vote of confidence, conflict was in the offing, and another spiritual battle was getting underway.

In the meantime I signed the contracts that formalized my role in Poco. While relations among members of the band were very cordial at first, there were signs of strain just below the surface. I had made a cameo appearance on the previous Poco studio album, 1984's *Inamorata,* but I didn't have a sense of the politics involved with the group until I said it would be cool if we could involve Paul Cotton and Timothy B. Schmit in the reunion. To me, they were big parts of Poco's history, and I felt that getting them into the mix would be a nice complement to the original lineup. But this suggestion was shot down so quickly that it made me wonder if there had been more friction behind the scenes than I realized.

In an attempt to avoid any similar misunderstandings, I was up-front from the outset about my faith. Because I was the pastor of a church, I told everyone I didn't want to sing or perform any songs that would put me in a place of compromise or make me feel that I was sending the wrong message.

Everyone in the band, as well as Allen Kovac, assured me that I wouldn't be forced into any awkward situations.

A PROBLEMATIC SONG LIST

It turned out that keeping that pledge would be much easier said than done. Predictably, the first signs of discord arose over the songs themselves. Kovac had chosen a high-profile producer to oversee the album: David Cole, who, with partner Robert Clivillés, would go on to form C+C Music Factory, which had a string of dance-pop hits in the early nineties. David was a very talented person who died far too young. In 1994 he passed away due to complications from spinal meningitis.

Even though Poco had always been a band filled with great singer-songwriters, Kovac and Cole were determined to put outside material on the record, including "Nothin' to Hide," a song co-written by none other than Richard Marx. That may explain why they couldn't muster much enthusiasm for the songs Scott Sellen and I wrote for the occasion. We came up with several strong compositions, but Kovac and Cole initially accepted only one, "If It Wasn't for You." Fortunately, Scott and I completed another song, "When It All Began." The song was the perfect way to kick off the new album, since it looked back nostalgically at the group's origins with such lines as "The kids came dancin', and their hearts were romancin'. And the music was live Poco."[2]

My first chance to hear the other songs chosen for the album came during a rendezvous at Jimmy's ranch near Ojai, California. Ostensibly, the purpose was to get a feel for playing together again after so many years apart, but I think Jimmy and Rusty both wanted to make sure that everybody could still cut it. I'm sure I was one of their main concerns since I hadn't done much playing or singing outside of churches for years. Jimmy, in particular, insists on performances of the highest caliber, as is evident from the recent Loggins and Messina reunion tour, which I joined for a date in Minneapolis. I feel that way too, so it put us both on the same page.

On the other hand, I had a real problem with a song Jimmy wanted us to include on the album. The lyrics were about a fellow who worked from nine to five during the week so that he could go out on the weekend and raise hell. I wanted to be a role model for the people in my congregation and for Christians in general, and when I heard the lines Jimmy was singing, I knew I had to say something. I really felt I was being challenged and tested. So I brought the song to a stop and gathered everyone in a circle for a talk.

"I'm starting to sense that this isn't going to work," I told them. I explained that I didn't want to put everyone in the position of having to rethink all of their lyrics, but that I couldn't sing something that contradicted my values. We had a good conversation that carried over to dinner at an upscale restaurant Jimmy loved, and by the end of the evening, we agreed to give things another try. I left feeling confident that Jimmy and the others understood the limits I placed on myself.

Of course, the outside songwriters brought in by Kovac and Cole weren't part of these conversations, and I had major complaints about a couple of their tunes. The first was "Call It Love." Its melody and backing track were terrific, but the original lyrics were another story. Before they were altered, they bordered on being pornographic. Lyrically, this was not Poco—it was someone else's idea of how to sell records. A similar difficulty cropped up with "The Nature of Love." I remember two lines from the original version, before the lyrics were changed: "Some people find it on their wedding day. Some people find it in the backseat of a Chevrolet."[3] Now *you* tell me what he's talking about.

I don't want to come across as a prude. I'm the composer of "Kind Woman" and other songs that have a sensual side. But on those occasions I was writing about love in a committed relationship, not sex in a casual or extramarital affair. Just as important, none of the other Poco songwriters had ever gone down this path. The first incarnations of "Call It Love" and "The Nature of Love" were not only offensive to me personally, but they flew in the face of the band's style and tradition.

Taking this position put me at odds with everyone else in the band, with the surprising exception of Randy, who agreed that I had a point. Still, the other band members paid attention to my arguments, and Jimmy ended up trying to play the peacemaker. Kovac, too, was polite, at least when we were face to face. He took out his frustrations on Mark Ferjulian, my manager, using a highly abrasive tone. I felt bad for Mark, who proved his loyalty and friendship, sticking by me despite being subjected to so much verbal abuse.

In the end, "The Nature of Love" disagreement was resolved with a phone conversation between me and Van Stephenson, who co-wrote the song. He was a skilled musician who went on to have a long career in the modern-country band Blackhawk, and like David Cole, he died before his time, losing a battle to cancer in 2001. On this occasion, Van and I went round and round about the song's themes. "I'm a Christian too," I remember him saying. "What's the matter with those lyrics?" He did eventually change some of the lines to make them more acceptable, and although the song never became a favorite of mine, I was able to deal with it.

I couldn't get to the same level of acceptance with one other song: Jimmy's "Look Within." This time my objection wasn't over explicit lyrics. Instead, I was troubled by its new-age philosophy. Rather than recognizing the unique-ness of the God of the Bible, it seemed to say that all of us *are* God and that awakening the God-consciousness within is all one has to do to be on par with Him. But people who look within for God won't find Him there unless He has first been invited into that person's life. Since, in my view, Jimmy's song didn't do anything of the sort, I chose not to sing it.

I know choices like this have caused Christians to be labeled as narrow-minded. *What's the big deal?* many people wonder. But all gods are not the same. Other religions would try to diminish the uniqueness of Jesus by trying to lump Him into the just-another-of-many category. But He made the dis-tinction that He is "the way, the truth, and the life" and that "no one comes to the Father except through Me."[4] So I had to take a stand.

I know my decision hurt Jimmy, adding to the strain that cropped up during the studio sessions. Everything went well overall, but there was often a bit of tension in the air—even during some recording that took place on my birthday. I went in to sing "If It Wasn't for You," which turned out to be a real challenge. The chorus is extremely high, so high that when I play the song today, I sing it in a different key. But on that day I was struggling to tackle one of those hard-to-reach parts. I'll bet I sang the same line for ninety minutes, and I was getting frustrated to the point where I'm sure other people noticed it. When at last they told me I'd gotten it right, I wanted to take a break—but that wasn't in the cards. There were twenty people waiting inside the control room to wish me a happy birthday, and it turns out that one of the reasons they'd kept me singing for so long was to sneak everyone in without my noticing. Their intent was good, and in retrospect I appreciated it. But I would have enjoyed it a lot more at the time if they hadn't tortured me for an hour and a half beforehand!

MEANWHILE, BACK AT THE CHURCH

While I was struggling with certain aspects of the Poco reunion, I could sense that an undercurrent of discontent was rippling through my congregation in Colorado. The first sign of an impending crisis took place while I was in Kansas City for a prerelease junket to radio stations around the country. Late on a Friday night, I received a phone call from one of the church's board members. He told me that the entire church was in an uproar over the Poco reunion, and after detailing what he described as widespread dissension, he gave me an ultimatum: I needed to make up my mind whether I was going to be a pastor or a member of a rock-and-roll band.

I was stunned. True, I had an inkling that some people in the church had concerns, but I couldn't believe the situation had grown so dire. I had done everything I could to reassure the members of the congregation about the reunion, telling them I had no intention of leaving the church. But if what this person said was accurate, my words had fallen on deaf ears.

Even before the board member had finished his account, I knew I had to get to the bottom of the dispute. I told him I would return to Colorado the next day and asked him to pass the word among board members that we would discuss the reunion issue then. Following my return on Saturday and the meeting with the board, Nancy and I spent hours talking and praying about this dilemma, and the Lord led me to the obvious conclusion. Sure, I had signed contracts in connection with the reunion, and if I suddenly dropped out, I would be breaking my word and inviting a lawsuit. Yet if I was forced to choose between Poco and the church, I would pick the church. There is great wisdom contained in the gospel of Matthew: "Seek first the kingdom of God and His righteousness, and all these things shall be added to you."[5] This passage tells us to put Christ first in our lives, and I had no intention of suddenly turning my priorities upside down. I knew my motives were righteous before God, but some of the confusion still needed my attention.

At the same time, I didn't think God wanted me to completely reject my past. I was called not to be a monk but to testify of Jesus' love and His power to change lives. Some people believe that Christians, and especially pastors, should be isolated from earthly concerns. By this way of thinking, any kind of secular activity should be condemned. Of course, Christians need to be careful that the kind of information they're consuming is in keeping with what the Bible teaches, just as we should make sure our place of employment is above board in all its business dealings. But that doesn't mean we should reject all of society. What's important is to strike a balance, as I had been trying to do with the Poco reunion.

For me, the apostle Paul puts everything in perspective in these verses from the New Testament:

> It is required in stewards that one be found faithful. But with me it is a very small thing that I should be judged by you or by a human court. In fact, I do not even judge myself. For I know of nothing against myself, yet I am not justified by this; but He who judges me is the Lord. Therefore judge nothing before the time, until the Lord comes,

who will both bring to light the hidden things of darkness and reveal the counsels of the hearts. Then each one's praise will come from God.[6]

While these verses bolstered me, I still spent a sleepless night prior to that Sunday morning's church service. I had determined that I would call for a special all-church meeting after the sermon so we could get to the bottom of the problem.

The next morning, after delivering the message I'd prepared, I told the congregation that an important meeting would take place half an hour after the service ended. At that meeting I talked about reports of conflict over my involvement in the Poco reunion. I reiterated my reasons for temporarily rejoining the band and pointed out that everything to date had gone as I had predicted. I hadn't been away from the church more often than I thought I would, and there was no indication that a greater commitment of my time would be in the offing. Then I went around the room and asked each person if he or she were troubled by my taking part in the reunion.

Each member of the congregation spoke up, and at the end of this process, a grand total of three people protested: one woman, one man, and the board member who'd phoned me in Kansas City. Most in the congregation had been unaware that there was any sort of controversy at all, let alone that the whole church was in an "uproar." They had been taken care of while I was out of town, ministered to by pastor friends of mine. The three who voiced opposition just wanted to stir up trouble. When it became clear that the rest of the congregation had no intention of rallying to their cause, the three critics chose to go their separate ways. I told the rest of the congregation that since no one else seemed to object, I planned to keep my commitments to the band.

THE TENSION BETWEEN TWO WORLDS

With that behind me, I was even more concerned than before that nothing I did in Poco would reflect negatively on my testimony as a Christian. And sure enough, another incident soon brought my beliefs and my work with the band into conflict. This time the source of the trouble was a video that was to air on VH1. RCA had hired Michael Bay, the future director of violent feature films, such as *Bad Boys* and *Bad Boys II,* to put together a music video for our first single.

Given how provocative many music videos had become, I was concerned that I could be pushed in directions I didn't want to go. For this reason, I'd insisted that the band have complete artistic approval over everything we did—both our music and the videos. Knowing that this clause was in our contract, I phoned Bay and told him I wouldn't appear in any video that clashed with my values. Predictably, he told me not to worry. He had just filmed a video with Donny Osmond, he said, and since Donny had been fine with what he'd done, he couldn't imagine I would be unhappy. As if that was going to make everything all right.

I took Bay at his word, and the portion of the video I appeared in didn't raise my hackles. He simply filmed the five of us playing and lip-synching to "Call It Love" and "Nothin' to Hide." Even so, I knew some kind of video narrative would be added after the fact, and it concerned me that no one ran the particulars past me. Allen Kovac and the other members of the band told me I shouldn't worry.

Then about two weeks prior to RCA's national convention in Nashville, where we were scheduled to perform, I received a copy of the "Call It Love" video. With anticipation and excitement, I popped it into my VCR and sat down with Nancy to watch. After all, this was the band's first video. But Nancy and I were startled by what we saw. The story portion of the video took place in a little shack in the desert, and the men inside were hosing down a bunch of women. It looked like a wet T-shirt contest.

Even though the imagery offended me, we screened the video several times so I could make notes about every image or sequence I found offensive. When I was done, I had jotted down twenty-one different items. The sheer (no pun intended) number made me despair. Again and again throughout the Poco reunion process, I was in the position of having to fight against things that would have put me in a place of compromise.

I was definitely upset when I called Allen about the video, which may explain why he lost it with me. He snapped that he had personally gone over the video and removed anything that could possibly have bothered me. If I still had a problem, he added, I needed to call the people at RCA—so I did. The RCA executive I reached seemed to acquiesce. She told me that Jimmy and Rusty were scheduled to be in the offices soon, and that the three of them would go over the video and make any cuts or changes necessary to make it acceptable to everyone. She also promised that she would show me the finished product at the convention, and furthermore, she said it wouldn't be released without my approval.

I probably should have insisted that I see the video before the convention. But time was tight and the executive appeared to be sensitive to my concerns, so I agreed to the timetable.

THE BIG SURPRISE

Although a tremendous thunderstorm was lashing the area when I arrived at my Nashville hotel, it was nothing compared to what would follow. The guys in the band were all in a good mood as we sat down for a musical warmup, and everything went smoothly. We sounded great—maybe even better than we had in the old days—and I was excited to perform in front of a live audience. But as time passed I found myself wondering what had happened to the RCA executive. I assumed that she'd be at the hotel to greet us and fill me in on the edits. But she was nowhere to be seen, and no messages were waiting for me in my room.

Finally, Jimmy called my room to tell me that the RCA executive wanted to meet with us. I went downstairs, where everyone else in the band was waiting for me. Moments later the executive told me that none of the changes I'd requested had been made. When I asked about the timetable to get it taken care of, I sensed a check in my spirit as she danced around the question. Then she confirmed my worst nightmare: It was already on the air.

In a way, the meeting was a setup. I think the executive thought that with

Jimmy, Rusty, George, and Randy in the room with her, I would swallow my complaints about the video and move on. Instead, I went back to my room and called Mark Ferjulian, who had just heard about the video from Greg Laurie, of all people. Greg had seen it on VH1. Armed with that news, I phoned Allen and told him there was no way I'd sing at the convention. "You guys don't seem to get the point," I said. "We talked about this, and if talk is cheap, I need to take some action." Thunderstorm or no thunderstorm, I had to get out of Nashville. Out of courtesy for the guys, I left messages letting everyone know that I wouldn't be going to the convention. And then I was on my way to the airport.

I suppose some people might accuse me of doing the same thing Neil Young had done back in the Buffalo Springfield days—disappearing and leaving the rest of his bandmates in the lurch. To me, there are major differences. For one thing, I let everyone know I wouldn't be participating in the convention and why. For another, I didn't take a stand because of restlessness or creative differences or any earthly reason. I did it for principle.

These words from the New Testament explain my motivations: "All things are lawful for me, but all things are not helpful. All things are lawful for me, but I will not be brought under the power of any."[7] The apostle Paul was saying that as Christians we need to pick what is right and wrong based on what God has revealed to us in His Word, because our actions and behavior influence those around us. We are responsible for our decisions and actions, and we will one day give account before the throne of God.[8] This doesn't mean that we must live our lives in isolation, but it does mean that we must be ready to face challenges as well as the opposition of the world when we're confronted.

GOING ON TOUR

Because of what happened in Nashville, I wasn't sure if I would join the tour promoting *Legacy,* Poco's new album. I was angry with RCA and Allen Kovac, especially. But after some delicate negotiations, I agreed to play with the group for the six-week tour that was in my contract.

We got a lot of national exposure, performing on two episodes of *The Tonight Show,* one hosted by Johnny Carson and the other by Jay Leno. We also appeared on the late-night programs starring Arsenio Hall and Pat Sajak. These appearances helped "Call It Love" become one of the Top 20 singles in the country and boosted sales of the album. Likewise, the tour with Richard Marx was a success, selling well at most dates.

Unfortunately, what should have been a tremendously satisfying experience turned into something of a test. Richard Marx's audience was dominated by young girls, and he did his best to get them excited in ways that certainly made me uncomfortable. In addition, everything that had taken place leading up to the tour created rifts with some of the guys in the band. Randy, who had sided with me when I complained about some of the song lyrics contributed by outside writers, was much less sympathetic when I balked at singing a line about having a girl in a car from "Hearts on Fire," his biggest solo hit. Communication broke down between Jimmy and me as well.

By the end of six weeks, I think everyone was happy when I headed home. The rest of the band continued on for another leg of the tour, and I joined them for one date, playing a show in Winter Park, Colorado, as a favor to the promoter, Chuck Morris. Not knowing better, Chuck, a longtime friend, had advertised that I would be on the bill, and I didn't want to make it look as if he was pulling a fast one.

After the Winter Park concert, I refocused specifically on my church duties. It was so good to be back home again with my family. The church's membership may not have been growing at a rapid clip, but it was stable, and spending time alongside them brought a sense of peace to my heart. Soon it was evident that I was developing and maturing as a pastor, which made me a better teacher of the Word.

One of the tools still available to me in this mission was music, the universal communicator used in our contemporary worship services. Scott and I wrote new worship songs on a regular basis, and we were able to share them during Sunday services and also on those occasions when I joined Greg Laurie for some of his radio events and the evangelistic crusades he was conducting at the time. Greg's popularity had grown to the degree that he was able to put on three-day events at places like Anaheim Stadium. Being asked to be a small part of these outreaches was a tremendous honor.

IN MY FATHER'S HOUSE

Then in 1995 another door opened for me. I was given the opportunity to make an album called *In My Father's House* with the help of Calvary Chapel. For many years Calvary Chapel had operated its own record labels, beginning with Maranatha Music. Later other labels arose, including Asaph Records, but they had relatively short life spans. Although I knew many of the people involved with these projects, none of them ever asked me to work with them. Things picked up again when Pastor Chuck Smith gave my friend Tom Stipe the go-ahead to start a new label, Calvary Music. Tom asked Randy Rigby, a musician we both knew well, to find songs for a compilation disk. Randy asked me if I had any material, and when Scott and I played him some of what we'd written, he realized that we had enough tunes for an entire album.

In short order I was at Quadraphonic Sound, a state-of-the-art Nashville studio, with producer-engineer John Macy and some of the most gifted musicians in the world. Drummer Dennis Holt has kept time for a who's who of Christian musicians, including Phil Keaggy. Bassist Michael Rhodes's résumé includes albums by Dolly Parton, Kenny Rogers, Rodney Crowell, Reba McEntire, and many other country stars. Keyboardist Pete Wasner made his name in Vince Gill's band. And Chris Leuzinger's guitar can be heard on most of Garth Brooks's recordings, not to mention CDs by everyone from George Jones to Toby Keith.

These musicians never failed to amaze me. They would listen two or three times to a demo tape Scott and I had assembled, and then they would instantly write arrangements that would have taken most other performers weeks to produce. They knocked out songs like "In My Father's House," "Hallel," and "Wake Up My Soul" in three days.

Randy was so excited by the songs that he suggested we put together a band to perform at some church events in California. In short order we assembled a lineup that included Dennis, Scott, Randy, John Macy, Don Garberg, Brenda Harp, Jim Fletcher, and Ed Edwards. Our performances went so well that when Kenny Weissberg, my old friend from Boulder, asked if I wanted to play a show at Humphrey's by the Bay, the beautiful outdoor venue in San Diego that he books, I jumped at the chance. Kenny scheduled us to open for Emmylou Harris, and everything went so well that we decided to perform at other secular venues.

Following a show at the Coach House in San Juan Capistrano, a longtime fan named Andy Somers approached me. Andy is a very successful agent, and he offered on the spot to book more shows and tours in the future—a proposal I gladly accepted. Arguably the most meaningful of these dates was one at the Fox Theatre in Boulder. People traveled from across the country to see the show, and a lot of them came to church the next day, which was extremely gratifying. At the Fox Theatre show—just as I do at every other venue—I was able to tell about my life, from the Springfield and Poco to *In My Father's House*.

The new album wasn't a big success commercially because the distribution lined up by Calvary Music never came together. (*In My Father's House* was later reissued; a 2004 deluxe edition on Friday Records features live performances from the Fox Theatre show.) But the tour to promote the disk was something of a breakthrough for me. After more than twenty years of trying to combine my love of rock and roll with my faith, I'd found the right blend.

I realized then that my ministry extended far beyond the four walls of my local church. I could play my songs to my own congregation. I could play them in churches and at Christian outreach events across the country. I could even play them in clubs, theaters, and arenas like the ones where I'd performed early in my career and still be true to myself and my faith in Christ. In all of these settings, I was able to be a light in the world, letting people discover how the love of Jesus, which transformed me in every way possible, could do the same for them.

Becoming a member of the Rock and Roll Hall of Fame, as I did a year or two later, put me in the company of performers who are often referred to as musical immortals. But I aspire to a far more profound kind of immortality—the eternal life that can only be found through faith in Christ. There's only one word to describe how it feels to serve Him. Blessed.

The Lord and Me

Being inducted into the Rock and Roll Hall of Fame was the honor of a lifetime, but the years since then have been some of my most fulfilling and rewarding. That's especially true when it comes to my family. My love for Nancy grows deeper and richer every day. Our relationship is much healthier for having survived such difficult challenges so many years ago.

As for our daughters, they were quite literally a Godsend, and they've grown into wonderful adults. Timmie is married to Dave Aragon, who heads up a program for minority engineering students at the University of Colorado and serves alongside me in the ministry at Calvary Chapel in Broomfield. They have three children, Jackson, Luke, and Kendall. Katie is married to Vincent Rodriguez, who just earned his architectural license (first try) here in Colorado, and they have been blessed with their first child, a daughter named Parker Lily. Our third daughter, Polly, is still single—and she'll be quite a catch for someone! Our youngest daughter, Jesse, got married a few years back to Tom Lynch, and they live in New York City. All of our children have a living faith in the Lord, which is the greatest blessing for Nancy and me, since we know we'll be together in the next world as well as this one.

Marvelous things have happened at our church, too. In 2002 we got our own building, and the process we went through refreshed and renewed the convictions of the entire congregation. We had spent eighteen years holding services in a school gymnasium. Twice a week, on Wednesdays and Sundays, we did our setup, bringing in equipment, a sound system, banners, and a couple hundred chairs. Then we'd have to tear everything down. None of that would have been necessary if we'd had a permanent space.

And, as always, some major obstacles stood in the way of our obtaining a church home. Property in Boulder is extremely expensive. In addition, Boulder is a white-collar town with a high percentage of residents working in high-tech jobs, and it tends to attract people with an interest in fringe religions. Our church, in contrast, has always appealed to folks from a more traditional, blue-collar background, and the cost of living forced many of them into communities that border Boulder, including Broomfield, Arvada, Westminster, Longmont, and Louisville. With so many families making long treks to attend our services, I began to wonder whether we should move closer to where the majority of our congregation lived.

In the midnineties we thought we had found a solution. A church in Broomfield was looking to expand, and when that congregation relocated to its new building, we thought we'd be able to move into the old one. After much discussion, we put this space under contract, but at the last minute, our finances broke down and the deal fell through. Several years passed before we had another chance to resettle, and, coincidentally, the opportunity involved a property we'd looked at years earlier. Miramonte Lodge consisted of two buildings on a piece of land in a pretty Broomfield neighborhood. It had been too pricey for us back then, but in the intervening time, one of the structures became available for lease. This solution was a lot more cost-effective than buying the entire property.

We didn't want members of our congregation in Boulder to think that we were abandoning them, and fortunately a couple of additional options opened up. My assistant pastor, Michael Patrick, felt the call to start a Calvary Chapel in Longmont, and a young man from Washington State planned to move to Boulder to keep a church going there after we moved. In a sense, our decision to go to Broomfield spawned two new churches. As it turned out, some members stayed in Boulder (although not enough to keep a fellowship going over the long run) and others headed to Longmont. But the majority of folks came with us to Broomfield.

Since our first service in Broomfield in November 2002, our membership has fluctuated between 150 and 225 people. Those numbers let me get to know everyone personally and to be there for them whenever there's a need. In that sense, it's the perfect size for a church.

I know now that the Lord put me where He felt I could do the most good, but I don't hesitate to reach out to people beyond Colorado when compelled by the leading of the Holy Spirit. That's exactly what I did following the attacks on the World Trade Center on September 11, 2001. During my early years as a musician, I lived in New York City, and I returned quite often in subsequent years. That was especially true after my daughter Jesse moved to Manhattan to attend the American Musical and Dramatic Academy and then chose to stay on to pursue a career in entertainment. For those reasons, the tragedy of 9/11 was very personal for me. In its wake I called my friend Mike Finizio, who pastors the Harvest Christian Fellowship in New York. I asked Mike what I could do, and he responded by inviting me to help him in his efforts to minister to the people of the city.

That October, Nancy and I flew to New York. Over the following week we conducted numerous outreaches to the brave men and women of the police and fire departments, as well as to anyone else who had a need. We made ourselves available day and night, encouraging everyone who was touched by these devastating events and reminding them about the comforting arms of the Lord. I returned again in December to participate in a firefighters appreciation breakfast along with Chaplain John White, the organizer of a group called Firefighters for Christ.

A year and a half later, in March 2003, I was among the pastors invited to go to Washington DC, where I was part of the largest group of evangelical Christians ever to be invited to the White House. We were unable to meet with President Bush because the Iraq War had just gotten underway, but we did get a chance to hear the thoughts of several cabinet members, including

Attorney General John Ashcroft and Secretary of Commerce Don Evans. The gathering served as a reminder that even at such a difficult time, there are a lot of influential people standing up for Christian values.

I AM SURE

From a musical standpoint, I've been busy as well. Scott Sellen and I have spent a lot of time writing songs together, and by 2004 we had enough tunes to complete another devotional album titled *I Am Sure*. We decided to finance the project personally rather than seek the support of a record label. Based on my concert appearances in church and secular settings, I know my songs continue to touch people who are young, old, and in-between. So, rather than have to deal with the biases of a record company, if I have something to say musically, I'll find a way to say it on my own.

With the recording of *I Am Sure*, the Lord made it possible for me to get that same great cast of players to help out. In addition to the core group of musicians who contributed to *In My Father's House* (Michael Rhodes, Chris Leuzinger, Pete Wasner, Dennis Holt, and producer John Macy), I worked with Dan Dugmore, a great guitar and pedal-steel player who appears on some of the most popular music coming out of Nashville. Dan played on my 1979 album *I Still Have Dreams*, and it was great to be able to work with him again. The disk also featured cameos by Jimmy Messina, Rusty Young, Paul Cotton, Chris Hillman, bluegrass star Sam Bush, and three members of the Nitty Gritty Dirt Band: Jimmy Ibbotson, Bob Carpenter, and Jeff Hanna. Just as special, my daughter Jesse sang on six of the tracks. She's an excellent vocalist with a big future ahead of her.

With such accomplished performers behind me, I was able to convey a message of hope and faith in song. The chorus from the album's title track, "I Am Sure," is a good example: "We are set apart to proclaim His holy Name. We are set apart in His righteousness. We are set apart—I am sure of this thing."[1]

Only a few months after I completed *I Am Sure*, I tackled another project: my first new collection of mainstream songs in more than twenty years. It's called

Heartbeat of Love. Once again, the same band helped out, but I also had a broad cast of characters contributing as guests. Neil Young supplies a guitar part and a vocal on my new version of "Kind Woman." I couldn't get him on the song thirty years ago, but persistence pays off. Kenny Loggins sings on "Kind Woman" as well. Steve Stills sings on "Callin' Out Your Name," a new song that I wrote with Jim Mason. Rusty Young plays Dobro on "Dean's Barbecue," another new song written in tribute to the summer barbecues thrown by Dean Fearing, a famous chef and good friend, at the Mansion on Turtle Creek in Dallas. Al Perkins and Sam Bush are on that one too. Paul Cotton sings on the title track, "Heartbeat of Love" and adds a guitar solo to "In the Still of the Night." Mark Volman of the Turtles sings on "Real Love," Jeff Hanna of the Dirt Band does likewise on "Forever with You," and Timothy B. Schmit did all the background vocals on "My Heart's Cryin' Tonight." And when you add my daughter Jesse, who sings with just about everyone, you have a real supergroup.

I'm quite comfortable these days when it comes to sharing every facet of my life and music, whether it be in churches or at shows where I team up with Poco or when I share the stage with Jimmy Messina. I enjoy having the opportunity to get together with the friends who have supported me over the years. Collecting the love songs I've written over recent years is a natural extension of this philosophy, and it was a lot of fun, too. I'm a romantic through and through, and I make no apologies for writing love songs that send a positive message, inspire people, and hold out hope for the future.

Two of my favorite songs on this latest project were composed for the weddings of Timmie and Katie. Scott and I collaborated on "Forever with You" for Timmie and Dave, and when I found out that Katie and Vincent were getting married, she asked me to write a song for them as well. The result: "Only to You."

THE LORD AND ME

The love I have for the Lord couldn't be stronger. Through all the challenges and difficulties of my life, I have never let my faith waver, even when temptation was at its greatest. After I was born again, many well-meaning people told me not to talk about my Christian beliefs and to keep any hint of religion out of my songs, or else I'd be finished as a performer. The easiest course would have been to take their advice, but I couldn't do it. The changes I'd experienced had been so profound that I wanted to share them with the world.

Here's a good example. In 1974 my friend Peter Knobler called. He is a best-selling author who has written or co-written books about a wide range of famous people, from billionaire Sumner Redstone to basketball legend Kareem Abdul-Jabbar. But back then he ran *Crawdaddy,* one of the best music magazines of the day, and he was asking major music figures, and even some sports stars, to contribute essays about what it was like to turn thirty. Since I was thirty-three at the time, Peter thought I'd have some good insights about reaching this milestone.

I agreed to tackle the assignment, but I probably shouldn't have. I was in the midst of my marital crisis, and I was so focused on getting Nancy back that it was difficult to concentrate on anything else—and I also had just been born again. Finally, with my deadline nearing, I called Peter and told him I wouldn't be able to complete the essay. He said not to worry about it, because about three-quarters of the people he'd asked hadn't finished either. He gave me a new deadline, and I promised that I wouldn't let him down, even though I had no idea what I was going to write.

The answer came to me in a flash. The Lord's inspiration began coursing through me, and a bold testimony began flowing out of me. In the strongest words I could find, I wrote about how I'd been transformed by Jesus Christ. I began with these words:

> I'd just like to share with you a little bit about the love of God. For those of you who don't know, I'm speaking about Jesus Christ. If you're wondering what that has to do with this article and growing up, well, it has a lot to do with me and growing up.
>
> You see, I didn't come to the Lord until I was thirty years old. That

is approximately the same age Jesus was when His ministry fully matured and was appreciated by believers. I'm by no means comparing myself to God, but, simply, I have reached my maturity at thirty. Until that time my life had been one unfulfilled desire after another. Everything I thought I ever wanted was covered with my ego and the lusts for it. I thought cars, land, hit (gold) records, possessions—literally anything money could buy—were the ultimate one could attain for happiness. Oh, sure, you're probably saying, "What a messed up guy." But what are *you* living for? If your sights aren't on the ultimate—Jesus Christ—then you're falling short of what life is all about!... You see, the Lord gave me 30 years to show Him what I could do with my life, and all I could do was keep falling short, never quite making it. All the success you may think I've had has never brought me true happiness! I know now that true peace of mind is found only in the Lord God Jesus Christ, and without Him, one only fails.

I continued in this vein for four pages, ending with a simple thought: "Think about it—what do you have going for you? God is love."[2] Then I sent my essay to Peter, knowing that I had honestly conveyed the truth that had been revealed to me.

Three days later he called and said, "Richie, I can't print this."

"What do you mean?" I asked.

"If I print this," he replied, "it's the end of your career."

"Pete, this is who I am," I told him. "You have to print it."

To Pete's credit, he did as I asked, and despite his prediction, my career survived. Sure, there were hard times and frustrations and injustices along the way. But they pale in comparison with what the Lord has given me, including the hope He has promised through faith in Him, which has sustained me through good times and difficult times. He offers the same thing to all who call upon His name: the blessing of everlasting life. Besides, it's important to keep focused on what's ahead of us, not what's receding in the rearview mirror.

From the moment I accepted Christ, my faith never fluctuated. Drugs, alcohol, and everything negative in my life went by the wayside. All that remained was my desire to serve the Lord faithfully, and in return I've been given more than I could have ever dreamed—the love of my wife and my family, plus the opportunity to live my life for the Lord and to tell others about Jesus Christ. I couldn't have imagined when I was growing up in Yellow Springs, Ohio, that I would not only enjoy a musical career on par with so many of my heroes, but that I would also be given the precious gift of eternal life, and that it was there just for the asking.

I've lived my dreams as a musician, a husband, a father, and a servant of the Lord. I can go into churches and minister to the body of Christ through the worship songs God gives me. But I also find people outside church settings who are interested in my story, and they're just as receptive to "In My Father's House" as they are to "Kind Woman" and "A Good Feelin' to Know."

I identify with the apostle Paul, who went through changes far greater than mine. He was a well-known, well-respected religious leader of his day. In one passage he referred to himself as a Hebrew of the Hebrews, a leader who kept all the religious laws. As the passage continues, however, Paul cast aside all of these accomplishments:

> But what things were gain to me, these I have counted loss for Christ. Yet indeed I also count all things loss for the excellence of the knowledge of Christ Jesus my Lord, for whom I have suffered the loss of all things, and count them as rubbish, that I may gain Christ and be found in Him, not having my own righteousness, which is from the law, but that which is through faith in Christ, the righteousness which is from God by faith; that I may know Him and the power of His resurrection, and the fellowship of His sufferings, being conformed to His death, if, by any means, I may attain to the resurrection from the dead.
>
> Not that I have already attained, or am already perfected; but I press on, that I may lay hold of that for which Christ Jesus has also laid

hold of me. Brethren, I do not count myself to have apprehended; but one thing I do, forgetting those things which are behind and reaching forward to those things which are ahead, I press toward the goal for the prize of the upward call of God in Christ Jesus.[3]

I believe every one of these words, just as I believe that Someone high above the heavens planned the journey of my life. When I was a full-time musician, playing in cutting-edge bands like Buffalo Springfield and Poco, I lived for the moment and traveled around the world first class. I performed at the Hollywood Bowl and Carnegie Hall and Madison Square Garden. I stayed at the Ritz in Paris. I achieved a great deal of personal success. In one sense, I lived my dreams, but in another way, my experiences far exceeded anything I'd ever hoped for. Yet I was never quite satisfied. These dreams, though, were only a beginning of what was to come. It's nice to realize that I left a mark on music that's still being felt today. And I continue to feel that Poco deserves to have its name enshrined in that room of honor upstairs at the Rock and Roll Hall of Fame because of the influence the band had on the Eagles, on country rock music, and on American music in general. Even so, this kind of recognition would pale in comparison to the knowledge that my name is written in blood in the Lamb's Book of Life.

Some people say that Jesus Christ is either the Savior of humankind or the biggest lunatic and liar to ever walk the earth. Well, I've staked my life on my belief that He is Who He said He was, and I have confidence in the Word of God that I'm right. I have tried to live my life as honorably and with as much integrity as I can. Sure, I've fallen short, just as every human does, but I've picked myself up and tried to do better. I hope the people who hear my testimony will be challenged to think about the ultimate decision of what life is all about.

My purpose for writing this book is to share the love I have for Jesus Christ, my family, and you. My life has been fulfilled in so many ways. No one should have been blessed as much as I have. To make it all the more satisfying would be to know that I'll be seeing you in eternity, after our lives here are finished, because you have made a personal decision for Jesus Christ in your life. If you've been challenged to look deeper into your life, and if you want to pray to be born again, here's a prayer you can say in your heart to receive Christ today:

> Dear God, I'm going to take a step of faith today and trust Jesus Christ as my personal Lord and Savior! I confess to You that I haven't really given this a lot of thought, but I'm tired—just worn out from trying to make all the pieces of my life fit together. I believe that You, Jesus, are the Piece that's going to make it all work, giving real meaning and purpose to my life. I confess that I need You and I want You. Forgive me of my sin, be my Lord and Savior. I believe that You died at Calvary for me and that the "power of God to salvation"[4] is through Your sacrifice and Your blood that was shed for the forgiveness of my sin. Thank You, Jesus, for pickin' up the pieces of my life.

If you prayed this prayer, Jesus has made a place for you in His heavenly kingdom. Thanks for reading my book. May the grace of the Lord Jesus Christ be upon you.

Discography

The Au-Go-Go Singers
They Call Us Au-Go-Go Singers, 1964, Roulette Records. CD reissue, 2000, Collectors' Choice Music.

Buffalo Springfield
Buffalo Springfield, 1967, Atco Records. CD reissues, 1990, Atco Records, and 1997, Elektra/Asylum Records.

Buffalo Springfield Again, 1967, Atco Records. CD reissue, 1990, Atco Records.

Last Time Around, 1968, Atco Records. CD reissue, 1990, Atco Records.

Retrospective: The Best of Buffalo Springfield, 1969, Atco Records. CD reissue, 1990, Atco Records.

Expecting to Fly, 1970, Atlantic Records.

Buffalo Springfield (collection), 1973, Atco Records.

Buffalo Springfield, Star Collection, 1973, WEA Records (import).

Buffalo Springfield Box Set, CD Box Set, 2001, Rhino Records.

Poco
Pickin' Up the Pieces, 1969, Epic Records. CD reissue, 1995, Epic/Legacy Records.

Poco, 1970, Epic Records. CD reissue, 1990, Epic Records.

Deliverin', 1971, Epic Records. CD reissue, 1990, Epic Records.

From the Inside, 1971, Epic Records. CD reissue, 1991, Epic Records.

A Good Feelin' to Know, 1972, Epic Records. CD reissue, 1989, Epic Records.

Crazy Eyes, 1973, Epic Records. CD reissue, 1995, Epic/Legacy Records.

Cantamos, 1974, Epic Records. CD reissue, 2003, Wounded Bird Records.

The Very Best of Poco, 1975, Epic Records. CD reissue, 1999, Epic/Legacy Records; reissued 2002, Beat Goes On Records.

Songs of Richie Furay, 1980, Epic Records.

Legacy, 1989, RCA Records. CD reissue, 2001, BMG Special Products.
The Forgotten Trail (1969–1974), 1990, Epic Records.
From the Inside/A Good Feelin' to Know, 2002, Beat Goes On Records.
Pickin' Up the Pieces/Poco, 2004, Beat Goes On Records.
Keeping the Legend Alive, CD and DVD, 2004, Madacy Records.
The Essential Poco, 2005, Epic Records.
Crazy Love: The Ultimate Live Experience DVD, 2005, Purple Pyramid
   Records.

The Souther-Hillman-Furay Band

The Souther-Hillman-Furay Band, 1974, Asylum Records. CD reissue, 2002,
   Wounded Bird Records.
Trouble in Paradise, 1975, Asylum Records. CD reissue, 1994, Line Records;
   reissued 2002, Wounded Bird Records.
S-H-F, 1997, Line Records.

The Richie Furay Band

I've Got a Reason, 1976, Asylum Records. CD reissue, 2003, Wounded Bird
   Records.

Richie Furay

Dance a Little Light, 1978, Asylum Records. CD reissue, 2003, Wounded
   Bird Records.
I Still Have Dreams, 1979, Asylum Records. CD reissue, 2003, Wounded
   Bird Records.
Seasons of Change, 1982, Myrrh Records.
In My Father's House, 1997, Pamplin Records.
I Am Sure, 2005, Friday Music.
Heartbeat of Love, 2006 (upcoming release).

Notes

Acknowledgments

1. John Einarson and Richie Furay, *For What It's Worth: The Story of Buffalo Springfield,* rev. ed. (New York: Cooper Square Press, 2004). For fans who want to check out this book, it's distributed by the National Book Network, 1-800-462-6420.

Prologue

1. Neil Young, fax sent to the Rock and Roll Hall of Fame, May 1997, quoted in Denise Sheppard, "Neil Young Speaks His Mind to the Rock and Roll Hall of Fame," May 8, 1997, www.chartattack.com/damn/050897.html.
2. Tom Petty (speech, Rock and Roll Hall of Fame, Cleveland, Ohio, May 6, 1997).
3. See John 15:19; 17:14-16.
4. Richie Furay, "Pickin' Up the Pieces." Words and music by Richie Furay. Copyright © 1971 (Renewed) WB Music Corp. and Little Dickens Music. All rights administered by WB Music Corp. All rights reserved. Used by permission.
5. Richie Furay, "I've Got a Reason." Copyright © 1976 by Song Mountain Music Publishers. Administered by WB Music Corp. (ASCAP).

Chapter 3

1. John Sebastian, Mark Sebastian, and Steve Boone, "Summer in the City," copyright © 1966 by Alley Music and Trio Music.
2. See David Edwards and Mike Callahan, "The Roulette Story," April 18, 1998, www.bsnpubs.com/roulette/roulette.html.

Chapter 5

1. Richie Furay, "Seasons of Change," copyright © 1982, Song Mountain Music Publishers. Administered by WB Music Corp. (ASCAP).

Chapter 6

1. Tim Sendra, All Music Guide, biographical information on Arthur Lee, Artist Direct, www.artistdirect.com/nad/music/artist/bio/0,,457537,00 .html#bio (accessed October 11, 2005).

Chapter 7

1. Genesis 2:18.
2. Song of Solomon 8:7.

Chapter 8

1. Richie Furay, "A Child's Claim to Fame." Words and music by Richie Furay. Copyright © 1967 (Renewed) Cotillion Music Inc., Ten-East Music, Springalo Toones, and Richie Furay Music. All rights reserved. Used by permission.
2. Richie Furay, "Kind Woman." Words and music by Richie Furay. Copyright © 1968 (Renewed) Cotillion Music Inc., Richie Furay Music and Springalo Toones. All rights reserved. Used by permission.

Chapter 9

1. Richie Furay, "Crazy Eyes," copyright © 1973, Little Dickens Music. Administered by WB Music Corp. (ASCAP).
2. Philippians 2:3-4.
3. Amos 3:3.

Chapter 10

1. Stephen Stills, "Love the One You're With," copyright © 1970 by Sony/ATV Music Publishing.
2. Proverbs 5:15-18.
3. Hebrews 4:16.

Chapter 11

1. Richie Furay, "In the Still of the Night," copyright © 2005, Always An Adventure Music. Used by permission.
2. Romans 1:16.

Chapter 12

1. 2 Corinthians 5:17.
2. Carole King and Gerry Goffin, "Will You Still Love Me Tomorrow?" copyright © 1995 by Warner/Chappel Music Publishing.
3. 1 John 4:19.

Chapter 13

1. Jim Gordon, biographical information, Drummerworld, www.drummer world.com/drummers/Jim_Gordon.html (accessed October 11, 2005).
2. Isaiah 40:1.
3. See Malachi 2:16.
4. See Matthew 19:1-9.
5. Psalm 4:6-8.
6. Richie Furay, "Pickin' Up the Pieces." Words and music by Richie Furay. Copyright © 1971 (Renewed) WB Music Corp. and Little Dickens Music. All rights administered by WB Music Corp. All rights reserved. Used by permission.
7. Luke 1:37.
8. Richie Furay, "For Someone I Love." Word and music by Richie Furay. Copyright © 1992 Warner-Tamerlane Publishing Corp. Administered by Alfred Publishing Co. All rights reserved. Used by permission.
9. Isaiah 55:8-9, author's paraphrase.
10. Romans 8:28.
11. See Ephesians 5:25-29; 1 Peter 3:7.

Chapter 14

1. See Luke 9:62.
2. Acts 9:6.
3. Psalm 27:14.

Chapter 15

1. See Hebrews 10:24-25.
2. Isaiah 28:10.
3. Ephesians 6:10-11.

4. 2 Corinthians 10:4.

5. 1 Corinthians 4:2.

6. Psalm 16:8.

7. Zechariah 4:10, author's paraphrase.

8. Psalm 23:1.

9. Matthew 13:57.

Chapter 16

1. 1 Peter 3:15.

2. Richie Furay, Scott Sellen, Stephen Mark Pasch, Anthony Krizan, "When It All Began," copyright © 1989, Rockwood Music, Straight Gate Music, Warner-Tamerlane Publishing Corp. (BMI).

3. These lines were dropped from the lyrics of "The Nature of Love" before the song was recorded for the Poco album *Legacy.* Lyrics by Jeff Silbar and Van Stephenson, copyright © 1989 by Lorimar Music A Corporation and Silbar Songs/Lorimar Music.

4. John 14:6.

5. Matthew 6:33.

6. 1 Corinthians 4:2-5.

7. 1 Corinthians 6:12.

8. See Romans 14:11-12.

Epilogue

1. Richie Furay and Scott Sellen, "I Am Sure." Copyright © 2005 Always An Adventure Music. Used by permission.

2. Richie Furay, "A Good Feeling to Know," *Crawdaddy,* June 1975, 52, 53.

3. Philippians 3:7-14.

4. Romans 1:16.

Index

ABC Records 122
Abdul-Jabbar, Kareem 236
"Act Naturally" 118
Acuff, Roy 120
Adler, Lou 80, 102
Adventures of Ozzie and Harriet,
   The 24
Aerosmith 158
"After Loving You" 41
Allman Brothers, the 119, 184
Allman, Duane 119, 159
Allman, Gregg 119, 121, 159
Almost Famous 109
American Bandstand 77, 93
American Dreams 77
America Sings 42
"And Settlin' Down" 154
Antioch College 12, 14, 27
"Anyway Bye Bye" 140
Aragon, Dave
   (Timmie Furay's husband) 231
Ashbaugh, Noel 22
Ashcroft, John 234
Association, the 61
Asylum Records 155, 171, 183,
                       191, 193-98
Atco 81, 82, 87, 92, 111
Atlantic Records 3, 81, 94, 108,
                   127-28, 136, 138, 183
Au Go-Go Singers, the 32, 43,
      45-48, 50-51, 55, 81, 84, 105, 109
Axton, Hoyt 126
"Baby Don't Scold Me" 83, 92
Back Porch Majority, the 60

Bad Boys 224
Bad Boys II 224
"Bad Weather" 150
Baker, Ginger 80
Bakersfield Sound, the 118
"Ballad of Johnny Collins,
   The" 29, 39
Barons, the 25
Batstone, Bill 195
Bay, Michae 224
Bay Singers, the 41, 51, 52
Beach Boys, the 3, 5-6, 59, 108,
              110, 117, 125, 158, 191
Beatles, the 62, 82, 102, 110, 118
"Be-Bop Baby" 24
Beckham, Virgil 193
Bee Gees, the 1, 3, 5, 216
"Believe Me" 163
Berra, Yogi 193
Berry, Chuck 74, 133
"Best of My Love" 156
Big Brother and the
   Holding Company 91, 103
Billboard Hot 100 93
Bingham, Diane 24
Bitter End, the 39, 52, 133
"Bittersweet Love" 192
Black, Bill 18
"Black Is Black" 85
Black Oak Arkansas 184
Blease, Jack 202-3
Blew Mind 90
"Bluebird" 92, 103, 107
Blues Image 165

Blues Project, the 103
"Blue Suede Shoes" 74
"Blue Water" 158
Boenzee Cryque 101, 121-22
Bond, Johnny 157
Bono, Salvatore Philip
    ("Sonny") 80, 82
Booker T and the MGs 102, 148
Boston Tea Party, the 133
Bowie, David 127
Box Tops, the 108
"Brass Buttons" 53, 121, 158
Brewer and Shipley 61
Brewer, Mike 61, 64
Brittan, William 105
"Broken Arrow" 107
Brooks, Garth 228
"Brown Eyed Handsome Man" 74
Bruce, Jack 80
Buckley, Tim 40
Buffalo Springfield 53, 62, 66,
                        67, 83, 87, 92
Buffalo Springfield Again 25, 40, 61,
                104, 105, 107-8, 111
*Buffalo Springfield
    Box Set, the* 60, 83, 94, 112, 128
Buffalo Springfield Roller
    Company 71, 130
Buffalo Springfield, the 1-6, 25, 53,
        59-62, 66-67, 69-79, 81-82, 84, 88,
        90-92, 94, 96, 98-115, 117-18,
        122-29, 134, 138, 141, 147, 154, 156,
        158, 163, 175, 194, 210-11, 214,
        216-17, 226, 229, 239
Buffett, Jimmy 191
Bunky and Jake 38
"Burned" 83, 87, 93
Burrito Deluxe 120
Burton, James 24

Bush, President George W. 233
Bush, Sam 234, 235
Butterfield Blues Band, the 102
Byrds, the 5, 55-56, 69, 71-73, 75,
                79, 82, 119-20, 156
Café Au Go-Go 42-43, 50
Café Bizarre 42
Café Wha? 32, 39, 42
Cale, J. J. 158
"Calico Lady" 51, 128
Callen, Micki 112
"Callin' Out Your Name" 235
"Call It Love" 219, 224, 227
Calvary Chapel
    Broomfield, CO 2, 231-33
    Costa Mesa, CA 163, 175,
                201, 204-5, 228
    Denver, CO 209
    Longmont, CO 232
    Nederland, CO 204
    Riverside, CA 201
    South Bay, Gardena, CA 204
Canned Heat 102, 115
"Can't Keep Me Down" 62, 128
Captain Beefheart
    (Don Van Vliet) 75
"Carefree Country Day" 112
Carnegie Hall 143, 239
Carpenter, Bob 234
"Carrie Anne" 127
Carroll, Diahann 46
Carson, Johnny 100, 227
Cassidy, David 166, 193
Cat Mother and the All Night
    News Boys 40-41
Cavaliere, Felix 6
Chad and Jeremy 85
Chad Mitchell Trio 52
Charles, Ray 81

"Child's Claim to Fame, A" 106-7, 113, 147

Chin, Charlie 40

Clapton, Eric 80, 114-15, 159, 184

Clark, Gene 56

Clarke, Michael 56

Clivillés, Robert 218

"C'mon" 151, 195

Cochran, Eddie 17

Cofrin, Paige 120

Cole, David 218-20

Coltrane, John 81, 183

Columbia Records 127, 136, 143, 148, 150-51

Columbus School for the Blind 29

Commander Cody and the Lost Planet Airmen 157

Como, Perry 43

Concert for Bangladesh 102

Conrad, Don 51, 57

"Consequently So Long" 128

Cook, Dale 16

Cooke, Sam 43

Cooper, Alice 153, 158

Cooper, Bill 165

Cotton, Paul . . . 102, 147-48, 150, 154, 158, 209, 217, 234

Country Joe and the Fish 115

country rock 1-2, 53, 83, 106-7, 117, 120, 124, 140, 147, 153, 155-56, 197, 239

C+C Music Factory 218

Crawdaddy magazine 236

Crazy Eyes 54, 157-58

"Crazy Eyes" 121, 157-58

"Crazy Love" 209

Cream 80, 114

Creatore, Luigi 43-44

Creedence Clearwater Revival 133

Crests, the 25

Cropper, Steve 148-49, 153, 190

Crosby, David 5-6, 56, 102, 127

Crosby, Stills, and Nash 1, 5, 7, 127-28, 137-38, 155, 159

Crosby, Stills, Nash, and Young 59, 138

Cross, Christopher 190

Crowe, Cameron 109

Crowell, Rodney 228

Daily Flash, the 102

Dance a Little Light . . . 153, 192-95, 197

Davis, Clive 127-28, 136-38, 150-51, 191

Davis, Dickie 58, 60, 78, 87, 89, 96, 108, 110, 125, 135, 137-38

"Dean's Barbecue" 235

"Deep, Dark and Dreamless" 162

Deliverin' 143, 147, 151

Densmore, John 74

Denver, John (Henry John Deutschendorf Jr.) . . . 52

Derek and the Dominos 159

Dickson, Jim 69, 71, 79

Diggs, David 198

Dillards, the 69

Diltz, Henry 44

DiMucci, Dion 25

Dion and the Belmonts 25

"Dock of the Bay, (Sittin' On) The" 94, 148

Doerge, Craig 196

Doerson, Bob 36

"Do I Have to Come Right Out and Say It" 83, 84

Dolenz, Micky 59

"Don't Let the Rain Come Down" 41

Doobie Brothers, the 189

Doors, the 63, 74-75, 80, 104, 133

Douglas, Chip 44, 166

Douglas, Michael 5, 107

Dowd, Tom 183

"Do You Feel It, Too" 128

draft board 48, 68

drugs (including alcohol, hashish LSD, marijuana, and pills) 54-55, 85-86, 91, 109, 114-15, 174, 188, 204,238

Dugmore, Dan 196, 234

Dunhill Records 80

Dwyer, Bruce 26

Dylan, Bob 3, 30, 39, 56, 107

Eagles, the 124, 154-55, 162, 173, 196-97, 239

Eckroad, Kippy 26

Ed Sullivan Show, the 46

Edwards, Ed 229

Electric Flag 103

Elektra Records 80

Ellis, Don 150

"Endless Flight" 198

Epic Records 128, 136, 139, 148, 150, 153, 164

Ertegun, Ahmet 3, 81-82, 91-92, 110, 127, 138, 150, 191

Evans, Don 234

"Eve of Destruction" 189

Everly Brothers, the 3

"Everybody's Wrong" 83, 87

"Everydays" 61, 107

"Expecting to Fly" 107, 110

Ezrin, Bob 158

"Fallin' in Love" 163, 165, 178

Faryar, Cyrus 44

Fearing, Dean 235

Feelin' Glad 122

Ferjulian, Mark 210-11, 220, 226

Fielder, Jim 61, 64, 86, 96, 109

Fifth Dimension, the 100

Fillmore Auditorium, the 91

Firefall 153

Five Satins, the 17

Fletcher, Jim 229

"Flight of the Dove, The" 163

Flo and Eddie 89

Flying Burrito Brothers, the ... 56, 120, 156, 159

"Flying on the Ground Is Wrong" 83, 84

Foley, Red 120

"Fool's Gold" 157

Forever Changes 74

"Forever with You" 235

Forgotten Trail, The 129

"For Someone I Love" 183, 185

Forssi, Ken 96, 109

"For What It's Worth" 1, 92-93, 100, 104

Four Winds, the 32, 35, 39, 40, 45

Frampton, Peter 158

Frampton's Camel 158

Frayne, George 157

Frazier, Dallas 140

Frey, Glenn 124-25, 156

Friedman, Barry (Frazier Mohawk) 60-62, 64-67, 69, 71, 79-81, 104

Friedman, Jim 44-46, 60

From the Inside 128, 148-51

"From the Inside" 150

Furay, Jesse (Mrs. Jesse Lynch) (Richie's daughter) 1, 44, 197, 231, 233-35

Furay, Judy (Mrs. Judy Hugli) (Richie's sister) 12, 14, 19, 22-23

Furay, Katie (Mrs. Katie Rodriguez)
  (Richie's daughter) 1, 182, 186,
                        191-92, 231, 235
Furay, Nancy Jennings
  (Richie's wife) 1, 3, 5-6, 77-79,
    89-90, 97-99, 101, 112, 114-15, 123,
    134, 141-45, 149, 152, 155, 163-67,
    169-73, 175-78, 180-86, 188, 191-92,
    197, 199, 202, 222, 224, 231, 233, 236
Furay, Naomi Coffman
  (Richie's mother) 8, 11, 13, 14,
    16-19, 21-23, 26, 48, 53, 98, 143
Furay, Paul Charles
(Richie's father) 11-12, 14-21,
                        23-24, 26
Furay, Polly
  (Richie's daughter) 1, 192, 231
Furay, Timmie Sue (Mrs. Timmie Sue
  Aragon) (Richie's daughter) 1,
    141-42, 152, 154, 165-67, 171, 177,
    181, 183-85, 192, 204, 231, 235
Gabriel, Peter 158
Garay, Val 196
Garberg, Don 229
Geffen, David 2, 127-28, 137-38,
    140, 155-56, 158, 161, 163,
    171, 176, 183, 189
Geiger, Fred (Rick) 41, 44, 52
"Gettin' Through" 188
Gibb, Maurice 5
Gibney, Dee 204-5
Gibney, Doug 204-5
Gibney, Pat 204-5
Gibson ES295 18
Giglio, Steve ("Bugs") 175, 186
Gill, Vince 228
Glad 122
Go 99
"Go and Say Goodbye" 83-84, 154

Good Feelin' to Know, A 83, 153-54
"Good Feelin' to Know, A" ... 154, 238
"Good Old Rock and Roll" 40
"Good Time Boy" 105
Goodwin, Skip 51, 128
Gordon, Jim 159, 162, 173-74
GP 120
Graham, Billy 157
"Grand Junction" 128
Grant, Amy 199
Grantham, George 101, 124, 148,
                        152, 193, 215-16, 226
Grateful Dead, the 90, 139
Greenbaum, Norman 189
Green, Charlie 80-82, 85, 94-96,
                        101, 107, 112, 122
Greenwich Village 30, 32-33,
                        39-40, 42, 59, 94
Grievous Angel 54, 120-21
Grillo, Nick 110, 115, 125
Guercio, Jim 183
Guess Who, the 153
Gurney, Ann 51, 78
Gurney, Jean 41, 51-53, 94
Gustafson, Nels 8, 28, 30, 35,
                        38-39, 46-47, 50, 94
Guthrie, Woody 3
Haggard, Merle 117
Hall, Arsenio 227
"Hallel" 229
"Hallelujah" 198
Hammer of the Gods 142
Hanna, Jeff 234, 235
"Happy Together" 89
Hardin, Tim 40, 62
"Hard Luck" 147
Hard Times, the 90, 93
Harmelink, Bob 8, 28, 30, 35,
                        38-39, 44, 46-47, 50, 94

Harp, Brenda 229

Harris, Emmylou 120, 229

Harris, Paul 159, 161

Harvest Christian Fellowship,
    New York 233

Hastings, Doug 101, 103-4

Hathaway, Dick 26

"Headin' South" 195

"Hear Our Song" 39

"Heartache Tonight" 162

Heartbeat of Love 157, 235

"Heartbeat of Love" 235

"Hearts on Fire" 227

Hendrix, Jimi 3, 40, 70, 77,
                                    103, 148

"Here We Go Again" 158

Herman's Hermits 98

"Hey Joe" 77

"High Flying Bird" 43

Highwaymen, the 54

Hillman, Chris 56, 73, 89, 120,
                        155-59, 161-63, 165, 176,
                        184, 193, 234

Hollies, the 94, 127

Holly, Buddy 109

Hollywood Bowl, the 85, 100,
                                    102, 239

Hollywood Palace 96

Holt, Dennis 228, 234

"Home to My Lord" 198

"Honky Tonk Downstairs" 140

Hopkins, John 32-33, 35

Horizon Christian Fellowship,
    San Diego, CA 204

"Hot Dusty Roads" 83

"Hot Rod Lincoln" 157

"How Do You Feel" 61

Huey, Buddy 197

Hughes, John 26

Hugli, Tony 12

"Hung Upside Down" 107

"I Am a Child" 111

I Am Sure 234

"I Am Sure" 234

Ian, Janis 191

Ibbotson, Jimmy 234

"I Can See Everything" 154

"(I Can't Get No) Satisfaction" 94

"If It Wasn't for You" 218, 221

"If You Want Love
    in Your Heart" 74

Illinois Speed Press, the 101-2, 147

Inamorata 217

"Incense and Peppermints" 108

In My Father's House 228, 229, 234

"In My Father's House" 229, 238

International Submarine
    Band, the 53, 119-20

"In the Hour of Not Quite
    Rain" 112

"In the Midnight Hour" . . . 70, 94, 148

"In the Still of the Night" 149, 235

"I Put Away My Idols" 25

Iron Butterfly 82

"Island Love" 195

I Still Have Dreams 6, 195-97, 234

"I Still Have Dreams" 195

"It's So Hard to Wait" 112

"I've Been Lonely Too Long" 6, 195

I've Got a Reason 149, 187-91, 193

"I've Got a Reason" 10, 188

"I've Got a Tiger by the Tail" 118

Jackson 5, the 1, 6

Jacobs, Allan 38

James, Etta 43

James, Rick 64

Jefferson Airplane 61, 91, 103

"Jesus Is Just Alright" 189

Joey Dee and the Starlighters 43
Johnston, Jim 22, 47
Jones, Davy 59
Jones, George 228
Joplin, Janis 91, 103, 127
Jorgenson, Steve and Marie 206
"Just for Me and You" 149-50
"Just in Case It Happens,
     Yes Indeed" 118
Kaye, Chuck 62
Kaylan, Howard 88-89
Keaggy, Phil 228
"Keep on Believin'" 140
Keith, Toby 228
Kelly, Walt 126, 130-31, 137
Kemp, Allen 122
Kennedy, President John F. 44
"Kind Woman" 112-13, 118, 122,
          147, 157, 219, 235, 238
King, Kathy 41, 46-47
Kingston Trio, the 8, 28
Kleinow, Sneaky Pete 120
Knobler, Peter 236-37
Koblun, Ken 63-65, 96
Kovac, Allen 216, 218-220,
          224, 226
Krieger, Robby 74
Kunkel, Russ 196
L.A. Confidential 68
Last Time Around 111, 113-14
Laurie, Greg 175, 201-2, 204,
          208-10, 226
"Lawdy Miss Clawdy" 74
"Layla" 159
Lazarus, Bill 105
"Leave" 83
Leaves, the 77
Led Zeppelin 142
Lee, Arthur 74, 75, 77
Lee, John 181
Legacy 226
Lennon, John 107
Leno, Jay 227
"Let's Dance Tonight" 157
"Letter, The" 108
Leuzinger, Chris 228, 234
Levy, Morris 43, 44, 46
Lindsey, Hal 164
"Lion Sleeps Tonight, The" 43
Lithgow, John 12
Live Aid 102
Live 8 102
Loggins and Messina 218
Loggins, Kenny 147, 235
"Lonely Surfer, The" 83
Longbranch Pennywhistle 124, 156
"Look Within" 220
Los Bravos 85
"Loser" 62
Love 74, 96, 109
Love, Mike 3, 110
Love Story 99
Lovin' Spoonful 52, 94
Lynch, Tom
     (Jesse Furay's husband) 231
MacIntosh, Mike 204
Macy, John 228-29, 234
Madison Square Garden 239
Maglieri, Mario 73, 74
"Magnolia" 158
"Make Me a Smile" 128
Mamas and the Papas, the 80, 102
Manassas 156, 159
"Man Like Me, A" 151
Manzarek, Ray 74
"Marrakesh Express" 137
Martin D28 . . . . 28, 165-67
Martin, Dean 92

Martin, Dewey 1, 6-7, 69-70, 76,
        78-79, 84, 94-95, 98, 105-6, 211-13
Martin, Steve 133
Martin, Vince 40
Marx, Richard 216, 218, 227
Mason, Jim 153, 192, 235
Mason, Proffit 190
Mastin and Brewer 61, 64, 86
Mastin, Tom 61, 64, 86
"Maybelline" 74
Mayberry R.F.D. 126
Mays, Steve 204
McCartney, Paul 4
McEntire, Reba 228
McGinnis, Pat 27
McGuinn, Roger 56
McGuire, Barry 61, 189
McQueen, Steve 92
Meader, Vaughn 44
Mehler, John 175, 187
Meisner, Randy 102, 122-24,
        129-30, 134-36, 141, 148,
        196, 215-16, 220, 226-27
"Memphis" 74
"Merry-Go-Round" 112
Messina, Jim (Jimmy) 51, 107,
    109-12, 117-21, 123-24, 128-30, 134,
    139-41, 147-48, 156, 193, 215-16,
        218-20, 225-27, 234-35
Michaels, Roy 41, 43, 52
"Mighty Maker" 188
Miles, Buddy 70, 148
Miller, Eddie 41-42, 44
Miller, Eleanor 23
Miller, Michael 97
Mingus, Charles 183
Mitchell, Joni 1, 138
Mitch Ryder and
    the Detroit Wheels 93

Moby Grape 91
Modern Folk Quartet 44
Mojo Men, the 62
Monkees, the 40, 44, 59, 166
Monks, the 28-30, 35, 38, 41, 50
Monterey International
    Pop Festival 102, 104, 127
Morris, Chuck 227
Morrison, Jim 74
Morrison, Van 107
Mothers of Invention, the 61
Motown Records 64
"Mountain of Love" 74
"Mr. Pitiful" 94
"Mr. Soul" 92, 94, 107
Mr. Tambourine Man 56
Mundi, Billy 61, 64, 67-69
"My Heart's Cryin' Tonight" 235
"My Kind of Love" 94, 95, 128
"My Lord and My God" 198
Mynah Birds, the 64
Myrrh Records 197-99
Nash, Graham 6, 127-28
Nashville 89, 139, 224-26
"Nature of Love, The" 219-20
Neil, Fred 40
Nelson, Ozzie and Harriet 18
Nelson, Rick (Ricky) 24
Nesmith, Michael (Mike) 59
New Christy Minstrels 41, 44,
        60, 189
"New Kid in Town" 162
Night Owl Café 39, 94
Nitty Gritty Dirt Band, the
    (The Dirt Band) 128, 234-35
Nitzsche, Jack 83, 100, 107
"Nobody's Fool" 128
"Nobody's Fool/El Tonto
    de Nadie Regresa" 139

Noone, Peter 98
Northeim, Lois 18
"Nothin' to Hide" 218, 224
"Nowadays Clancy Can't Even
    Sing" . . . 53, 62-63, 66, 83-85, 87, 93
Nyro, Laura 127, 161
Ocean 189
"Ol' Forgiver" 150
Omartian, Michael 190
On Broadway Tonight 46
Ondine's 92-93
O'Neal, Ryan 99
"One Toke Over the Line" 61
"Only to You" 235
"On the Line" 183
"On the Way Home" 111
"Ooh Dreamer" 192
"Oooh Child" 197
Osmond, Donny 224
Otterbein College 8, 12, 27-31, 35,
                    37-38, 48, 50, 55
"Out of My Mind" 83
Owens, Buck 117, 118
Pajama Game, The 27, 29, 50
Palmer, Bruce 1, 6-7, 64-67, 70, 76,
            84-86, 95-96, 98, 101, 103,
                    109, 115, 211-13
Pandora's Box 91
Parks, Van Dyke 59-60
Parliament-Funkadelic 1
Parsons, Gram 49, 53-56, 119-21,
                        156, 158
Parton, Dolly 228
Partridge Family, The 166
Patrick, Michael 232
"Pay the Price" 83
"Peppermint Twist, The" 43
Peretti, Hugo 43-44
Perfit, Ronald 185

Perkins, Al and Debbie 159-61,
        163-64, 167-71, 175-81, 190,
                    193, 198, 235
Peter, Paul, and Mary 27, 30
Petty, Tom 6-7
Phillips, John 102
Pickett, Wilson 70, 148
Pickin' Up the Pieces 9, 133,
                    136-37, 139
"Pickin' Up the Pieces" 9, 181
Pink Floyd 158
Pioneer Chicken 65
Poco 139-40
Poco (Pogo) 2, 9, 51, 53, 70, 83,
        101-2, 107, 113, 125-26, 128-31,
        133-36, 139-41, 143, 147-51, 153-59,
        162-64, 168, 175, 193-95, 199, 209,
        215-19, 221-23, 229, 234-35, 239
Poconuts 168
Podolor, Richie 151, 153, 164-65
Poor, the 102, 122
Presley, Elvis 24, 41, 43
Prestidge, Eric 192
"Pretty Girl Why" 112
Pryor, Richard 44
"Pushin' Too Hard" 96
"Put Your Hand in the Hand" 189
"Railroad Days" 150
Randall, Rob 18
Rascals, the 1, 6, 195
Rawls, Lou 102
RCA Records 216, 224-26
"Real Love" 235
Reardon, Charlie 196-97
Redding, Otis 70, 94, 102, 148
Redstone, Sumner 236
Reed, Lou 158
Rhinocerous 104
Rhodes, Michael 228, 234

Rich, Don 118

Richardson, Jack 153, 157-58

Richie Furay Band, the 187, 193

"Ride, Captain, Ride" 165

"Ride the Country" 154

Rigby, Randy 228-29

"Right Along, A" 158

Rinehart, Bill 77, 78, 97

Riot on the Sunset Strip 91

Ritter, John 19

Ritter, Keith 175-76, 180, 182, 202

Rivers, Johnny 74, 100

Rock and Roll

    Hall of Fame 1, 3-5, 7, 81,

        230-31, 239

"Rock and Roll Woman" 92

"Rockin' Pneumonia

    and the Boogie Woogie Flu" 74

Rocky Mountain Christian

    Fellowship, Boulder, CO 207

Rodriguez, Vincent

    (Katie Furay's husband) 231

Rogers, Kenny 228

Rolling Stone magazine . . . 109, 189, 211

Rolling Stones, the 85, 94, 197

Ronstadt, Linda 196

Rose, Biff 127

Rothchild, Paul 104

Roulette Records 43, 46-47, 50

"Rustic Dance, The" 18

Ryle, James 207

"Sad Memory" 62, 105

Safe at Home 53, 119-20

Sajak, Pat 227

Sam and Dave 148

Sams, Ronnie 36-37

San Francisco 57, 90, 99-100,

        102-3, 152

Santana 127, 133

Sarkisian, Cherilyn ("Cher") 80

Satan Is Alive and Well

    on Planet Earth 164

"(I Can't Get No) Satisfaction" 94

"Satisfied" 195

"Satisfied Mind, A" 120-21

Schaub, Dale 22

Schmit, Timothy B. . . 122, 124, 134-36,

        140-41, 147-48, 150, 154, 158,

            193, 196, 217, 235

Schnee, Bill 190

Scott, Mike 41, 52, 109

Screen Gems 62

Seasons of Change 198

"Seasons of Change" . . . 60-61, 198, 201

Sebastian, John 39

Seeds, the 96, 100

Sellen, Scott 209, 218, 228-29,

        234-35

Serendipity Singers, the 41, 44

Serling, Rod 12

Serpico, Frank 204

Shanahan, Pat 122

Shipley, Tom 61

Shirelles, the 169

Siegel, Doc 82

Silverstein, Shel 44

Sims, Judy 100

"Sit Down I Think I Love You" 62

        78, 83

"(Sittin' On) The Dock

    of the Bay" 94, 148

Sklar, Leland 196

Sky, Patrick 40

Sledge, Percy 113

Smith, Chuck 163, 203-5, 228

Smither, Chris 113

Smith, Joe 191

Smith, Johnny 206

Snively, John 54

Solomon, Howard 42-47, 50

"Someone Who Cares" 192

Somers, Andy 229

Sonny and Cher 80-81

Souther-Hillman-Furay Band, the 2, 56, 159, 161-62, 164, 166-67, 170-71, 173-75, 183-85, 187, 193-94

Souther-Hillman-Furay Band, The 162-65, 178

Souther, J. D. 56, 155, 161-63, 176, 184, 196

Southern rock 119

Sparks, Mike 26

Sparks, Randy 60

"Special Care" 70

Spector, Phil 3, 82

"Spirit in the Sky" 189

Squires, the 53, 63, 67

"Stand Your Guard" 192

Starr, Ringo 118

Stephenson, Van 220

Steppenwolf 151

Stewart, Rod 158, 190

"Still Rolling Stones" 189

Stills, Stephen (Steve) 1, 5, 32, 40-41, 44, 49, 52-53, 56-60, 62-67, 69-70, 76, 83-87, 91-92, 95-96, 98, 101, 105, 107, 109-12, 114, 127-28, 137-38, 142, 148, 154, 211-13, 235

Stills, William 57

Stipe, Tom 175, 187, 228

Stone, Brian 80-82, 85, 94-96, 101, 107, 112, 122

Stone, Sly 210

Strait, George 113, 140

Strawberry Alarm Clock 108

"Suite: Judy Blue Eyes" 137

"Summer in the City" 39

Summer, Donna 189

Sunset Strip (the Strip) 6, 65, 73, 87-88, 91, 93, 194

"Super Freak" 64

Supremes, the 100

Surrealistic Pillow 61

Swaton, Pam 78, 89-90

Sweetheart of the Rodeo 56, 120

"Sweet Lovin'" 154

"Take It Easy" 154-55

Taylor, James 196

"Teenager in Love" 25

TeenSet 100

Them Changes 148

"They Call the Wind Mariah" 28

They Call Us Au Go-Go Singers . . . 43-44

Third I, the 88

Third Rock from the Sun 12

"This Magic Moment" 192, 195

Thomas, B. J. 199

Thomas, Miles 113, 122

Three Dog Night 126, 151

3's a Crowd 64-65

Tickner, Ed 69, 71, 79

Tiny Tim 126

Tokens, the 43

"Tomorrow" 51, 128

Tonight Show, The 100, 227

Tork, Peter 40, 59

Troubador, the 58, 60, 71, 125, 133, 135, 215

Trouble in Paradise 185

Truax, Jay 187

Turtles, the 44, 88-89, 166, 235

Twilight Zone, The 12

"Uno Mundo" 112

Valens, Ritchie 77, 109

Valentine, Elmer 73-74

Vallee, Rudy 46

Van Vliet, Don
  (Captain Beefheart) 75
Vaughn, Sarah 43
VH1 . . . . 3-4, 224, 226
Vincent, Gene 17
Vinton, Bobby 41
Volman, Mark 88-89, 123, 235
Wachtel, Waddy 196
Wagner, Robert 46
"Wake Up My Soul" 229
Wall of Sound 82
Walsh, Joe 173
Wasner, Pete 228, 234
Weintraub, Fred 52
Weissberg, Kenny 181, 229
"We'll See" 94, 188
"What a Day" 128
"What If I Should Say
  I Love You" 149
"What's the Matter, Please?" 195
"When It All Began" 218
"Where I'm Bound" 43
Where the Action Is 90, 93
Whisky A Go-Go 6, 73-79, 81,
                          87, 89, 93, 109
White, Chaplain John 233
Who, the 103, 133
"Willow Weep for Me" 85
"Will You Still Love Me
  Tomorrow" 169

Wilson, Brian 5, 59, 108
Wilson, Carl 110
Wilson, Dennis 108, 114
Wilson, Flip 44
WING-AM 17
Winter, Johnny 133
Wonder Boys 106
Woodstock 102, 137-38
"Woodstock" 138
Yellow Springs, OH 8, 11-16,19-20,
                  26-27, 30-31, 35, 50, 71, 238
Yes 158
"Yesterday's Gone"
  (Chad and Jeremy) 85
"Yesterday's Gone"
  (Richie Furay) 192
Yester, Jerry 44
Yogi, Maharishi Mahesh 110-11
"You Better Think Twice" 140, 147
Young, Neil 1-5, 49, 53, 62-67,
          70, 76, 83-87, 92, 94-96, 98, 100-1,
          103-5, 107, 109, 110-12, 138,
                211-13, 225, 226, 235
Young, Rusty . . . 101, 113, 118, 120-23,
          128, 135-37, 139-40, 144, 148, 152,
          154, 159, 193, 209-11, 215-16, 218,
                225, 226, 234-35
"You're the One I Love" 188
Zappa, Frank (The Mothers
  of Invention) 61, 75-76, 89

Printed in the United States
by Baker & Taylor Publisher Services